AUTOBIOGRAPHY AND IMAGINATION

AUTOBIOGRAPHY AND IMAGINATION
Studies in Self-Scrutiny

John Pilling

Lecturer in English Language and Literature
University of Reading

ROUTLEDGE & KEGAN PAUL
London, Boston and Henley

First published in 1981
by Routledge & Kegan Paul Ltd
39 Store Street,
London WC 1E 7DD
9 Park Street, Boston, Mass. 02108, USA and
Broadway House,
Newtown Road,
Henley-on-Thames,
Oxon RG9 1EN
Printed in Great Britain by
Biddles Ltd, Guildford, Surrey
© John Pilling 1981

British Library Cataloguing in Publication Data

Pilling, John
Autobiography and imagination
1. Autobiography
I. Title
809'. 93592   CT 25

ISBN 0-7100-0730-2

For Cathy

This your Narcissus
can no longer be seen
in the mirror
because he is the mirror itself

Antonio Machado, *Proverbios y Cantares* (1919), vi

CONTENTS

ACKNOWLEDGMENTS

I wish to thank my old teacher Professor Frank Kermode, now
of the University of Cambridge, for his stringent but helpful
criticisms of an earlier version of my chapter on Nabokov;
Dr Angela Livingstone of the University of Essex for her encouragement and refinement of my interest in Pasternak;
Professor Ian Fletcher of my own university for furnishing me
with his unpublished notes on Yeats's 'Autobiographies', and
Mr Adrian Caesar for his shrewd appraisal of the shortcomings
of my first approach to Yeats; Dr David Gervais and
Dr Patricia Righclato of the University of Reading for sharing
their respective ideas on Henry James with me, and sharpening
the focus of an earlier version of chapter 2; Mr Richard Read,
also of Reading, for taking time to make the writings of
Adrian Stokes yield up their secrets; Professor Anthony
Stephens of the University of Sydney for convincing me that
a consideration of Rilke's 'Notebooks of Malte Laurids Brigge'
should not form part of this book; and Professor Shirley
Neuman of the University of Alberta for giving me permission
to quote from 'Some One Myth: Yeats's Autobiographical Prose'
(Dolmen Press, 1981). This book is a reflection of my debt
to them, while any shortcomings are entirely my responsibility.

I should also like to thank the library staff of the Univers-
ities of Reading, London and Oxford for providing me with
materials otherwise difficult of access, Professor Graham
Falconer of the University of Toronto for a copy of an article
that proved beyond even their combined capabilities, Mr James
Hansford and Mr Paul Buck for similar acts of kindness, and
Miss Catherine Wardale for help with the typing and her
support throughout the writing of this book. I am particularly
grateful, finally, to Monsieur E.M. Cioran for convincing me
that writing it was worth while.

J.P.
University of Reading
March 1980

INTRODUCTION

It was Herbert Read who, in introducing a distinguished but
by no means outstanding addition to the genre, complained
that no category of literature was so poor in masterpieces as
autobiography.(1) As with many of Read's most stimulating
remarks, one is at once struck by both its brilliance and its
simplicity, or, to put it another way, impressed by the possibility that one might be induced to believe it and disappointed
that there is no supporting argument. In the absence of such
an argument, it is bound to seem as if Read has suffered a
temporary mental aberration and forgotten Augustine, Abelard,
Petrarch, Cardan, Montaigne, Casanova, Cellini, Rousseau,
Goethe, Chateaubriand, De Quincey, Stendhal, Tolstoy and
Gide, to name only them. One had better have good reason for
passing over such a wealth of impressive writing, and reason
seems temporarily to have deserted Read here. And yet the
very recital of these names commits one to a recognition of one
of the crucial problems inherent in any critical approach to
the genre in question, namely that it is a much more lawless
and various one than those with which we customarily have
to deal(2) (poetry, the novel, drama) and that – to adapt the
remarks of a writer on tragedy – we have to do here not so
much with a uniform model as with an unruly heap of autobiographies. In the absence of a thriving critical literature
on the subject, one might be tempted to alter Herbert Read's
remark to: 'no category of literary criticism is so poor as that
which deals with autobiography.' But this would be to ignore
the surprising explosion of interest in this area in recent
years, and to refuse to engage, however tentatively, in certain
rudimentary methodological discriminations.

Now I think it is clear that the term 'autobiography' –
apparently first used by Robert Southey in 1805 – tends to be
rather liberally applied to any kind of personal writing which
has to do with the facts of the author's life, irrespective of
whether the author has intended to create a continuous and
determinate work of self-portraiture. As a result, many sub-
genres tend to be included under a rubric of almost ideal
elasticity, among which the memoir, the confession, the apology,
the diary and the 'journal intime' are clearly the dominant
species.(3) There is also another shadowy area obtaining
between the autobiography (however defined) and the novel
which is known, for one reason or another, to take its life
from the facts of its author's life. It is possible to argue that

1

these various kinds of writing do not so much obscure the genre as define it, i.e. that they are in fact constitutive of a genre rather than pendants to it. And whilst I do not myself propose to do this, I feel bound to acknowledge that I am concerned with what I take to be an observable species existing within the bounds of a more or less ill-defined genre.

In the literary criticism that has, possibly in default of anywhere else to turn, grown up around the autobiographical impulse in recent years, it is rare to find anyone who will deny pride of place to the pioneering study by Roy Pascal,(4) although increasingly it has come to be realized that Pascal's analysis is less foolproof than it looks and is in need of some remedial attention, in terms of both theory and practice.(5) For my present purposes it is sufficient to point out that Pascal was the first to see what followed from opposing notions of 'truth' to notions of 'design', without being tempted to propose that there was an absolute need to drive a wedge between them; rather he was intent on asserting that truth might partake of design and that design might embody truth. No subsequent study can remain entirely uninfluenced by Pascal's and indeed no subsequent study can lay claim to a similar eminence. But more recent studies have attempted less to map out the ground than to raise certain edifices upon it, and have concerned themselves with a more concentrated, less speculative, approach than Pascal's. In recent years there has been a decisive swing towards what Jean Starobinski - in a paper whose importance makes it perhaps the only serious rival to Pascal's book - has called 'the style of autobiography'.(6) The proliferation of studies that concern themselves with 'versions of the self', 'metaphors of self', 'the art of life', 'the voice within' and 'autobiographical acts'(7) are, like this one, notes towards a definition rather than attempts to enunciate rules. All these books contain valuable discussions of particular autobiographies (and also some works that seem to me miscalled autobiographies) and if the peculiar difficulties of talking about the subject, plus a certain amount of dissatisfaction, remain in a reader's mind after reading any or all of these - as also with respect to the special numbers of three avant-garde periodicals devoted to the subject(8) - this is no doubt a salutary reminder of how intractable the whole business is.

I have tried to diminish this intractability, first, by confining myself to a manageable period of time within which certain continuities may be presumed to exist, and, second, by confining myself to works that, if they may be said to be autobiographies at all, are so only in the special sense of Wordsworth's 'Prelude', the 'growth of a poet's mind'. To compensate for this narrowness, I have included studies of authors contributing to four literatures and have not worried unduly about any disparities in status between those at present considered 'great' and those who are (in my opinion) unforgivably neglected. This may give the impression that certain chapters - in particular the appendices - are 'causeries', although it seems to me that the real 'causerie' is on behalf of the genre to which these books contribute, rather than on behalf of the authors themselves. The authors and the books must obviously be their own advocates; but it would be foolish to deny that the context in which I place them is designed to make each individual case more powerful.

Any reader will immediately be struck by the fact that almost all of the authors in question are better-known for works of theirs that I do not deal with, that three (and possibly four) are distinguished novelists, two are outstanding poets, and four are masters of discursive writing (in history, art criticism, anthropology and philosophy). Only one, Michel Leiris, is primarily associated with the genre of autobiography, and his reputation outside France makes him arguably the most unfamiliar of them all. In so far as I was striving to isolate a neglected genre, and to articulate, however tentatively, a kind of morphology of the genre, this did not, and does not, strike me as surprising, nor even very important (except in so far as the works I do not deal with have tended, very understandably, to mask those I am concerned with). Much more important, to my mind, is to see why these works, without being robbed of their individuality or idiosyncrasy, benefit from being seen in the same plane, and tell us something of inestimable value about autobiographical writing in all its forms in the twentieth century.

It must be admitted at once that there is no one common denominator that will explain why a particular book has taken the shape it has, except perhaps the fact that, in each case, the author has stamped his personality on his work by means of a distinctive, sometimes very demanding verbal surface, and, a corollary of this, the fact that each reader is forced, by the difficulty of the work before him, to become an active participant in the creative act. There may be something of a paradox here, in so far as the life which forms the basis of the narrative is by definition a private one, and yet is revealed to the public by methods that might have been presumed to make it even more private. Certainly none of these authors conforms to the assumption that all modern autobiography is essentially footnotes to Rousseau,(9) not even Henry Adams (who is the only one who openly admits to keeping Rousseau in mind). Self-exposure is, in fact, only a secondary, or even tertiary aim in each case, even where the expressed intention (as, for instance, with Leiris) is 'to lay bare one's heart, to write the book about oneself in which the concern for sincerity would be carried to such lengths that . . . "the paper would shrivel and flare at each touch of his fiery pen".'(10) Quite unlike Rousseau, each of the authors in question is concerned, at a particular point in their lives, with the formulation of an image of themselves that is not contaminated by subjectivity. Michel Leiris (who, with Yeats and Pasternak, is something of an exception to the general rule that most of the authors chosen are not compulsive autobiographers) provides us with a useful description of his aims when he says that he has chosen 'a tone as objective as possible, trying to gather my life into a single solid block (an object I can touch. . .).' (11) This is precisely what all the other authors are intent on, even an author of apparently limitless egotism, like Vladimir Nabokov.

It is not so much the history of a life that these authors are concerned with as what James calls 'the history of . . . imagination'.(12) They are orientated outwards not inwards. It is no accident that we find Henry Adams explicitly concerned with those who will follow after him; W.B. Yeats concluding his first sustained attempt at prose autobiography with a reference to 'all life weighed in the scales of my own life'; an irritated Pasternak reminding the reader that 'Safe Conduct' is not a biography; Michel Leiris 'trying to find in my neighbour less a judge than an accomplice'; Adrian Stokes turning his personality 'inside out' in order 'to find the themes of human nature' and 'a certain relation to the external world'; Sartre concluding with the image of 'a whole man, made of all men' – and so on, each author revealing a very complex and individual personality, and yet each of them more concerned with the shape of the work they are writing. 'Between artists', Henry Adams wrote to a friend, 'or people trying to be artists the sole interest is that of form'; and in a letter of four years previously, 'Every man is his own artist before a work of art.'(13)

Now there is no point in pretending that the works I have chosen to deal with are easy of access; however, they are not, I think, esoteric, except perhaps in the sense that Henry Adams hoped all future literary art would be. Adams spoke of a literature that would be 'freer and happier for the sense of privacy and abandon',(14) and it is clear that the works I deal with are immensely 'abandoned' without in any way losing their essential 'privacy'. Paradoxically, one comes to know these authors as well as, and in some cases better than, one knows the compulsive autobiographers of the nineteenth century, Stendhal and Tolstoy for example. Whilst no one could deny the intense interest of studying the personal writings of these two huge figures, nor indeed the compelling drama of diarists like Kafka(15) and Pavese from the present century, I think it is clear that in all these cases one is left ultimately with only a heap of brilliant fragments, each intrinsically fascinating and most of them shedding light on the life or the work or the relationship between life and work. By contrast, in the works with which I deal, I am concerned with showing how the fragments have been artfully composed into a unity. I am tempted to see the contrast I am making here in terms of a distinction

basic to the oeuvre of one of the authors I study here: the
'carving' and 'modelling' traditions as defined by Adrian Stokes.
Richard Wollheim's description of these is the clearest account:
> in the last analysis, the 'modelled' work of art can be
> thought of as the mirror-image of the 'carved' work of art.
> Examine the characteristics of each, and we see that they
> are those of the other in reverse. So, in the 'carved'
> work of art there is a lack of any sharp internal differentia-
> tion: the individual forms are unemphatic, and the transitions
> between them are gradual. . . . And the reward for this
> is that the work of art as a whole asserts its distinctness
> or otherness from the spectator. By contrast, in the
> 'modelled' work of art, there are sharp transitions and
> considerable internal differentiation; the forms are distinct
> and individuated. . . . And the price that is paid for this
> is that the work of art as a whole tends to merge with or
> envelop the spectator.(16)

This is a suggestive, indeed brilliant, method of classifying
the divergent and yet convergent impulses that find embodiment in the work of art, and there is much to be gained from
aligning the works I consider here with the 'carving' tradition
as defined by Stokes. But his analysis of the 'modelled' work
of art is also extremely relevant to works like 'Safe Conduct',
'Reveries Over Childhood and Youth' and 'Speak, Memory',
each of which manifests 'sharp transitions and considerable
internal differentiation'. Indeed all nine of the works I deal
with may be said to tend to 'merge with or envelop the
spectator.' In the end, as Stokes himself seems to have recognized, it is not a matter of recommending one method and
denigrating the other: the dualism turns out to have been a
unity after all. And this is why I think there is a certain
appropriateness in the epigraph which I have taken from a
poem of Machado's, for 'the mirror itself' can only assert 'its
distinctness or otherness from the spectator' at the same time
as it 'tends to merge with or envelop' him.

No doubt there are other authors in the twentieth century
who could have proved my case for me - Gide, for example,
or Julian Green, or Genet - and thus disproved Herbert
Read's contention that ' no category of literature is so poor
in masterpieces as autobiography.' Yet even then I think one
would be struck by the fact that the most canvassed twentieth-
century writers - Proust, Joyce and Thomas Mann in prose,
Rilke, Eliot and Valéry in poetry - have only contributed to
the genre indirectly and have thus, to some extent, ensured
its neglect and partial impoverishment. There is, of course,
an intense self-scrutiny involved in writing such works as
'A la Recherche du temps perdu' and 'Die Aufzeichnungen des
Malte Laurids Brigge', and it may have been perverse of me
to decide that such works are 'autobiographical novels' and
thus beyond my self-imposed restrictions. The Rilke text, in
particular, would have formed a most useful base for much of

what I say about Pasternak and Adrian Stokes, and the Proust text has influenced almost all French writing subsequent to it. Both works outline what Paul Nash, in his own preface to the book which Herbert Read was introducing, called 'the development of an artist's life, a development which, on looking back, appears to have a curious "inevitable" quality, like a line of fate in the palm of the hand.'(17) Yet they are surely not, in the last analysis, autobiographies in the same sense that the works discussed here may be said to be. It is true that Rilke's 'Malte' formed the kind of 'prelude' to later composition that Wordsworth's long poem was intended to be; but the parallel case in Proust's development was the writings that have come to be known as 'Contre Saint-Beuve', and neither of these texts (the latter an inevitably synthetic one) seem to me to demand inclusion in a study of this kind to the exclusion of any one of my nine examples.

There is, in short, a 'finished' quality about all these texts that seems to be one reason why they can provide a permanent stimulus and a continuing satisfaction. As even the most devoted of its readers must admit, and as the most subtle of its commentators has demonstrated, Rilke's 'Malte' remains a bifurcated and disunified work.(18) It enabled Rilke to clear away the rubble in his personality preparatory to making the first assault on the 'Duino Elegies'. But it is a much less complete work than the 'Elegies' themselves, and much less complete than any of these texts. These too were written at points of crisis, sometimes in the full awareness that they might be 'preludes' to composition (although in no less than three cases they are more obviously 'postludes' coming at the end of a career); but owing to the skill and concentration with which they were written, they compel us, as readers, to see them as compositions in their own right.

The primary points of contact between my examples are, therefore, formal and stylistic, although there are certain incidental resonances which accrue from juxtaposing these works in this particular way.(19) My purpose has been to make each section sufficiently self-contained to make sense to someone who wants only to read that section and yet also to ensure that each section may be, in the words of someone who has written on a theme similar to mine, 'a mirror which may reflect other works.'(20) It should at all times be clear that I am by no means attempting a history of autobiography in the twentieth century, but rather seeking to contemplate certain transformations of one particular kind of autobiographical writing. I am much less interested in making general statements about the autobiographical mode than in making particular statements about particular works of art which happen to be 'autobiographical'. However, at the same time, such an investigation compels one to test one's conclusions against the best that has been thought and said on autobiographical literature generally, so in my conclusion I have tried to move beyond particular examples into a more abstract area, where it is doubtful if there will ever be unanimity, and no doubt undesirable that there should be.

1 HENRY ADAMS:
'The Education of Henry Adams' (1907)

In a letter of 1903, the year in which he began to write the
book for which he is best known, Henry Adams commended
his erstwhile compatriot Henry James for a book that is now
largely forgotten: 'William Wetmore Story and his Friends'.
'You have written', Adams told him, 'not Story's life, but your
own and mine, - pure autobiography.'(1) Four years later
Adams sent out the first of a hundred privately printed copies
of his own version of his life, 'The Education of Henry Adams'.
As early as 1883, in a letter to his lifelong friend John Hay,
Adams explained in the ironical manner that was now second
nature to him the advantages of the genre:
> I am clear that you should write autobiography, I mean to
> do mine. After seeing how coolly and neatly a man like
> Trollope can destroy the last vestige of heroism in his
> own life, I object to allowing mine to be murdered by any
> one except myself. Every church mouse will write auto-
> biography in another generation in order to prove that it
> never believed in religion.(2)

Despite his fondness for literature that was more or less
autobiographical (he seems not to have drawn a distinction
between biography and autobiography) Adams regarded it, as
he came to regard almost everything, with suspicion and
scepticism. Adams's letters are peppered with splenetic out-
bursts against biographies, all predicated on the fact that he
'never knew a mere biography that did not hurt its subject.'(3)
His feelings were, not unnaturally, at their most intense where
members of his family were concerned:
> I've been trying to read my brother Charles's Life of our
> father. Now I understand why I refused so obstinately to
> do it myself. These biographies are murder. . . . They
> belittle the victim and the assassin equally. They are
> like bad photographs and distorted perspectives . . . I
> have sinned myself . . . [but] I did not assassinate my
> father.(4)

The image of biography as a kind of murder was habitual to
Adams, whether it was Morley 'taking' Gladstone's life or the
hypothetical biographer of John Hay as a strychnine poisoner.(5)
And yet, as Adams admitted in the letter quoted above, he had
often played the role of biographer himself. In 1879 he published the 'Life of Albert Gallatin'; a biography of John Randolph
followed in 1882, the same year in which he prepared a biography

of Aaron Burr that was never published. In 1893 he printed
privately his free adaptation of the memoirs of Queen Marau
of Tahiti, later revised and enlarged for another private
printing in 1901. His last major enterprise was 'The Life of
George Cabot Lodge' published in 1911.

Adams had indeed 'sinned' so persistently against his own
beliefs that it may seem difficult to absolve him of duplicity
in the matter, especially when in March 1907 he wrote to
Elizabeth Cameron that he would not write a memoir of his
friend John Hay,(6) and yet in the following year a twenty-
two page memoir by Adams (unsigned) appeared as a preface
to Hay's widow's compilation of her husband's letters and
diaries. The truth would seem to be that, whilst Adams had
genuine enough intellectual objections to this kind of literature,
he never entirely freed himself of an emotional attachment to
it that was endemic in the culture of his family.(7) His range
of reading was so wide, so encyclopedic almost, that it would
be wrong to single out personal literature as his particular
obsession, but his suspicion of the various forms that such
literature might take was clearly grounded in more than a
nodding acquaintance with those forms. As a historian his
commitment to written records of past lives could not be less
than total, even if he later affected a devil-may-care attitude
to facts and details. And when it came to writing a version of
his own life, he was hyper-conscious of the formal problems
that had attended previous enterprises in the genre, as perhaps only someone with a profound knowledge of such literature
could have been.

Adams's preference in the genre of personal literature seems
to have been for 'memoirs'. As early as 1869 we find him
writing to his English friend Gaskell: 'I am myself preparing
a volume of Memoirs which may grow to be three volumes if
I have patience to toil. It is not an autobiography - *n'ayez
pas peur*. An ancient lady of our house has left material for
a pleasant story.'(8) The hostility to autobiography that is
evident here surfaces again in the letter to John Hay already
quoted, and is an inseparable part of Adams's distrust of
egoism in all its forms. 'The ego may pass in a letter or a
diary', he told his brother Brooks, 'but not in a serious
book.'(9) This takes up an idea mooted in a letter of 1882,
to Henry Cabot Lodge ('If we could only be impersonal, our
books would be better than they are. . . .')(10), and prepares
us for the most striking feature of the 'Education', Adams's
rejection of the first person in favour of the third. By the
time of the 'Education' Adams had come to believe that 'annihilation of self' was 'the first condition before absorption in a
higher unity,'(11) but it is clear from the John Hay letter
that self-slaughter also had a less altruistic component in it.
A very similar note is struck in a letter to Henry James a
quarter of a century later, referring specifically to the
'Education': 'The volume is a mere shield of protection in the

grave. I advise you to take your own life in the same way,
in order to prevent biographers from taking it in theirs.'(12)
It is clear from this letter that, for Adams, 'annihilation of
self' did not preclude a pre-emptive strike of self-creation.
Indeed, as a number of commentators have noted, the adoption
of a third-person form in the 'Education' thrusts 'Adams'
before us more decisively than a first-person form would have
done.(13)

A corollary of Adams's stance of anti-egoism was his belief
that the subject (in the sense of subject-matter) was more
important than the subject in a narrowly grammatical sense.
In an early letter to his eldest brother, Adams sees the two
as interdependent:

If I write at all in my life out of the professional line, it
will probably be when I have got something to say, and
when I feel that my subject has got me as well as I the
subject.(14)

Fifteen years later the dominance of the one over the other
had become an article of faith: 'I cannot conceive how any
rule of prose can be made that shall not require the subject
to stand first. This is a general law. . . .'(15) At the same
time Adams was aware that this might lead to monotony and
was careful to 'insist on the law of variety',(16) particularly
where the length of sentences was concerned.(17) This in
no sense committed Adams to a belief in ornamentation for
its own sake:

the reader ought to be as little conscious of the style as
may be. It should fit the matter so closely that one should
never be quite able to say that the style is above the
matter - nor below it.(18)

Adams was not, as this makes clear, opposed to the development of a personal style. But he certainly believed that the
austerity and refinement of 'styleless' writing was an ideal to
be aimed for. (His love-hate relationship with Carlyle pretty
obviously originates from this.) Anything that might bring
this ideal close to realization - in particular the erasure of
superfluities - earned his strong commendation. 'Writing is
only half the art,' he wrote to Gaskell in 1867, 'the other
being erasure';(19) 'you will find', he told Henry Cabot Lodge,
'it pays also to try to condense your sentences';(20) 'I am
a little toqué about condensation,' he told Lodge six years
later;(21) and as late as 1904, when the 'Education' was being
written, he reminded Sarah Hewitt: 'When you come to writing,
I can recommend only one rule:- Strike out every superfluous
sentence, and, in what is left, strike out relentlessly every
superfluous word.'(22) It may seem quixotic that a man who
was clearly convinced that 'what one leaves out contributes
more to success than what one leaves in' should have written
a nine-volume history that is probably read, when it is read
at all, in an abridged form. But Adams did not confine his
strictures on condensation to writers other than himself. When

Henry Cabot Lodge turned Adams's own weapon against him
after reading 'The Life of Albert Gallatin', Adams readily
agreed with him: 'You are quite right in regard to Gallatin.
Pruning would improve it. I think fifty pages might come
out, to great advantage, and perhaps a hundred could be
spared.'(23) There are those who would say the same of the
'Education', of course, and even in the absence of a manuscript version it is difficult to believe that Adams followed
his own advice especially as, in the words of Ernest Samuels,
'he wrote [it] with what must have been furious speed.'(24)

Adams's emphasis on condensation is of a piece with his
stress on the avoidance of egoism, and both are part and
parcel of a very bifocal attitude to literature. Writing to Henry
Cabot Lodge in 1880, whilst at work on his 'History', Adams
told him: 'I get into a habit of working only for the work's
sake and disliking the idea of completing and publishing. One
should have some stronger motive than now exists for authorship.'(25) In the same year he published his first novel,
'Democracy', anonymously, and protected himself from those
who guessed his authorship by visiting it upon other authors.
Adams's ambivalence in regard to the question of authorship
is memorably expressed in a letter of 1882, to John Hay:

I neither want notoriety nor neglect, and one of the two
must be imagined by every author to be his reward. My
ideal of authorship would be to have a famous *double* with
another name, to wear what honors I could win. How I
should enjoy upsetting him at last by publishing a low
and shameless essay with woodcuts in his name! . . .(26)

In 1884 Adams came close to realizing this ideal by publishing,
this time not anonymously but pseudonymously, his second
novel 'Esther', a book that he described to the publisher as
an 'experiment . . . [in] whether authorship without advertisement was possible'(27) but which he always thereafter considered to have been written 'in one's heart's blood'.(28)
In the last twenty years of his life Adams attempted not so
much 'authorship without advertisement' as 'authorship without
audience', confirming his self-fulfilling prophecy that he had
'printed volume after volume which no one would read'(29) by
making it difficult, if not impossible, for anyone not personally
selected by him to read his work at all. He could not keep
his promise of 1892 that 'I will never again appear as an author,
but I don't mind writing anonymously'(30) but he did what
he could - in an external sense at least - to become as anonymous as possible.

As early as 1867 we find Adams telling Charles Eliot Norton
'I have suffered so much from publicity that I prefer over-
caution'(31) and it is clear that his desire for 'impersonal'
books was conditioned by his need of what he later called 'a
shield of protection'.(32) In one remarkable letter concerning
a book ('John Randolph') that was clearly far from 'impersonal',
Adams went to great lengths to provide himself with a shield
after the fact:

My John Randolph is coming into the world. Do you know,
a book always seems a part of myself, a kind of intellectual
brat or segment, and I never bring one into the world
without a sense of shame. They are naked, helpless and
beggarly, yet the poor wretches must live forever and
curse their father for their silent tomb. This particular
brat is the first I ever detested. He is the only one I
never wish to see again; but I know he will live to dance,
in the obituaries, over my cold grave. Don't read him,
should you by chance meet him. Kick him gently, and let
him go.(33)

It is important to recognize that this complex amalgam of self-
disgust and self-aggrandizement dates from before the tragic
suicide of his wife Marian, after which it is not so much images
of birth as images of death that cluster around the fact of
book-making for Adams. But the germ of the post-suicide
Adams, when he came to believe that 'all books should be
posthumous except those which should be buried before
death'(34) can be discerned in his letters from before the time
of his marriage, as he develops a stoical indifference to his
disenchantment with politics and contentedly predicts that his
career will be a failure. Literature offered a respite from his
disappointed dreams of statesmanship, just as politics had
ousted the law as a possible career. But literature - under
which head Adams would have included the writing of articles
on economics and books on history - soon revealed itself to
him as a medium that was almost as unsatisfactory as those
he had left behind, and before he had completed his 'History'
he had lost confidence that it 'would be what I would like to
make it.'(35) Although he was congenitally incapable of main-
taining the silence which he felt to be the only adequate
response to life,(36) he grew more and more aware, especially
when in the South Seas with his painter friend John La Farge,
of the shortcomings of words in the face of reality. 'Tahiti
is not to be described. Don't expect me to do it,' he told one
correspondent,(37) and only with paradoxes could he describe
it to another: 'I cannot get expression for the South Seas.
Languor that is not languid; voluptuousness that is not
voluptuous; a poem without poetry.'(38)

It was on the death of John La Farge that Adams, once
again facing the question of biography that had so much
haunted him, gave most memorable expression to what he saw
as the inevitable failure of literature:

The task of painting him is so difficult as to scare any
literary artist out of his wits. The thing cannot be done. It
is like the attempt of the nineteenth-century writers to
describe a sunset in colors. Complexity cannot be handled
in print to that degree. La Farge used to deride his own
attempts to paint sea and sky and shadow in the South
Seas. . . . At a certain point of development, the literary
artist is bound to fail still more, because he has not even

color to help him, and mere words only call attention to
the fact that the attempt to give them color is a predestined failure.(39)
In another letter to the same correspondent Adams developed
his theme, adding to his analysis of the literary artist's problems the motif of self-protection that even the 'Education'
had not been powerful enough to exorcise:

Luckily, the painter's world is relatively compact and
organised, and within its limits will probably be worth
living for. I wish I could say as much for the literary
artist's world; but I see no hope of organised self-defence
there.(40)

This is perhaps as poignant an admission as Adams ever made,
especially when we consider that he had by this time written
not only a history of America that will survive comparison
with his beloved Gibbon, but also the two books on which his
literary fame will always depend: 'Mont Saint-Michel and
Chartres' and 'The Education of Henry Adams', both in their
own way as true a 'cry of the heart' as the song of Richard 1
that he translated for chapter eleven of the former.(41) The
fascination, particularly of the latter, consists in their being
at once both an exemplification of Adams's literary beliefs and
a disproof of them, and at the same time, depending on one's
angle of vision, both a masterpiece and a resounding failure.

It is crucial, in approaching a work that has never attained
in England the status of a classic that it enjoys in America,
to be aware of the background against which any just assessment of the book must figure, and Adams's voluminous letters
provide a matchless introduction to that. But Adams's sense
of his own achievement in the 'Education' is so various as to
threaten the removal of the ground from under our feet. What
is quite clear is that he did not himself consider it an 'autobiography' and would have rejected the subtitle added by the
publisher of the best-selling posthumous trade edition. Adams
had, however, to some extent encouraged this misnomer by
beginning his preface to the 'Education' with a reference to
Rousseau's 'Confessions' and also mentioning Benjamin
Franklin's classic unfinished 'Autobiography'. A more accurate
literary analogue is offered in the editor's preface, also
written by Adams himself despite the signature of Henry Cabot
Lodge. This refers to Adams's ambition 'to complete St. Augustine's *Confessions*', the work which, in letters written after
the private publication in 1907, Adams came to think of as
'my literary model'.(42) Adams pursued the analogy with increasing fervour. His first explicit allusion to it occurs in a
letter of 1908 to the philosopher William James:

Did you ever read the Confessions of St. Augustine, or of
Cardinal de Retz, or of Rousseau, or of Benvenuto Cellini,
or even of my dear Gibbon? Of them all, I think St. Augustine alone has an idea of literary form, - a notion of writing
a story with an end and object, not for the sake of the

object, but for the form, like a romance. I have worked
ten years to satisfy myself that the thing cannot be done
today. The world does not furnish the contrasts or the
emotion.(43)

Only nine days later he was writing to another correspondent
not of Augustine's success but of his failure 'as artist'.(44)
A year later Adams expands this, reintroduces Rousseau and
articulates his notions of failure more clearly:

When I read St. Augustine's Confessions, or Rousseau's,
I feel that their faults, as literary artists, are worse than
mine. We have all three undertaken to do what cannot be
done - mix narrative and didactic purpose and style. The
charm of the effort is not in winning the game but in playing it. We all enjoy the failure. St. Augustine's narrative
subsides at last into the dry sands of metaphysical theology.
Rousseau's narrative fails wholly in didactic result; it subsides into still less artistic egoism. And I found that a
narrative style was so incompatible with a didactic or
scientific style, that I had to write a long supplementary
chapter to explain in scientific terms what I could not put
into narration without ruining the narrative. . . .(45)

Adams adopts here the stance of literary artist, and is more
preoccupied with style than perhaps, given his earlier beliefs,
he should have been. But the continuation of the letter indicates that it is not a purely literary matter. It is essentially
a cultural lack that has caused his particular enterprise
to fail:

With St. Augustine's background, or Benvenuto's, or
Saint-Simon's, the failure would be less perceptible than
mine. Do what we please, the *tour-de-force* of writing
drama with what is essentially undramatic, must always be
unpleasantly evident . . . if I could have had a dramatic
setting like St. Augustine or Benvenuto or even Fanny
Burney, I could have made it a success.(46)

'Background' is, of course, ambiguous here, with at least two
meanings that make good sense: (a) the perspectival sense,
as of a painting; (b) the broader educational and cultural
sense. 'What is essentially undramatic' is also more ambiguous
than it looks, since although in the context of this letter it
appears to refer to the incommensurable didactic and scientific
elements, it is clearly related to what Adams said in an earlier
letter to William James, in which he again saw his enterprise as
a tour de force: 'It is the old story of an American drama. You
can't get your contrasts and backgrounds.'(47) The peculiar
poverty of 'an American drama' is only obliquely present in the
later letter, where all Adams's contrasts are with European
autobiographers. But this does not resolve the ambiguity of
the word 'background'. For the letter to James (as later a
1909 letter to Henry Osborn Taylor)(48) is couched in plainly
pictorial terms. (The implication that literature is inferior to
painting is spelled out, as we have seen, in the letters on the
death of La Farge.)

The ambiguities cannot be resolved one way or the other. They are testimony to the way a multi-faceted man saw a multi-faceted book. Adams told William James that the book interested him 'chiefly as a literary experiment'(49) analogous to the novels of James's brother Henry, and in a letter of the same year (1908) he impressed upon Whitelaw Reid that 'an experiment like this volume is hazardous, not as history, but as art.'(50) But in other letters, often addressed to the same correspondent, he stressed the book's historical preten-sions, seeing it as a twentieth-century pendant, 'a companion study', to his more effective study of the twelfth century, 'Mont Saint-Michel and Chartres'.(51) One of Adams's choicest strategies was to relate his book to his career as an academic historian and to see it as 'my closing lectures to undergraduates in the instruction abandoned and broken off in 1877.'(52) But as time wore on Adams came, characteristically, to think of it as addressed less to others than to himself: 'it has at least served one purpose - that of educating me.'(53)

Modern commentators have decisively, and without question sensibly, stressed the book's claims on us as a work of art. This would have appalled the younger Adams who was so intent on recommending the 'subject' or the 'matter' as the primary focus of a literary work. But by the time of the 'Education', as we have seen, the whole of Adams's emphasis had switched to questions of form. 'What kind of matter is suited to the public,' he told his brother Brooks in 1899, 'I do not know. . . . All that concerns me is the cooking and the service.'(54) Adams restates this in a less cavalier fashion in a letter of 1908:

> Between artists, or people trying to be artists, the sole interest is that of form. Whether one builds a house, or paints a picture, or tells a story, our point of vision re-gards only the form - not the matter. . . . Now that I have the stuff before me - in clay - I can see where the form fails, but I cannot see how to correct the failures.(55)

Adams's concentration on formal problems was certainly conditioned by the special difficulties he was forced to confront in writing his two late masterpieces. He admits as much in another letter of 1908, in which he links his interest in form with his lifelong interest in education: 'In the effort to give form to thought, one's object is not so much to teach as to learn.'(56) It is usual to view Adams's adoption of the role of pupil with some scepticism, and it is difficult to believe that Adams published the 'Education' privately merely in order that it might be corrected, like a schoolboy's essay. (A striking feature of Adams's letters on this question is that they are concerned far less with form than with matter, although Adams repeatedly professed to 'care very little whether my details are exact, if only my *ensemble* is in scale.')(57) In the event he seems to have received very few corrections, and in pre-paring the text for a trade edition he confined himself almost exclusively to spelling errors and other trivial corrections. But

however sceptically we may view Adams's claim to be among the
ranks of the taught rather than the teachers, it would be
wrong to distrust it altogether. In the face of a universe that
had increasingly come to seem a multiverse, Adams abandoned
a unitary or fixed point of view in favour of a relativistic and
perspectival science of aspects. This necessarily had repercus-
sions on his understanding of the relationship between art
and its audience, and it is unfortunate that his most explicit
letter on the subject is to be found not in the three volumes
of letters in his own name but hidden away among the 'Letters
of Mrs. Henry Adams':

   All considerable artists make a point of compelling the public to think for itself, and their rule is to require each
   observer to see what he can, and this will be what the
   artist meant. To the artist the meaning is indifferent. Every
   man is his own artist before a work of art.(58)

This remarkable letter dates from 1904, by which time the
'Education' was in the process of being written, and it is an
invaluable document for anyone who finds the 'Education' itself,
or indeed Adams's letters about the book, difficult to come to
terms with. In absolute contradiction to his earlier view that
matter and meaning must be the most important concerns of
the artist, Adams is here - already perhaps aware that no
amount of his own artistry will save the 'Education' from ultimate failure - shifting the burden of responsibility from the
shoulders of the artist and openly inviting the imaginative
collaboration of the reader. In the letters dating from after
the private publication of the book, Adams becomes the reader
(and therefore the artist) of his own work of art, aggressively
attacking it as a formal object but at the same time defending
it against its apparent forbears. But even without the figure
of Adams as his own interpreter, it would be difficult, if
not impossible, to interpret the 'Education' in any definitive
way; with such a book the paradoxes multiply almost to
infinity. 'Taking one's own life' stands revealed as a pre-
emptive act, 'a shield of protection in the grave'(59) in more
than a merely metaphorical sense - and yet an enterprise in
which any reader may have a part to play, an unexpectedly
creative act therefore.

   The 'Education' is the kind of book that only a monograph
can hope to do justice to, and even then it remains elusive and
intractable. The approach through form which seems such a
promising one (even allowing for Adams's acknowledgment that
'the form fails') is hedged round with all kinds of problems,
at least in so far as 'form' is taken to mean 'structure'. Melvin
Lyon's book summarizes the critical debate on this in a manner
that clearly indicates his sense of the futility of this approach:

   Critical discussion of the structure of the 'Education' centres
   upon whether it has two or three major parts. Levenson,
   Samuels and Chalfont all say three. All view 'Chaos' and/or
   'Failure' as the end of the first part; they disagree as to

where the third part begins . . . Sayre seems to return
to the three-part division but considers the second part
to be the omitted twenty years. . . .(60)
(Interestingly enough, in a book published a year previously
to Lyon's, Vern Wagner proposes a six-part division in an
attempt to reconcile 'manner' and 'matter'.)(61) It would be
difficult to find a more convincing demonstration of the truth
of Adams's claim that 'every man is his own artist before a
work of art' than in this structural approach, where every
critic seems to possess a finer sense of structure than the
author himself.

Lyon's own approach is through 'symbol' and 'idea' and
originates in a letter Adams wrote in 1912, which does not
refer to the 'Education' at all:

Symbolism is a wide field. It is, in fact, the whole field
of art. No artist ever thought of anything else until the
Dutchmen came down to portraits and landscapes in their
own Dutch spirit. You have a sort of symbolic monument in
every picture that the Italians ever painted, and every
statue the Greeks ever sculpted. Every coin was a symbol,
and every line an idea.(62)

Without surrendering entirely to Adams's pardonable overstate-
ment, Lyon identifies what seem to him the key symbols and
investigates how they interact to produce a meaning, or
meanings that ultimately may be seen to relate to one another.
This approach has certain obvious advantages over that which
wants to divide the book into more or less clearly defined
sections, although it inevitably runs the gauntlet of confusing
images with symbols and setting up more exact correspondences
than the book itself seems prepared to sustain. In particular
it leaves itself open to the objection that 'The Education of
Henry Adams' was not conceived as a Symbolist poem and
cannot be approached as if it were.

The great merit of Lyon's study is that it establishes the
need for what might be called a 'perspectival' reading of
Adams's most ambitious book. In such a reading no one chapter,
or pair of chapters - not even the chapters Quincy and
Boston with which the book begins - would dominate any
other but rather each would be seen as distinct in character,
whilst nevertheless contributing to the whole. It is doubtful
if any first-time reader of the 'Education' would come away
with an impression of unity. But at the same time no sensitive
reader could regard it as a random collection of atoms. Adams
proceeds somewhat like a surveyor engaged in triangulation
work, who maps first one area and then the area adjacent to
it and then the one after that, and so on until he has created
a network of relationships. But there is no one fixed point
from which Adams takes his bearings, and even though certain
dates (and to a lesser extent certain places) assume a relative
fixity, Adams always leaves himself room to alter the perspective and thus to reveal an unsuspected aspect. It is in this

respect that the otherwise very suggestive comparison of the
'Education' to a late Gothic cathedral(63) ultimately must be
abandoned, for if Adams had built spatially as he built his
two great literary edifices, the building would have fallen
down.

The multiplicity of aspects from which Adams views his life
is announced in the table of contents which he added for the
trade edition of 1918. (In the privately printed 1907 edition
the chapters had no titles, only dates.) Five of the first six
chapters are given the names of towns or cities, but only one
chapter thereafter (chapter twenty-two) is honoured in this
way. One chapter is named after a real human being (President
Grant), another after a fictional one (the protagonist of
Carlyle's 'Sartor Resartus', Teufelsdrockh). Several chapters
have single abstract nouns as titles: Treason, Diplomacy,
Eccentricity, Chaos, Failure, Silence and so on. Others have
abstract notions, such as Political Morality or The Perfection
of Human Society. Some chapters are mirror-images: The
Height of Knowledge and The Abyss of Ignorance, Vis Inertiae
and Vis Nova. Others still fall into no particular category, as
is the case with Twenty Years After which contrives to be
both a statement of fact and an oblique allusion to a historical
novel by Alexandre Dumas Père. This considerable heterogeneity
exacerbates the already heterogeneous time-scheme of the book,
in which a majority of chapters purport to deal with a single
year, others purport to deal with two consecutive years or a
four-year period or (in the case of the first two chapters
only) longer periods - and none at all confines itself to the
years it is ostensibly dealing with. The eccentricity of the
book is not unfairly represented by the fact that there is a
gap of twenty-one years between chapters twenty and twenty-
one, as if to justify the numbering of the latter.

'The Education of Henry Adams' is not the only book whose
real contents are only hinted at by the table of contents. The
titles which Adams provides are as various as those found in
most biographies, and it is as a biographer that Adams pretends to proceed, at least until the pretence proves untenable
or simply dispensable. As biography, it is unreliable to the
point of distortion, especially in the early chapters; has a
huge lacuna in the middle; and towards the end abandons
facts for theories of history. Indeed, from the point of view
of biography, the 'Education' is much more deserving of
criticism than the biographies Adams claimed to dislike, an
irony that was doubtless not lost on him and must have pleased
him. But the biographical stance is only one of Adams's many
roles, a partial perspective only, displaced in favour of other
roles that qualify it and ultimately throttle it. These other
roles are analogous to the biographical role in that they all
involve Adams, to a greater or lesser degree, in playing the
part at which he was most expert: that of historian. This enables Adams to dramatize the political conflicts and social

changes that affected a whole generation of Americans and
altered, or in Adams's view, ought to have altered, their
attitude to the nature of things in the widest sense. There
are times when the figure of 'Henry Adams' occupies so min-
uscule a position in the background that it is almost as if he
has effectively ceased to exist. But the figure is an immensely
resilient one, heroic in its own helplessly passive way, and
is never quite killed off, least of all when the 'biographer'
speaks, Chateaubriand-like, from beyond the grave.

Adams belittles his titular hero from the beginning, describing
him in the preface as a 'manikin', a little man or, worse, an
inanimate dummy. 'The object of study', Adams writes, with
an emphasis designed to make us forget the existence of a
'subject', 'is the garment, not the figure.'(64) The unimportance
of the figure is obliquely reaffirmed in the first paragraph of
the first chapter, a single serpentine sentence at the end of
which, oppressed by all that has preceded it (literally, as
well as linguistically), a child gets born and named. This is
the first of the many births and deaths that stud the book,
and it is both dwarfed by history and at the same time high-
lighted by it in a paradoxical manner that sets the tone for
everything that follows. The Adams figure is from this point
on perpetually ending the world and beginning it again, which
is why the 'biographer' begins his second chapter with another
account of Adams's birth from a slightly different perspective.
This foregrounded motif which accompanies what is really
'background' information, is a way of planting, without explanation, the seeds of what will later be A Dynamic Theory of
History, without reference to, but obviously enough the product of, personal experience. But it is more than a motif; the
very structure of the book is a matter of beginning and ending,
which is one reason why it seems so atomized at first reading.
In each chapter(65) the Adams figure begins the world anew,
traverses a limited part of it, reaches a kind of terminal
point,(66) and then either lapses back towards the point of
origin or tries to turn this terminal point into a new kind of
origin.

In this way Adams sets up peculiar resonances between
chapters, in lieu of a more obvious formal structure. The
last sentence of chapter three - 'He knew not even where or
how to begin' - is echoed in the last sentence of chapter four -
'Education had not begun.'(67) Sometimes the resonances are
distributed over a wider area. The last sentence of chapter
six - '. . . he started with mixed emotions but no education,
for home' - is recalled at the end of chapter eight - 'He
meant to go home.'(68) At the end of chapter fifteen Adams
actually goes home, only to go away again, to return home
again in chapter twenty-one, again at the end of chapter
twenty-five, again at the end of chapter twenty-nine and finally at the end of the last chapter. The fractured structure
of the 'Education' is of a piece with its metaphysical message.

But a longer perspective discloses a simpler pattern: the boy begins at home (in one of the most celebrated and privileged American homes), experiences, like Wilhelm Meister, his 'Wanderjahre',(69) and returns home (the sense of the word having now changed to 'native country') at the end. But the end is also a beginning: 'the new man', Adams writes, 'could be only a child born of contact between the new and the old energies.'(70)

The pattern of deaths and entrances links the personal life of Adams to the public life of his time. The network of relationships is so complex in this area that only a full critical 'triangulation' could hope to reproduce them all. The news of the assassination of President Lincoln reaches Adams in Rome; confronted with 'a world so changed as to be beyond connection with the past' he has no option but to 'spin a new web in some new place with some new attachment'.(71) The news of a serious and ultimately fatal accident to his sister reaches Adams in London; as a result of her death Adams has to 'recover his balance in a new world'(72) in which first nature and then mankind are revealed as 'a chaos of anarchic and purposeless forces'. Only in the second half of the book, where all the downward curves of the first half strive to turn tail upwards, is the Adams figure strong enough to resist the buffeting and keep on course. The news of President McKinley's assassination reaches him in the Arctic Circle and 'upset[s] for the moment his whole philosophy of conservative anarchy'.(73) Instinctively, he turns towards Russia, whose inertia seems at the furthest remove from this 'marvelous' acceleration, and immediately he has to come to terms with a new perspective: 'To recover his grasp of chaos, he must look back across the gulf to Russia, and the gap seemed to have suddenly become an abyss. Russia was infinitely distant.'(74) And yet with the very next sentence the perspective changes again, and he sees 'in full vision' the glacial ice-cap of the North Cape, 'ready at any moment to advance', the very opposite of inertia. At moments of climax in the 'Education' almost no two consecutive sentences have the same point of perspective. And when the subject of inertia returns again three chapters later the context is quite different, the network of relations entirely new and the educational value inestimable, in both senses of the word.

The unfolding drama of the 'Education' is kaleidoscopic: no sooner has one configuration been established than another rushes in to take its place. Every reader of it, as Adams hinted, recreates it for himself. Like his friend Henry James, Adams believed that 'really, truly, relations stop nowhere' and the 'Education' is his most ambitious attempt at drawing the circle in which, in James's words, 'they shall *appear* to do so.'(75) It would be possible to begin one's interpretation of the book with a sentence like 'Rome was actual; it was England; it was going to be America,'(76) or with a group of paragraphs

like those describing Garibaldi(77) as anarchist, sphinx, wild
animal, 'type', patriot and pirate, all of them descriptions that
might be applied, and most of which are applied, to Adams
himself. The life of the manikin is always breaking into halves,
but the art of the writer is always keeping the fragments in
relationship with one another. Sometimes, as in the Rome-
England-America remark, the very syntax has a bifocal quality
to it, connecting and disconnecting at once. The same reason
prompts Adams to exploit the potentialities of individual words,
not only with the word 'education' (where he plays on the two
Latin roots of 'educo-', to rear and to lead out) but also with
words like 'prehistoric' (meaning 'before the birth of Adams'
as well as its more usual definition), 'term' (meaning 'limit'
and 'period of schooling'), 'secular' (meaning 'of the centuries'
as well as the opposite of sacred) and 'standard' (the centre
of a whole complex of moral, economic and military meanings).(78)
The writer who claimed to care little for details provided his
ensemble was in scale evidently wrote the 'Education' with a
passionate attention to small-scale, as well as large-scale,
effects. This is why the 'Education' is at once a difficult and
a simple book. In precisely the same way that the figure
'Henry Adams' learns from Garibaldi 'the extreme complexity
of extreme simplicity'(79) (and then reverses the terms when
it comes to teaching his readers his Dynamic Theory of
History), so the reader learns to expect that there will be
simple answers to baffling questions and difficult responses
to what had seemed on the surface simple.

It is not sufficient, then, to say of Adams, as T.S. Eliot
did, that 'he was perpetually busy with himself.'(80) In the
'Education' he concerns himself quite as much with his reader
as with himself. 'Everyone must bear his own universe',
Adams says on the second page. But he reminds us at the
same time that 'most persons are moderately interested in
learning how their neighbours have managed to carry theirs.'(81)
It seems probable that the reader who is as sceptical as Adams
himself will derive the most pleasure from his book. For he
will not be fooled into believing, as Adams would have him
believe, that the story 'has no moral and little incident'.(82)
Nor will he credit Adams's repeated claim that his book is
the story of an education and not a kind of an adventure
story. The adventures are as manifold as those encountered
by a knight in pursuit of the Holy Grail, and as tangled as
the interlocking narratives of a medieval romance. Adams
plays with his reader in the full knowledge that his reader
will play with him. The charm of the effort, as Adams told
a correspondent, is not in winning the game but in playing it.
In the very important passage describing the St Gaudens
bronze cast in memory of Adams's wife, he does his best to
help his reader see the game for what it is. Adams creates
here a kind of verbal equivalent of the mirror-image with
which the passage ends:

The interest of the figure was not in its meaning, but in
the response of the observer. As Adams sat there, numbers
of people came, for the figure seemed to have become a
tourist fashion, and all wanted to know its meaning. Most
took it for a portrait-statue, and the rest were vacant-
minded in the absence of a personal guide. . . . Like the
others, the priest saw only what he brought. Like all
great artists, St. Gaudens held up the mirror and no
more. (83)

This unconsciously prescient appraisal of what the 'Education'
has become is more attractive and a good deal more accurate
than some of Adams's other prophecies. The book has become,
for American critics at least, 'a tourist fashion', and for most
readers it will remain a kind of 'portrait-statue'. But in a way
that is peculiar to unclassifiable books of the kind I am concerned with here, it concentrates one's attention on the mirror
rather than on the figure of Narcissus. The scrutiny of self,
as we shall see in subsequent chapters, is squarely bound up
with the construction of an art-object that, by virtue of its
multi-faceted perspectives, turns the relationship between
author and reader inside out and gives renewed intensity to
the 'auto' of autobiography.

2 HENRY JAMES: 'A Small Boy and Others' (1913)

Despite a massive amount of critical activity devoted to the explication of what has come to be known (since F.O. Matthiessen's pioneering study) as 'the major phase' of Henry James's writing career,(1) there has been almost no consideration given to a book that is, in its own way and in its own right, as important as 'The Ambassadors' or 'The Wings of the Dove' or 'The Golden Bowl' - the 'attempt to place together some particulars of the early William James and present him in his setting': 'A Small Boy and Others' (1913). This is no doubt partially due to a widespread critical nervousness when confronted by autobiographical literature, but must also have been affected by the intrinsic difficulty of the text and by the misleading opening statement which implies that the book is more concerned with James's philosopher brother than with James himself. Almost all studies of James elect to treat his writing career as if it ended with 'The Golden Bowl', and as if the two unfinished novels ('The Sense of the Past' and 'The Ivory Tower'), the book of memoirs ('William Wetmore Story and his Friends'), the travel book ('The American Scene') and the three volumes of autobiographical writing (of which 'A Small Boy' is the first) were plainly inferior to what had preceded them. But to do this is to succumb to an artificial fragmentation of what is essentially homogeneous, and to fly in the face of James's own sense of his artistic career, memorably described in a letter to his friend Henry Adams in justification of his autobiographical volumes as 'an act of life'.(2) It seems odd that generations of critics, armed with James's celebrated dictum that 'it is art which *makes* life',(3) should have neglected the work that most consistently demonstrates the truth of this remark, and scanted a book that James himself, despite innumerable modest disclaimers, clearly and justifiably thought highly of. For although 'A Small Boy' is grounded in the facts of James's life, it is as self-conscious and deliberate a work of art as any of his more celebrated novels, an experiment as daring as 'The Awkward Age' and an achievement as satisfying as 'The Portrait of a Lady'.

The experimental qualities are perhaps what strike the reader first and give him the impression that James is unsure of what he is about and casting about desperately for a spar to cling to. For in the opening pages James's focus takes in an astonishingly large number of events, all described in daunting and seemingly irrelevant detail, and without any very

serious attempt being made to link one occurrence with
another. But the difficulty here is not merely formal, for the
book begins as a sustained and characteristic exploitation of
the notoriously complicated 'late' syntax that first surfaces
in parts of 'The Tragic Muse' and 'The Spoils of Poynton'
and which reaches its apotheosis in the last three completed
novels. This is the style that led Max Beerbohm to write his
two famous parodies(4) and to speak of three Henry Jameses,
'James 1, James 11 and James the Old Pretender'.(5) James
himself spoke in a letter of the 'mere twaddle of graciousness'(6)
which did service, on social occasions, for genuine communica-
tion, and critics antipathetic to the late James have fastened
on the phrase, appropriating it as a stick with which to beat
him. But whilst there is no gainsaying the fact that James
in his late years wrote - or dictated - in as mannered a prose
instrument as one can think of, it is remarkable how sensitive
and flexible a medium it can be, and it is striking how well-
adapted it is to James's purpose in 'A Small Boy and Others'.
The distinguishing features of this potentially unwieldy and
cumbersome prose have been expertly analysed by others,(7)
and I am not concerned here with isolating stylistic features
at the expense of seeing how James's language reinforces and
articulates his main aims throughout the book. For it is the
coherence of 'A Small Boy and Others' which gives it an
abiding claim on our attention, and which justifies James's
final realization that he had written an essay in the 'science
of aspects' and a portrait of 'the history of an imagination'.(8)

'A Small Boy and Others' is not so much a venture in the
egotistical sublime as 'a tale of assimilations small and fine'(9)
in which, as the title suggests, 'others' play almost as important a role as the child who is father of the man. The title,
for all its apparent casualness, is an accurate description of
the contents, and is more than a mere adjunct to the picture
it identifies. Even the simple connective 'and' is important
here, for what James is primarily concerned with is the
relationship between the unstructured facts of life and the
constructions which the imagination places upon them. The
self-abnegation of the title is an implicit acknowledgment on
James's part that it is not so much the minutiae of one particular life that are important as the manner in which these
minutiae are combined together by the imagination to create
configurations full of meaning. James contrives, in both the
title and the book that follows it, both to demonstrate that
the merely personal and subjective has a value all its own and
at the same time to show that the merely personal has to be
transcended. His avoidance of anything resembling egotism is
both deliberate and, in a sense, involuntary: deliberate in
that he knows that the book would be greatly impoverished if
he gave way to egotism (as any exceptional human being might
wish to do), involuntary in that many of the experiences which

shaped this particular sensibility actively discouraged self-aggrandizement. A dispassionate summary of the facts might satisfy our desire for objectivity; but a passionate selection of the crucial facts offers us something more rewarding: the creation and installation of a subject.

James admits, in chapter thirteen, that he is dealing with 'matters all of a usual cast',(10) as if half-aware that in his fiction-writing he has laboured endlessly to shake off all the dust of the merely 'usual'. Life, he suggests as early as the second page, is inevitably an 'abject little matter'(11) whose 'tiny particles'(12) require moulding and shaping before they can be of much interest to anyone else. But it is precisely out of this 'refuse', 'directly interesting', James reminds us, 'to the subject-victim only, the most branching vegetations may be conceived as having sprung.'(13) This is what James means when he speaks of 'assimilations small and fine', for the facts are both trivial and substantial (and therefore 'small'), attenuated and yet splendid (and therefore 'fine'). James means us to understand the word 'assimilations' in the widest possible sense; for him, as his book everywhere demonstrates, 'to assimilate' means not only 'to absorb' but also 'to be absorbed', not only 'to compare' like with like but also 'to make or become like' something. So the 'small' can at the same time, under the right pressure, be the 'fine', and fine in more than a merely aesthetic sense. In James's own words: 'I somehow feel morally affiliated, tied as by knotted fibres, to the elements involved.(14)

James's image of 'branching vegetations' indicates that, at least as far as he is concerned, his 'tale of assimilations' is essentially organic, one in which each of the elements involved grows out of the foregoing drama. But James's organicism is a controlled one, nature is supported by (and ultimately subservient to) art. James indicates this implicitly in his elaborate gloss on his phrase 'assimilations small and fine': 'Such are the absurdities of the poor dear inward life-when translated, that is, and perhaps ineffectually translated, into terms of the outward and trying at all to flourish on the lines of the outward. . . .'(15) Only the moral affiliation of which James speaks can save this translation from being pointless and self-gratifying, and even then it may be that the translation is ineffectual or absurd. The 'part played' by 'matters of a usual cast' is, in James's opinion, 'all but inexpressible',(16) partly because the memory is fallible and tends to colour the past with qualities it did not possess, and partly because the real complexity of the past is resistant to being categorized by the rational and deliberative present consciousness. At moments like this, James is openly foregrounding the technical difficulty of the task he is engaged in. But at the same time as admitting the difficulty, he is also effectively conquering it. The 'mere scrapings of gold dust'(17) may not, indeed clearly cannot, do service for a

total retrieval of the past.(18) But if the moral affiliation is
there - a much more powerful and more universal affiliation
than - that between son and father or brother and brother -
the scrapings may indeed be golden. In 'Notes of a Son and
Brother', the second volume of autobiographical writing,
familial affiliations interfere with the narrative of a 'fostered
imagination'(19) begun in 'A Small Boy and Others', and the
book seems to suffer from the 'terrible fluidity' of which
James spoke in the preface to 'The Ambassadors'. But in
'A Small Boy', precisely because of those moments in which 'my
father had again, characteristically, suffered me to dangle'(20)
and because the 'knotted fibres' of which James has just been
speaking are always in danger of unravelling, the material is
controlled and shaped into solidity.

It is very characteristic of James's practice in 'A Small
Boy' to embed his theoretical problems in the narrative he is
telling, and then to use them to return invigorated to his
narrative. This is one reason why the narrative, though often
interrupted for purposes of explanation or justification or
prefiguration or lamentation at the impossibility of the task,
has a tremendous forward momentum, a purposive impulse
that will not allow itself to be defeated by minor irritations
and insoluble problems.(21) James's purposiveness is actually
well-served by his apparent inability to resist digression.
There is what Wordsworth might have called a 'wise passive-
ness' about his procedure which only infrequently modulates
into frenetic activity. James indicates how important this
passivity is in a passage in chapter nine, where he once
again talks openly about his difficulties, and once again
conquers them by confronting them:

> The beauty of the main truth as to any remembered matter
> looked at in due detachment, or in other words through
> the haze of time, is that comprehension has then become
> one with criticism, compassion, as it may really be called,
> one with musing vision, and the whole company of the
> anciently restless, with their elations and mistakes, their
> sincerities and fallacies and vanities and triumphs, em-
> balmed for us in the mild essence of their collective sub-
> mission to fate.(22)

The great beauty of 'A Small Boy and Others' is that it
conjures up 'the anciently restless', not least the restless
'small boy' of the title, in full cognizance of the fact that
they are ghosts(23) who might better have been left in
peace, and then gently lays them to rest again. Although
James oscillates from uncertainty to uncertainty, between
extremes of pleasure and discomfort, he always resolves issues
into as tranquil a condition as they can support without falsifi-
cation. In this sense, 'A Small Boy' demonstrates what it is
here discussing, that compassion can be synonymous with
musing vision, and that comprehension and criticism are the
same. The author's vision, in the sense of what he sees, is

composed of 'particles'; but his vision, in the wider sense
of the word, is concerned with universals. The 'haze of time'
which makes vision in the first sense difficult, makes possible
vision in the second sense. For the 'particles' begin, under
the pressure of the artistic imagination, to compose a unity;
the integrity with which James records and evaluates each
particle leads ultimately to a synthesis in which every element
is integrated into a larger whole.

James obliquely advertises the crucial importance of what
is said in this paragraph by inviting the reader to dismiss it
and then revealing that, if he does so, he has missed the
point completely:

> Which reflections, in the train of such memories as those
> just gathered, may perhaps seem overstrained - though
> they really to my own eyes cause the images to multiply.
> Still others of these break in upon me and refuse to be
> slighted; reconstituting as I practically am the history of
> my fostered imagination, for whatever it may be worth, I
> won't pretend to a disrespect for *any* contributive
> particle.(24)

Here, as in his discussion of 'assimilations small and fine',
James's reflexive technique is at its most subtle, for the
'contributive' particle here is not so much a past fact as a
present reflection that operates retroactively upon past
facts.(25) This is important to the whole tone of the work,
because by this means James makes 'A Small Boy' appear to
be a self-generating work (and thus 'organic' in the strict
sense)(26) when it is inevitably predetermined by the facts
of what has happened. James is not simply constituting the
history of his imagination; he is reconstituting it by means
of an imagination that is still intensely alive. The imagination
operates, as James implies in the next sentence, in an un-
historical way, or rather, it can control the vision of the
past and arrest it for contemplative purposes: 'I left myself
just above staring at the Fifth Avenue poster and I can't but
linger there while the vision it evokes insists on swarming.'(27)
A complex effect is created here, in which two kinds of vision
are evoked, the retrieved image of the small boy of fifty years
previously, and the philosophical resignation of the contemporary
man who, on the author's own admission, has 'cause[d] the
images to multiply,(28) and swarm. 'I left myself' also means
more than its surface meaning, for in the course of the previous paragraph, James has indeed 'left himself' in order to
speak of 'we' and 'us' and a truth that he hopes will be uni-
versally acknowledged. It is by lingering with his imagination
that he retrieves himself again, and can proceed with his
'recherche du temps perdu'. Having looked with 'due detachment', he has not only comprehended 'the main truth'(29) but
also exemplified it. His reflections have taken on the status of
'criticism' and criticism has become, by virtue of the serpentine
syntax, 'one with musing vision'. Throughout 'A Small Boy and

Others', James is offering his reader dualisms that, properly
understood, form part of a single fabric; the 'palace of art'
and the 'house of life'(30) are ultimately seen to be different
aspects of the same thing. The business of 'translation'
threatens to disintegrate the seamless web; but the imagination
reintegrates and reconstitutes it.(31) The author's 'pressing
back' into 'a vanished world'(32) involves reciprocation and
interaction and ends in 'pressing pursuit rewarded',(33) the
most abiding reward being to find the past as alive and contemporary as the present. James dramatizes this with great
subtlety at the beginning of chapter eight:

> To look back at all is to meet the apparitional and to find
> in its ghostly face the silent stare of an appeal. When I
> fix it, the hovering shade, whether of person or place,
> it fixes me back and seems the less lost - not to my
> consciousness, for that is nothing, but to its own - by my
> stopping however idly for it.(34)

The gallery of 'ghosts' in 'A Small Boy and Others' is
extremely extensive, but much the most poignant of all these
'others' is a figure who is not really an 'other' at all: the
dream figure whom James encounters in the 'palace of art'
(the Galerie d'Apollon in the Louvre) and pursues - much
as he has 'pressingly' pursued his past in 'A Small Boy'. This
is the only section of 'A Small Boy' that has received anything like the volume of interpretation that the book as a
whole deserves,(35) which has had the unfortunate effect
of suggesting that none of the rest is worth extended study.
In fact this celebrated moment can only be made sense of in
the context of the whole book, and should not be separated
from it. For whatever else it may mean, in James's mind it
confirms that the continuity between his past and his present
selves has not been broken. James has been occupied up to
this point in chapter twenty-five with elaborating what Paris
.in the 1850s meant for him, and in particular with the role
the art galleries played in helping him to crystallize a sense
of 'Style' out of the ever-present atmosphere of 'mystery'.(36)
This crucial discovery is described in terms that connect it
with his discovery of 'Europe' at the end of chapter twenty.
In this first discovery the chance perception of an old peasant
woman makes 'a bridge over to more things than I yet knew'(37)
and Europe comes to seem a place of 'sublime synthesis' by
contrast with an America which has seemed to contain only
antitheses.(38) But only at the Louvre, the essence of Paris
as Paris is for him the essence of 'Europe', does James feel
himself 'most happily cross that bridge over to Style'.(39)
And only in the Galerie d'Apollon does James achieve 'a
general sense of *glory*'(40) that is far removed from the
sordid 'vie de province' which first awakened him to 'Europe'.
At the same time this new sense of a world 'raised to the
richest and noblest expression' is accompanied by an intensi-
fied awareness of the 'local present fact'(41) that has initiated

the whole process. It comes as something of a surprise, therefore, that James chooses this moment to describe 'the most
appalling yet most admirable nightmare of my life',(42) since
it not only runs counter to the 'local present fact' - being
a dream experienced 'many years later' in time - but also to
the sense of style that has been extracted from 'mystery' -
being quite as 'ineffable', 'inscrutable' and 'incalculable'(43)
as James's first experience of the paintings of Delacroix.

James's 'dream-adventure' is the only really 'extraordinary
experience' among the 'matters all of a usual cast' that are
the staple of his autobiography, and James makes no attempt
here, as elsewhere he almost always does, to offer a gloss on
what the experience means. This is because his primary purpose is to establish the Galerie d'Apollon as a much more
'splendid scene of things'(44) than any of the American 'scenes'
that have preceded it. But the absence of an interpretative
gloss is also intimately connected with the fact that he is for
a moment genuinely at a loss to know how best to confront
the decisive influences on his life:

> who shall count the sources at which an intense young
> fancy (when a young fancy *is* intense) capriciously,
> absurdly drinks? - so that the effect is, in twenty connec-
> tions, that of a love-philtre or fear-philtre which fixes
> for the senses their supreme symbol of the fair or the
> strange.(45)

The hallucination is not strictly speaking a 'source' (since it
is explicitly after the fact) but it is certainly a philtre which
fixes a symbol. At the same time it is in direct contact with the
source, not just because it is set in the place which first
gave James 'a general sense of glory', but because it is
'founded in the deepest, quickest, clearest act of cogitation
and comparison, act indeed of life-saving energy'.(46) James
hints here that the dream, despite its intense reality, is a
symbolic one between warring principles within himself, a
psychomachia in which his better nature triumphs and he saves
his life. And it is precisely in this sense that it is the most
important of the 'redemptive accidents'(47) James speaks of
later, dependent not on a considered and deliberate response
but rather on an 'inspired reaction'.(48) James stresses that
his behaviour, when confronted by his antagonist, is impulsive
and irrational, expressive of the deepest roots of his nature,
and he implies that, precisely in so far as the antagonist
'sped for *his* life'(49) so he, James, has pursued the figure
for his. The author sees himself first as defending the room
which has been a 'place of rest' for him against an intruder
and then turning aggressor by pursuing the intruder 'through
an open door'.(50) The image of the door recurs in the last
chapter of 'A Small Boy' when James speaks of how the experience of old Boulogne enabled him to think of himself as
something more than a small boy, and thus to discover 'a
part of myself previously quite unvisited and now made

accessible as by the sharp forcing of a closed door.'(51) The
dream, concerned as it is with a place that has been previously
visited, makes accessible to James not just a part of himself
but his whole self. The 'great point of the whole', James
writes, 'was the wonder of my final recognition,' and the final
recognition is that his 'young imaginative life . . . of long
before, the sense of which, deep within me, had kept it
whole' has not deserted him.(52) The element of circularity, of
self-fulfilling prophecy, with which James ends his account of
the dream, acts as a kind of proof of the unity and integrity
with which James has carried out his whole enterprise: 'The
"scene of something" I had vaguely then felt it? Well I might,
since it was to be the scene of that immense hallucination.'(53)
     James is exploring in the dream the idea that life is a drama
and an adventure which compels the artist, the possessor of
an 'intense . . . fancy' to engage wholeheartedly with it.
Throughout 'A Small Boy and Others' James indicates that the
consciousness of the small boy is constricted by agencies
over which he has little control, which prevent him from
actually being anything.(54) In the dream he engages in an
activity that indicates he has the chance to be something;
in this respect it is indeed an 'act . . . of life-saving energy'.
The 'final recognition' is that the 'imaginary life' need not
be a sterile and frustrating one, but rather a means of
creating life, one's own life most of all. The dream becomes
in a way the justification for writing the book at all, and is
left without comment because it must be allowed to speak for
itself. The act of writing 'A Small Boy and Others' stands
revealed as a re-cognition, with the end-product being as
much a matter of 'reconstituted history' as the paintings of
Delaroche that James had seen fifty or sixty years before in
the École des Beaux Arts.(55) It is no accident that James,
in writing of his discovery of 'form' in the Louvre, should
make us think, just previous to his account of the 'dream-
adventure', of the very book we are reading, and of how
subtle its artistry is:

> It was as if . . . [the forms] had gathered there into a
> vast deafening chorus . . . the influence rather of some
> complicated sound . . . than of such visibilities as one
> could directly deal with. To distinguish among these, in
> the charged and coloured and confounding air, was diffi-
> cult - it discouraged and defied; which was doubtless why
> my impression originally best entertained was that of those
> magnificent parts of the great gallery simply not inviting
> us to distinguish. They only arched over us in the wonder
> of their endless golden riot and relief . . . opening into
> deep outward embrasures that threw off the rest of monu-
> mental Paris somehow as a told story, a sort of wrought
> effect or bold ambiguity for a vista, and yet held it there,
> at every point, as a vast bright gage, even at moments
> a felt adventure, of experience.(56)

James's dream is one of those magnificent parts of his
book that do not 'invite us to distinguish'. And yet it leads,
like the door into the glorious hall, into 'deep embrasures'
which 'throw off' and throw into relief - in both senses of
the word - the 'told story' of an exceptional life. 'A Small
Boy' is full of these 'wrought effects' and 'bold ambiguities'
that are a 'gage' for the reader. And a 'gage' in both the
main senses of the word, for they are both a challenge to
the reader to make sense of them and a pledge deposited as
security that sense can be made of them; James's prose is
both monumental as befits a memorial, and mobile as befits
a 'felt adventure'. In chapter thirteen James describes a
journey by boat in which 'the great swing of picture and
force of light and colour were themselves a constant adventure'(57) and treats his childhood throughout as an adventure(58)
and a romance.(59) But it is the adult James who makes it so,
and who translates the facts of experience into a moving
picture. Earlier in the book James laments 'the lost art of
daguerreotype'(60) and remembers how inadequately dressed
he was for the exposure - another word used in more than
one sense - which followed. But he found in 'A Small Boy'
a more flexible art form, which makes the 'exposure' both
more enduring and less embarrassing. 'If one tries to evoke,'
he writes at the end of chapter five, 'one must neglect none
of the arts, one must do it with all the forms';(61) and it is
precisely because James uses all the forms of which he is
master that the book is such a remarkable evocation.

At the same time it is clear that the visual arts have a
special place in James's pantheon. 'A Small Boy' is full of
references to paintings and drawings, to the illustrators of
Dickens,(62) to Hogarth,(63) and to the young William James,
whom James belatedly retrieves drawing under the lamplight,(64)
only to lose him again almost immediately. (He retrieves him
again in a passage in which he discusses 'W.J.'s eclipses',
tries to suggest that he 'must again and again have delight-
fully lost myself',(65) and then finally forgets him.)
But what James is interested in is not so much the vision of
others - however much they may have helped him to visualize
London, Paris, Europe or America - as his own vision. The
early pages of 'A Small Boy' insist that we see the small boy
gaping in puzzlement and wonderment at the world(66) whilst
suffering from an 'inward blankness'(67) resistant even to
'incorrigible observers'.(68) This 'vague vision' is 'filled
in'(69) partially by books, especially by books that are themselves 'a state of vision'(70) and which impinge retroactively
on life, but 'filled in' more fully by the theatre (see chapter
nine, passim), by travel, and finally, and most importantly,
by life itself. There is an amusing passage at the end of
chapter thirteen in which a cousin of James's is reprimanded
for 'making a scene' which, like the other moments that to the
adult James seem like a 'door flung open' (the Galerie d'Apollon

and old Boulogne), reveals to him that 'Life at these intensi-
ties clearly became "scenes"; but the great thing, the immense
illumination, was that we could make them or not as we
chose.'(71) It is striking how, as the book proceeds, James
ceases to harp upon the idea of gaping at an out-of-focus
world and feelings of inward blankness, and gradually allows
a picture to come into focus, to become a 'scene' which will
give 'a sense of fulness without ever being crowded'.(72)
The important stages here are the moment when James first
'realizes' Fourteenth Street,(73) when he tries his hand with
a brush and devotes himself to 'the idea of representation',(74)
and when he 'realizes' Europe.(75) But really the whole book
is devoted to the subject, and the adult James cannot help
thinking in terms of frames,(76) landscapes,(77) and the neces-
sity of 'taking in' what is seen.(78) James links this with the
problems that surround translation of the inward life into the
terms of the outward and admits that his subject-matter has a
tendency to be '*any* particular point of the past at which I
catch myself (easily caught as I am) looking about me.'(79)
But he saves himself by supporting the predominantly visual
stimuli with other sensual perceptions until it does indeed
seem as if, as James claims later on in the book, that 'to
look or to listen or to touch . . . [are] somehow at the same
time to probe, to recover and communicate, to behold, to
taste, and even to smell.'(80) James is dramatizing here the
ultimate oneness of all experience, which is what his prose,
with its persistent mixed metaphors, strange alterations of
tone and labyrinthine syntax, has all along been demonstrat-
ing.

    Indeed one of the more important strategies of 'A Small
Boy and Others' is to present not only the private experiences
of the young James, but also the public experience of a generation. In this respect 'Notes of a Son and Brother' goes a
good deal further, although it is clear that even this first
volume of memoirs constitutes what Robert Sayre has called
'an autobiography of manners'.(81) In 'A Small Boy' James is
all the time juxtaposing large abstractions like America and
Europe, and seeking 'types' or 'cases' which will illustrate
a point about their respective customs and manners. This is
a reflection of the 'moral affiliation' discussed earlier, and
makes one think of 'The Education of Henry Adams' (1907),
otherwise so dissimilar a work(82) although it obviously provided enough of a negative stimulus to compel James to write
a different kind of book. James speaks time and time again
of his 'education' or lack of it, but never in the pessimistic
strain of Adams, and he clearly sees the education of his
eye, or rather the education of his taste, as the crucial
theme of his book. 'A Small Boy' is full of individuals who,
for James, have become 'types', from Mlle Delavigne, his
governess ('how large a sense of things her type and tone
prefigured'),(83) through the 'case . . . of being no case

at all' (the 'spectral spouse' of cousin Helen),(84) and so
on up to Monsieur Ansiot who 'impressed me as with an absolute ancientry of type, of tone, of responsible taste.'(85)
'My cases', James admits half-way, 'are of course given, so
that economy of observation after the fact . . . becomes
inspiring,'(86) and it is clear that he is using these types
and cases as organizing foci in much the same way as he had
used the 'données' of his short stories and novels. Indeed it
almost seems as if the very 'flatness'(87) of the American
scene(88) requires certain types(89) to be installed upon it,
in order that it should not seem entirely featureless.

Although it cannot be said to be James's primary purpose,
'A Small Boy' brilliantly reconstructs a society that is rootless
and shifting, where old and trusted values still peep through
from time to time but only as besieged outcrops of civilization.
The book is full of a nostalgia for a lost culture, tempered
by a determination to point the way towards a new one. James's
reference to the 'scrapings of gold dust'(90) is therefore
more than a mere metaphor; for the world he is depicting
still preserves traces of the 'golden age'.(91) At one point he
even speaks of his book as a 'sketch of a lost order',(92)
but he is clearly in a sceptical state of mind about this order,
and there is a moment in chapter eleven when he admits:
'if . . . ["Uncle"] hadn't so spoken of an order in which
forms still counted it might scarce have occurred to one that
there had ever been any.'(93) James's sensitivity to the 'lost
order' of American life had been sharpened by a return visit
to America, which led to the writing of 'The American Scene'
(1907), another immensely nostalgic book.(94) But the return to America seems to have stimulated him to reaffirm that
it was form that mattered most to him, and which ought to
matter most to others. This explains James's obsession in
'A Small Boy' with 'realities of relation',(95) realities which
are, for him, as a passage at the end of chapter two demonstrates, constitutive of true being:

I at any rate watch the small boy dawdle and gape again,
I smell the cold dusty paint and iron as the rails of the
Eighteenth Street corner rub his contemplative nose, and,
feeling him foredoomed, withhold from him no grain of my
sympathy. He is a convenient little image or warning of
all that was to be for him, and he might well have been
even happier than he was. For there was to be the pattern
and measure of all he was to demand: just to *be* somewhere -
almost anywhere would do - and somehow receive an impression or an accession, feel a relation or a vibration. He was
to go without many things, ever so many - as all persons
do in whom contemplation takes so much the place of action;
but everywhere, in the years that came soon after, and
that in fact continued long, in New York still for some time,
and then for a while in London, in Paris, in Geneva,
wherever it might be, he was to enjoy more than anything

the so far from showy practice of wondering and dawdling
and gaping; he was really, I think, much to profit by it.
What it all appreciably gave him - that is gave him in
producible form - would be difficult to state; but it seems
to him, as he even now thus indulges himself, an education
like another: feeling, as he has come to do more and more,
that no education avails for the intelligence that doesn't
stir in it some subjective passion, and that on the other
hand almost anything that does so act is largely educative,
however small a figure the process might make in a scheme
of training.(96)

James's 'strange sense for the connections of things'(97) is
one of the qualities that distinguishes him from the people
around him, and this is one reason why he thinks persistently
of himself and his family as 'queer' and 'weird' and 'odd'.(98)
But from his adult perspective it seems to him as if a concern
with connections and relations is almost a spiritual matter in
the context of the materialism that seems to dominate other
lives. This is why in 'A Small Boy and Others', James reveals himself as a determined enemy of 'art without grace' and
'presence without type'(99) - it is a characteristic Jamesian
conflation to suggest that they are essentially the same thing -
and an earnest advocate of things that will add 'a grace to
life'.(100) Late in the book James admires the way in which
the underprivileged of Boulogne 'make grace thoroughly
practical and discretion thoroughly vivid',(101) and throughout
the book he employs religious terms like 'consecrated'(102)
and 'beatitude'(103) to show that 'with a big installed conscience
there is virtue in a grain of the figurative faculty.'(104)

James is justifiably suspicious of what he calls a 'homeless
freedom',(105) because his 'small boy' experiences a multiplicity of homes in his early years. When, in Boulogne in the
last chapter, the small boy understands 'the opposition between
a native race . . . and a shifting colony',(106) James is
clearly expecting us to infer that his own native race had been
little more than a shifting colony. This is one reason why
James organizes his narrative around buildings: the houses
he has lived in, the houses he has visited, the schools he
has been educated at, the art galleries in which he has
educated his taste. In a book which is, in more than one
sense, a study of interiors, houses are used persistently as
an index of moral qualities, as in such novels as 'The Spoils
of Poynton'. And the recurrence of the motif allows James to
trace 'realities of relation' between 'the house of pain' and
'the house of delight',(107) or between 'places of confine-
ment'(108) like school, and places, like the Galerie d'Apollon,
where one breaks free from one's imprisonment. All these
buildings are mansions in what James calls 'the house of
life',(109) but it is clear that the house of life will collapse
without the 'palace of art'(110) to buttress it. R.W. Stallman
has spoken of 'the houses that James built'(111) and it is

common knowledge that James thought of certain houses as
'the great good place',(112) which makes it all the more
strange that one of his most imposing edifices, 'A Small Boy
and Others', in which the house of life and the palace of art
are in continual reciprocal relationship, should still be waiting
for appreciative readers to occupy it. For just as the house
on Fourteenth Street became for James 'a sort of adventure
of the spirit',(113) so 'A Small Boy and Others' - beginning
as an 'attempt to place together some particulars of the early
life of William James'(114) - became a way of anchoring his
imagination. 'Really, truly', James wrote in one of the prefaces
for the New York edition of his novels, 'relations stop nowhere,
and the exquisite problem for the artist is to draw . . . the
circle in which they shall *appear* to do so.'(115) In conquering what he at first saw as 'the drawback . . . of seeing the
whole . . . in each enacted and recovered moment,'(116)
James solved the problem so well that, as Percy Lubbock said
after his death, his life - both the life he lived and the
'life' he was writing - was not a mere succession of facts,
but rather 'a deeply knit cluster of emotions and memories,
each one steeped in lights and colours thrown out by the
rest.'(117) James himself wrote in a letter to his sister-in-law:
'The book I see and feel will be difficult and unprecedented
and perilous - but if I bring it off it will be exquisite and
unique.'(118) Unique and unprecedented it may not be;
perilous and difficult it certainly is. But in the last analysis
it is its exquisiteness that makes 'A Small Boy and Others'
one of James's great late masterpieces.

3 W.B. YEATS: 'Reveries Over Childhood and Youth' (1914)

As any reader of his 'Collected Poems' cannot fail to be aware,
Yeats practised the art of self-scrutiny with a vocational
diligence and rigour. But the most substantial testament to
Yeats's obsession with himself is inevitably the book known
in England as 'Autobiographies' and in America as 'The Autobiography of William Butler Yeats'. The slight, and yet crucial,
difference between these titles is a reflection of the peculiarly
undefined status of autobiographical writing which we shall
encounter again and again in this study. For although the
last edition seen through the press by Yeats offers itself to
the public, with the author's imprimatur, as a unified work,
the best authorities - even those who treat it as one work -
are agreed that it 'lacks unity of form',(1) despite Yeats's
subtle and persistent quest, as manifest in his prose as in
his poetry, to 'hammer [his] thoughts into a unity'. The
American title will no doubt continue to have its apologists
and adherents, but the English title recommends itself for
any number of reasons. First, the four sections which comprise the book were written at separate times and at one time
or another published separately; second, each section has its
own distinctive character quite unlike the other sections; third,
taken singly or collectively they hardly begin to satisfy the
expectations that 'the' autobiography inevitably arouses;
fourth, there is another work, the recently published 'Memoirs'
so-called, which covers some of the same ground as the first
two parts of 'Autobiographies'; fifth, and most important, the
English title uniquely conveys the feeling that was habitual to
Yeats, best expressed in the title poem of the volume 'The
Tower' in the words 'Myself must I remake'.

These writings have been, as Peter Ure said many years ago,
'strangely neglected'(2) although they were by all accounts
'most carefully composed'(3) and in Ure's opinion are 'worthy to
rank with Keats's "Letters" as one of the most remarkable and
explicit accounts of "the growth of a poet's mind" which we
possess'. They are certainly remarkable, though whether they
may be truly called explicit is more contentious, especially
in the case of the work I shall deal with here, the first (and
to my mind the most satisfying)(4) of Yeats's prose attempts
at confronting his life. Yeats began the book in the January
of 1914 and finished it (or at least dated his preface to it)(5)
on Christmas Day of the same year. He initially intended to
call his book after one of his brother's watercolours, a colour

36

reproduction of which was published in the first trade edition,
but 'Memory Harbour: a Revery of Childhood and Youth' gave
way to 'Reveries' and finally to the title by which it is known
today.(6) It is ironic that we should find Yeats vacillating
here between 'a revery' and 'reveries' much as he must have
done a quarter of a century later in collecting his autobiographies together and deciding, surely correctly in the first
case (if not the second), for the more accurate and more
evocative plural. More accurate, because the thirty-three
sections of the book, though tonally unified, offer themselves
as individual 'epiphanies'; and more evocative because the
word 'reveries' is being used by one of 'the last romantics'
as it had been used by one of the first, Rousseau, in his
'Reveries d'un promeneur solitaire'. But although Yeats is
very much a 'solitary' in his 'Reveries', he is never quite
so 'alone upon the earth'(7) as Rousseau felt himself to be,
in exile at the end of his life. And 'epiphanies', which
inevitably makes one think of Joyce's Stephen Dedalus and
his applied Aquinas,(8) is also perhaps a little misleading
in the context of a study that is intent on driving a wedge
between a certain kind of autobiography and the much more
familiar 'autobiographical novel'. But 'epiphanies' has at least
the virtue of reminding us of the deliberative and cerebral
aspect of what Yeats is engaged in, and thus alerting us to
the fact that 'reveries', derived from the French word for
a dream and in one of its senses connoting 'day-dreams',
also means, in both English and French, 'contemplations'.
These two meanings(9) of the word appear to point in opposite
directions; on the one hand, 'reveries' implies haphazard and
aimless experience of a passive kind, and, on the other, it
suggests active mental effort with a particular end in view.
The charm, and indeed the greatness of Yeats's 'Reveries'
resides in the way that Yeats makes these two meanings seem
but the two sides of a single coin. In the words of the epigraph to the important volume of poems 'Responsibilities' -
published in the same year in which 'Reveries' was written -
'In dreams begin responsibility.'
    It may, perhaps, be symptomatic of Yeats's bifocal attach-
ment to both these senses of the word that the book was first
published privately (as if the dedication - 'To those few people
mainly personal friends who have read all that I have written' -
was to be given its full, restrictive value) and then, a month
later, published in America and six months later in England. It
is difficult to think of a neater way of satisfying both the
impulse towards privacy (which the author could not have
been alone in feeling) and the need to present a public self to
the outside world. The dedication is in fact more important
(and more carefully worded) than such things usually are:
it offers the book to those close to Yeats, his family implicitly,
his personal friends explicitly, but also to anyone who has
felt sufficiently attracted to him to have read everything that

he has written.(10) This latter category is, as Yeats is sadly
forced to acknowledge, smaller than he would have liked,
although it cannot have been so small as he (perhaps deliberately erroneously and at the very least self-pityingly) imagined,
for the trade edition of 'Reveries' went into a second impression almost immediately. The usefulness of the dedication now,
when Yeats has, in Auden's phrase, 'become his admirers',
is to remind us that, to understand 'Reveries' fully, we ourselves should have read all that he has written. Yeats is
signalling, I think, beyond the immediate vicinity of his
family – who are at the same time being reassured that there
are 'few' readers beyond them – that the work we are to read
will make demands of us quite as severe as any of his more
obviously difficult poetry.

Yeats's preface is no less elaborately ingenuous than his
dedication. It consolidates the image of Yeats as an isolated
figure looking 'here and there' for 'someone to talk to',(11)
a Wandering Aengus indeed, but also – in so far as the book
seems to have exorcized certain obsessions – a Wandering
Jew.(12) But alongside this image we are obliged to place
the unnamed 'friend' that Yeats is intent on conjuring, unnamed because, unlike Wordsworth in his account of 'the
growth of the poet's mind', Yeats has no one specific in
mind.(13) In this preface Yeats is offering the reader the
opportunity of not reading his book if he does not want to,
but at the same time trying to establish what kind of book
it is, and delicately suggesting that the friend of his youth
who 'may remember something in a different shape' may not
be the optimum reader of 'Reveries'. Yeats contrives to seem
very timid, not wanting to offend the youthful friend whom
he has obviously lost contact with (for otherwise he could
have consulted him), and at the same time very self-possessed,
having 'changed nothing to my knowledge' but knowing all
the time that he 'must . . . have changed many things without my knowledge.' This is more than a mere admission of
fallibility designed to establish his credentials as a sincere
memoirist; it establishes at the very beginning of the work that
the author is not in complete control of his raw materials and
further that there is an element of mystery enveloping the
whole question of memory and knowledge. This mysterious
element, combined with the abrupt non sequitur of the opening
paragraph(14) (in which Yeats moves suddenly from the oral
medium to the written medium) and in the context of the sub-
merged suggestion that Yeats has been haunted by ghosts
that may never return again,(15) is obviously important in
preparing the reader for a narrative that will concern itself,
for much of the time, with things that do not have a rational
explanation, a narrative, in short, that is not so very far
removed from the wild and occult stories collected in 'The
Celtic Twilight' (1895) and 'Rosa Alchemica' (1897). The 'Celtic
Twilight' narratives are predominantly, as one title would have

it, 'dreams that have no moral,' concerned with legendary
figures of myth and fable, and 'Reveries', for all its patient
elaboration of a 'human, all too human' situation, which inevitably gives it a moral colouring, is ultimately concerned
with something not so very different from the life of the poet
as legend. Those few commentators who have paid the book
the attention it deserves have expressed some doubts as to
whether Yeats has achieved, by the end of it, the integration
of self that he seems to be seeking, and have pointed to the
sudden sadness of the final section as a disturbing element
in the fabric of 'Reveries'. But a vein of melancholy runs
throughout the book, and is even advertised in the preface,
which is also, of course, an 'afterword', in time if not in
space. The preface and conclusion of 'Reveries' are in intimate relationship one with another;(16) they represent a
reversion away from the quietly heroic self-aggrandizement
of life into legend, in a characteristically Yeatsian self-
criticism of an enterprise that has been effectively accomplished,
and thus make the book not simply a collection of 'dreams that
have no moral'(17) but also a systematic assemblage of what
we might call 'contemplations that have a moral.'
   Important as it is to understand these preliminaries, the
real interest of 'Reveries' is obviously in the thirty-three
sections of the book proper. These vary in length from the
very short (for example VIII, XVIII, XX and XXXIII, the
last and shortest of all) to the surprisingly long (for example
V, and those preceding it, especially the very first of all)
and it is clear that Yeats is deliberately exploiting the 'rhythm
and pattern' that this variation necessarily creates.(18) But
it is as much a matter of tone as of tempo, the 'bewildered'
child of section V giving way to the 'temperate' clergyman
headmaster of section VI, the mysterious cousin suffering
'remorse' at the end of section VII contrasting with the
'romantic excitement' of Yeats at the beginning of section
VIII.(19) It would indeed be difficult to find a better text
to illustrate Stephen Shapiro's contention that autobiography
is 'the art of juxtaposed perspectives'.(20) Much of its
vibrancy and dynamism derive directly from the unpredictability of its unfolding, its non sequitur quality. But together
with this there is also an implicit sequitur operating between
sections adjacent to one another and even between sections
that appear to have little to do with one another. Three
years later, in the second part of 'Per Amica Silentia Lunae',
Yeats wrote of how 'when all sequence comes to an end, time
comes to an end'(21) and it remained one of his abiding dreams
to experience his soul 'in an eternal possession of itself in
one single moment',(22) but despite the fractured sequence of
'Reveries' and the stress on the simultaneity of memories
(especially, but not exclusively, at the beginning of the book),
the book is ongoing in time, and not drastically unchrono-
logical.(23)

Yeats's later theory of history is helpful here, for his
belief that time moves in cycles does not allow him to believe
that men can ever be free of time. The late play 'Purgatory'
shows how even beyond the grave we may have to live over
certain events of our lives again, in the 'dreaming back' phase,
as 'A Vision' calls it.(24) 'Reveries' is by no means a book
designed to bring 'time . . . to an end', although the decision
to write it at all has obviously involved the author in treating
his past as something finished, an object of contemplation.
This is perhaps why Daniel Harris is moved to suggest that
Yeats 'holds . . . problems at arm's lengths by means of a
carefully gauged aesthetic distance'(25) in 'Reveries', and
it is certainly one of the most important strategies available
to Yeats in his attempt to transform the naturalistic minutiae
of life into a symbolic whole. But the total effect of 'Reveries'
is more complex than Harris suggests: the juxtaposition of
apparently unrelated mosaics of narrative not only creates
distances (between us and them, between Yeats and them, and
between each other); it also insinuates that there may be a
thread linking them all together and thus collapsing distances.
The narrative is never wholeheartedly naturalistic, but it
is also never unashamedly symbolic; its ingenuousness is
actually the product of a very considerable ingenuity. The
dreamlike unfolding of the narrative invests every element with
an aura of mystery which even repeated rereadings will not
entirely dispel. And since Yeats is seemingly unable, and more
than a little unwilling, to provide a gloss or an explanation,
the elements remain in a kind of glazed suspension one with
another. But unlike in an actual dream, where events succeed
one another without the agency of the dreamer, Yeats is all
the time exercising his faculty of choice and modelling the
whole in accordance with an implicit principle of selection
that will make sense of the whole.
    'Reveries' begins with an oblique sequence of recollections
from early childhood in which it 'seems as if time had not yet
been created.'(26) This arresting opening, where Yeats presents
memories that are 'fragmentary and isolated and contemporaneous'(27) (or at least would like us to believe them so), is
an attempt, as Daniel Harris has remarked, at 'mythification
of his origin'.(28) But it is only a tenative one, and one which
is abandoned almost at once in favour of actual 'thoughts
connected with emotion and place.' Like many of his most
famous poems, 'Reveries' is very much concerned with 'place',(29)
with Sligo and its environs cast in the role of Terrestrial
Paradise and London and its environs cast in the role of Hell.
But Yeats is never concerned with 'place' in isolation, always
with 'place' as it arouses or embodies 'emotion'. Every place
that Yeats refers to - Rosses Point, Knocknarea, Burnham
Beeches, Bedford Park, Hammersmith, Holland Park etc. - is
part of an education in sensibility, teaching the potential poet
that the world is more manifold and mysterious than some

people would have him believe. Most, though not all, of the
emotions of which he speaks are of the more painful kind,
from the 'night of misery' in the first section to the involuntary movements that Yeats experiences in the séance in the
last section but two.(30) And even when Yeats is almost too
young to know what emotion he is feeling - when, like the
'gaping' small boy of Henry James's first volume of autobiography, he is simply 'looking'(31) - the world reveals its
harsher aspects to him, 'a wall covered with cracked and
falling plaster,' 'a mastless toy boat with the paint rubbed
and scratched' and a boy in uniform about to blow up London.
In the second paragraph Yeats associates two separate acts of
'looking' (one 'out of an Irish window', the other 'out of a
window in London') but shifts in doing so from the past tense
to the present, which is then retained for the more prolonged
Sligo memory that follows. This strange shift of tense is
accompanied by an implicit contrast between an Irish house
in which 'some relation once lived' and a London one that
is on the point of being blown up by a boy that Yeats does
not know. All these details seem, at first glance, 'fragmentary
and isolated' but the total effect is so highly charged that one
begins to suspect there is more here than meets the eye. Why,
we are almost bound to ask ourselves, is Yeats living with his
grandparents rather than his parents? Why is he fascinated
by the 'long scratch in the stern' of the toy boat? What does
his gnomic utterance - 'It is further away than it used to
be' - really mean?(32)

Yeats nowhere explicitly answers these questions. But a
patient and imaginative reading of the rest of 'Reveries'
provides at least the glimmerings of an answer. In Section II,
for example, Yeats concentrates on a 'very fast and beautiful
ship'(33) that is fairly obviously related in some way to the
toy boat of the first section. These early sections are dominated by images of the sea and ships (as if in confirmation
of Yeats's later claim that 'All my dreams were of ships'),(34)
and it is only half the story to say, as Daniel Harris does,(35)
that 'Reveries' is 'a work dominated by houses, furnishing,
interiors,' which makes it sound more like a book by Henry
James. Nearly all the crucially important events of the book
take place in the open air. Yeats says at one point that he
had 'a literary passion'(36) for the open air, but it is clear
that his passion went somewhat deeper than this, and that he
saw the natural world as an escape from the enclosed and
claustrophobic world of his own family, a refuge in which he
could find infinite resources. In the very first section he
describes how he escaped from his grandfather's house at
night throught a back gate that was never locked;(37) in
section II he describes how his grandfather escapes shipwreck
in a steamer and how one of the Middletons designs a boat;(38)
later in the same section he tells of how he was first made
drunk;(39) in section XIV he describes how he made his home

in a cave;(40) section XVII describes in detail Yeats's Thoreau-like fantasies;(41) and the high point of section XXI is the description of a light moving at great speed up the mountain Knocknarea.(42) Yeats's first boat is only a toy, and a damaged toy, mastless and scratched; and only the kindly words of his great-uncle can console him for the irretrievable and irremediable loss of a plaything that epitomizes his need to escape. These are the first, and most poignant, of the many words of wisdom that Yeats hears and indeed expresses, and they are spoken by someone outside the purlieu of his immediate family. Yeats leaves these inferences to the reader's imagination for a number of reasons, uppermost among which is a feeling of guilt that is not confined to his feelings about his father. At the beginning of 'Reveries' it is not only the toy boat which is further away than it used to be; it is Sligo and the Ireland that he is intent on celebrating in the book he is writing. Yeats disguises this again at the beginning of section X when he speaks of an old woman who 'made me miserable',(43) ostensibly because of her nostalgia. But this old woman - who is, like the old woman at the beginning of 'Ulysses', an image of Ireland - is also to be found in the early and autobiographical story 'John Sherman', where she makes the hero miserable by saying 'Why don't ye stay among your own people?'(44)

It is clear, however, from the rest of 'Reveries', that it was Yeats's father who had obliged him to leave the country in the first place, so even here the father's role cannot be ignored. This is one of many areas in which he finds his father to be something less than perfect. It was very shrewd of one of Yeats's friends to bewail the fact that Gosse had already published his 'study of two temperaments' 'Father and Son', and to relate Yeats's 'Reveries' to it;(45) in both works there is considerable, if disguised, hostility between the two key figures. It becomes very clear, later in 'Reveries',(46) that his father's influence has been crucial and basically benign, but that it is an influence that he must ultimately transcend and leave behind if he is to be a figure in his own right. Yeats's feelings about his father are made as clear in 'Reveries' as his father's still being alive allows them to be, and will feature largely in my later discussion. But it is the third member of what Freud called 'the family romance', Yeats's mother, who had died in 1900, who remains a shadowy figure of almost indeterminable purport. There are two explicit references to her in section V: the first establishes her beauty, the beauty of Sligo (with which she is equated), her love of stories and the fact that 'her desire of any life of her own had disappeared';(47) the second describes nervously how she taught him to feel disgust for the way the English lacked sexual reserve.(48) Later, in section XIII, Yeats records how his father praised her 'intensity',(49) a quality that Yeats himself increasingly subscribes to in literary discussions with his father. There is nothing inherently suspicious in Yeats's apparent reluctance to talk about his mother, although any psychoanalytic account is likely to speculate on her effective absence. Brenda Webster, in the only such account that gives a sustained argument, has actually suggested that the mastless boat of the beginning is an unconsciously symbolic representation of Yeats's mother, whom he felt to be 'emotionally unavailable to him', and has interpreted the 'cracked wall' as part of a screen-memory of his mother.(50) It is true that almost all of Yeats's guarded discussions of sexuality bear his mother's Puritanical imprint. But to go much further, as Brenda Webster does, and to propose that at the opening of 'Reveries' Yeats is voyeuristically observing a 'primal scene' of parental intercourse, seems to be making an already oblique book into something of a cryptogram.

'It is further away than it used to be.'(51) This first utterance in 'Reveries' is very much the type and measure of all: first, in that it is spoken by Yeats - all the spoken words in 'Reveries', whoever says them, seem to have a Yeatsian quality about them and, second, in that it is uttered in a way that does not brook argument. Almost all the direct speech that Yeats chooses to remember has this quality, from the unexpected excursus into Gaelic in section V(52) to the remarks of his grandfather and his uncle in the penultimate section.(53) Since almost all of these utterances are isolated *aperçus* and not one of them gives rise to anything like a conversation, they have the effect of making Yeats seem even more isolated than he admits himself to be. But they also have another, and more positive effect: they are remarks made under the stress of great personal emotion, and have an intensity that makes them memorable and dramatic.(54) The child's attraction for passionate speech and the young littérateur's recommendation of intensity are clearly of a piece.

Yeats's ideas on 'intensity' derive directly from his father, as the conclusion to section XIII obliquely admits.(55) But the young boy obviously lived intensely before he responded to his father's theories and it seems fair to conclude that the theories simply confirmed the son's instincts. Later, Yeats says that he took his father's ideas further than his father wanted them taken by defining truth as 'the dramatically appropriate utterance of the highest man', and by preferring 'personal utterance' above everything.(56) 'Reveries' is full of 'dramatically appropriate' utterances of a personal kind, partly so that Yeats should be able to indulge his penchant for such things, but also to enable him to dramatize his theme. For the book is full of figures of authority, from the grandfather whom he confuses with God and, later, King Lear(57) (and whose death obliquely ratifies Yeats's increasing occultism) to the figure of John F. Taylor, the great orator, who dominates section XXVIII. Yeats is attracted by authority, but

also intent on escaping from any authority but himself. One
of the most dramatic moments in 'Reveries' is when Yeats
rounds on a putative professor of political economy and utters,
completely out of the blue, a damning sentence on his notions
of education. It comes as no surprise to find Yeats, in the
immediately subsequent section, reminding us that he 'wished
to become self-possessed' and was 'only self-possessed with
people I knew intimately';(58) the writing of 'Reveries' is
as much a struggle for self-possession and self-definition as
any of the more celebrated poems. This is one reason why
there are so many schoolmasters in the book: there is the
one who survives the shipwreck in section II,(59) the clergyman and paedophile of section VI,(60) the headmaster who is
vying with Yeats's father for control of the boy in section XI(61)
and who, like Yeats's father, is disrespectful of church and
clergy, and finally Professor Dowden, in whose drawing-room
Yeats almost re-encounters his old headmaster.(62) As the
pendant to this latter incident indicates, Yeats is determined
to define himself by his own ideas and beliefs and is happy
to bring about confrontations with authority that he thinks
he can win. As he says in the long genealogical third section,(63) 'I am delighted with all that joins my life to those
who had power in Ireland.'(64) In this sense, 'Reveries',
like the 'Responsibilities' volume that immediately preceded
it, is an assertion of power.

Yeats indicates as much in section XXVIII, when he contrasts the Fenian John O'Leary(65) with the academic Edward
Dowden. As a child, Yeats had thought he would 'like to die
fighting the Fenians';(66) but he ends up fighting the provincial academic:

He [O'Leary] had the moral genius that moves all young
people and moves them the more if they are repelled by
those who have strict opinions and yet have lived common-
place lives. I had begun, as would any other of my training,
to say violent and paradoxical things to shock provincial
society, and Dowden's ironical calm had come to seem but
a professional pose. But here was something as spontaneous
as the life of an artist.(67)

As spontaneous as the life of an artist, and yet *not* the
life of an artist, for 'he would speak a sentence . . . and
would forget it the moment after.'(68) Yeats is seeking a
more permanent form of utterance, for only then will he
achieve his desire to become 'the poet in the presence of
his theme'.(69) He is hypnotized by the great orator Taylor
and 'made a good many speeches' but, unlike Taylor, 'more . . .
as a training for self-possession than from desire of speech.'(70)

The idea of self-possession dominates the latter half of
'Reveries', but it is latent in Yeats the child as well, as when
he and his sister sit, 'very happy, drawing ships with their
flags half-mast high'(71) on the death of their younger
brother, Robert. It is, incidentally, striking how many Yeatses,

Pollexfens and Middletons either die, or are brought close
to death, in the narrative of 'Reveries',(72) and this alone
makes it permissible to wonder whether Yeats could really
have been genuine when he told his sister that the book
should be seen as 'some kind of an "apologia" for the Yeats
family'.(73) Although Yeats's happiness at his brother's
death can be perfectly satisfactorily explained as an instance
of the heedless amoral behaviour of a very young child, it
is also quite possible, in the context of the book as a whole,
to see it as a delight at the disappearance of a possible rival.
Yeats later pays his surviving brother Jack, the painter,
a great compliment, implying that Jack has been more successful in his chosen field than he has been in his. But Jack's
success very obviously exacerbates his tendency to melancholy,
and Jack is little more of a presence in the book than he was
in Yeats's life. The incident of his brother Robert's death
liberates Yeats in a way that will later prove very important.
Although Yeats remains afraid of death at the end of section
IV - and indeed is still afraid of it at the end of the book -
he plucks up enough courage to tell his grandmother that he
does not want to go with her when she visits bedridden people,
because they will soon die. There is an obvious defensiveness
here, but it is perhaps not too far-fetched to see the germ
of the 'cast a cold eye, on life, on death' philosophy surfacing
here as well.(74)

Yeats's account of the death of his brother Robert is also
important in the way it enables Yeats to introduce two other
themes that will be developed later in 'Reveries'. The first
is the spirit world, the second is sexual love. Yeats later, in
section XXV, acknowledges the influence on him as a young
man of psychical research and mysticism, and in section XXXI
describes in detail how he was affected at a séance. The day
after the death of his brother he hears 'people telling how my
mother and the servant had heard the banshee crying the
night before he died'(75) as if announcing the event. Yeats
clearly intends his readers to be as impressed as he himself,
as a young boy, was, by the widespread belief in magic among
the ordinary people of Sligo; there is little evidence in
'Reveries' of his later nervousness when asked whether he
actually believed in the forces of the occult. Indeed, in the
very first section of 'Reveries' Yeats suddenly jumps forward
in time to within six months of his book's composition, in
order to underline that he has retained, as an adult, the
ability to credit those moments when the real and unreal
worlds interact with possessing a miraculous power:

> Only six months ago my sister awoke dreaming that she
> held a wingless sea bird in her arms and presently she
> heard that he ['the youngest of my uncles,' William Middleton
> Pollexfen](76) had died in his mad-house, for a sea-bird
> is the omen that announces the death or danger of a
> Pollexfen.(77)

An analogous instance from the past is the 'supernatural bird' of the next section(78) which occurs in connection with the shipwreck of Yeats's grandfather. Other references to the cries of birds are less straightforward. Section XVI ends with the adolescent Yeats hearing birds at night crying 'as if in their sleep,'(79) with a spontaneous eloquence at the opposite remove from Yeats's desperate attempts to be wise and eloquent in society, against which behaviour they are no doubt obscurely warning him. In the middle of the following section (XVII) Yeats stresses how important it was to him to 'notice the order of the cries of the birds'(80) as the dawn broke over the Isle of Innisfree. Other references to cries that seem to have a part to play in this elaborate sub-text are the 'squeal' of the shot rabbit in section X(81) and the cry of the drunken child in section II.(82) It is almost impossible here not to be reminded of Yeats's 'Collected Poems'. The Tower ends with 'a bird's sleepy cry'; part three of Meditations in Time of Civil War ends with the scream of Juno's peacock;(83) part four of 'A woman young and old' ends with the shrieking of 'a miraculous strange bird'; Paudeen ends with Yeats longing for 'a sweet crystalline cry'; and throughout his later work he seems obsessed with the idea that a bird will cry out 'in a strange tongue' and announce the end of the world. The one common denominator in all these scattered references to birds is their annunciatory aspect, and it seems likely that the birds in 'Reveries' are performing a similar function. They are like emissaries from the spiritual world announcing his predestined dedication to poetry, warning him when he goes astray, and reminding him that, in the terms of one of his most famous poems, only 'an aching heart' can create 'a changeless work of art'.

Human voices, by contrast, seem to Yeats 'full of derision'.(84) Only inhuman voices like those he hears at the séance of section XXXI, are of assistance to him, or those voices which, as we have already seen, have a kind of disembodied absoluteness about them. The spirit world provides a solace for Yeats because it indicates a survival after death, for the dead return to have commerce (and even conversation) with the living, and thus are an intrinsic part of history.(85) It is interesting that the penultimate section should end with Yeats describing how the degradation of his grandfather's house began 'before he was dead':(86) it is almost as if life is more a matter of inevitable decay than actual demise. At the same time Yeats wants the reader to be aware of the deeper significance of the death of his grandparents. Yeats's grandfather did not in fact die until Autumn 1892,(87) six years later than the latest event recorded in 'Reveries' which, as Yeats told his father, takes the story up to 1886. The death of his grandfather, whom he has associated with God and sought, in his own way, to emulate, seems to sever him once and for all from Sligo and all that Sligo represents. (It is important to notice

that these are Yeats's maternal grandparents, with whom he
is living at the beginning of his narrative.) The very presence
of his grandfather at his grandmother's deathbed brings back
the 'childish fear'(88) so powerfully articulated in the very
first section of all, and thus inscribes a partial circle in
structural terms. It is no surprise to find Yeats, in the final
section, 'sorrowful and disturbed', for the mature unhappiness
of the end is bleaker than the childhood misery of the beginning, and there is no great-uncle to say a consoling word.
Yeats's reference to the recurrence of his 'childhood fear' is
not intended to indicate that history repeats itself and that
the circle can be closed; instead, history stretches out in
front of him, 'a freedom without meaning' (as Daniel Harris
has rather existentially put it), a series of incomplete
spirals.(89)

The death of his brother Robert is not the first death
in 'Reveries', but it is the first of the deaths that a chronological account would have dealt with, and the first death that
comes at all close to Yeats, even if he and his sister do not
allow it very close. It is, as Yeats tells us, his first 'realisation of death'.(90) But Yeats's narrative is more sequential
than chronological, and this allows him to create a more complex configuration than would otherwise have been possible.
In section IV his brother's death follows hard upon a paragraph that ends with 'the first breaking of the dream of
childhood'(91) at the discovery of the 'mechanism of sex'.(92)
Yeats is striving for a very complex effect here: he wants to
show us that the 'realisation of death' was not so great a
threat to the childhood world of reveries as sex was. But he
also wants to reassert, like the 'last romantic'(93) he is, the
close connection between sex and death. Subsequent references
to sex in 'Reveries' are equally ambivalent. Yeats cannot help
admiring the paedophiliac schoolmaster of section VI, because
he criticizes the school, because he is unashamedly anti-
English and because he believes the young Yeats to be clever.
But in the subsequent section (VII), where Yeats describes
himself as 'proud as a March cock'(94) at the thought that
he will one day be famous, Yeats darkens the mood by bringing
up the picture of the remorseful cousin who has 'speculated'
in a more mercenary, but equally damaging, way. Similarly,
section XIV begins with Yeats talking of 'the great event' of
a boy's life, 'the awakening of sex', and then almost immediately
shifting the focus, first to 'somnambulistic country girls',(95)
then to the realization that his solitude was necessary, and
finally bringing the focus to rest on a description of a cave
in the cliff that he would sometimes spend the night in. Yeats's
'content'(96) with his cave is ruined by the discovery of
lovers, presumably – though this is left to the reader to infer –
'in flagrante delicto',(97) and only the ghost of an evicted
tenant reappearing there soothes him. Yeats obviously sees
himself as the evicted tenant and, as in the case of the banshee

whose wailing led him indirectly to assert himself before his
grandmother, it is the spirit world that he has to thank for
the return of his cave.(98) Yeats contrives to make his own
agency in the matter both absurd and obscurely magical,
and it is difficult to believe that the sudden mention of
'eggs'(99) in close proximity to the lovers can be entirely
accidental: 'I had been trying to cook eggs, as I had read
in some book, by burying them in the earth under a fire of
sticks.'(100) This is quite possibly the same book that Yeats
has described himself reading at the end of section IV(101)
and like that book – an encyclopedia – it is both necessary
and unnecessary. It is necessary in the sense that it informs
the young Yeats of the facts of life, and unnecessary in that
he sees it as a useful buffer against the discomfiture of
sexuality,(102) although it is plainly inadequate in this respect.
In the latter part of 'Reveries' Yeats makes a poem – Shelley's
'Prometheus Unbound' – into his 'sacred book',(103) but by
this time he has unbound himself, 'conquered bodily desire
and the inclination of my mind towards women and love.'(104)

Yeats never allows us to forget that his interest in books
and the creation of literature has a peculiar relationship to
his fascination with sexual matters. In section XVII he mentions
how his uncle's servant mistook his nocturnal rambles for
sexual adventures, and then goes on to describe how these
rambles contributed to his first long poem, 'The Wanderings
of Oisin'. This follows on from a description of his uncle
George Pollexfen who is praised as a 'man of diligence and of
method, who had no enterprise but in contemplation' and whose
only experiences have been 'a voyage when a young man' and
'a love affair, not I think, very passionate'.(105) This uncle,
who is also interested in magic, is clearly an avatar of Yeats
himself, not least in his overwhelming melancholy; but Yeats,
by contrast with his uncle, is about to embark (as section XX
indicates) on his first passionate affair. This short section is
one of the climaxes of 'Reveries' but only achieves its full
resonance if we see it in the context of the two almost equally
dramatic sections which precede it (XVIII and XIX). The first
of these is a description of a play based on a fable that bears
some resemblance to 'The Player Queen',(106) the second a
collection of no less 'fabulous' anecdotes about courtesans,
English wickedness and the Queen of Sheba. The first re-
iterates the connection between sex and death; the second ends
oddly, with an account of how a heavenly angel saved a young
jockey from being 'led into temptation' and how the young
jockey then did 'something disgraceful about a horse'.(107)
Yeats's vagueness here – the word 'something' is left even more
undefined in the very last words of 'Reveries'(108) – is
obviously not merely a function of defective memory; he is
wanting to bring into relationship sex, death, writing and a
horse. In section XX, when Yeats describes his love for 'a
wild creature' who drives a pony-carriage and who has asked

him 'to ride beside her',(109) Yeats's only guardian angel is
the bad poetry that he writes to her and the intractable
circumstances of the woman's love-life.(110) Sections XVIII,
XIX and XX are all, in other words, closely related to each
other, without surrendering their intrinsic individuality. These
apparent non sequiturs are in reality subtle sequiturs.

By no means all the sequiturs of 'Reveries' are as oblique
as these. Section V, for example, ends with Yeats lamenting
the fact that 'we [i.e. himself] . . . cannot bring our flesh
to heel' and section VI begins with the clergyman schoolmaster who might have been supposed to be of some practical
value in achieving this aim.(111) Section VIII talks of pic-
tures(112) and section IX of poetry. Section XV ends with
Yeats junior and Yeats senior talking solely about style, and
section XVI begins with the young man making social gaffes as
a direct consequence of this extreme aestheticism. Rather as
in a collage, Yeats encourages us to think that elements in
close proximity or actually contiguous are related one to
another, however different they may seem. Even the deeply
puzzling last few words yield a meaning when they are considered in the context of the book as a whole: 'all life weighed
in the scales of my own life seems to me a preparation for
something that never happens.'(113) The 'something that never
happens' is that one's life cannot, even through the agency of
art, be made into a legend: the personality and the mask never
quite coincide. As Wolf Künne has suggested, the death of
Yeats's grandfather means the death of Yeats's myth of himself.(114) There is no finality in life, not even at the moment
of death.

In a letter written at the beginning of the month in which
he died, Yeats reiterated that 'Man can embody truth but
he cannot know it,' and in as early a story as 'Rosa Alchemica'
Yeats had realized that 'even in my most perfect moment I
[will] be two selves.'(115) In this early story Yeats dreams
of a book that would be 'a fanciful reverie over the transmuta-
tion of life into art, and a cry of measureless desire for a
world made wholly of essences.'(116) 'Reveries Over Childhood
and Youth' is clearly more than 'fanciful', and it ends pessimi-
stically with an absence of essence, and life stubbornly resistant
to being transmuted into art. But the dream of the writer of
'Rosa Alchemica' is at least partially satisfied in 'Reveries', for
its quality is of the kind that makes one think a kind of alchemy
has taken place.(117) It is like, as Yeats says elsewhere, trying to get a huge balloon into a narrow shed in a gale,
and the struggle can never be assured of success. Yeats returns to the task in his subsequent autobiographies. But the
more he tries to 'hammer [his] thoughts into a unity', the less
successful he becomes, at least in the genre of autobiography.
Only in 'Reveries Over Childhood and Youth' does 'the balloon
of the mind' seem secure in its narrow shed.(118)

4 BORIS PASTERNAK:
'Safe Conduct'
(1931)

> I wrote this book, not as one among many, but as if it
> were my only one . . . [it is] the most important thing of
> all that I have done . . . if [the reader] does not get
> interested in 'Safe Conduct', the rest of my work cannot
> and should not be of interest to him.(1)

A quarter of a century before the completion of the work by
which he is best known in the West, 'Doctor Zhivago', Boris
Pasternak wrote the first and most substantial of his 'autobiographical sketches',(2) 'Safe Conduct', published in 1931.
As an example of 'the prose of the poet Pasternak', as Roman
Jakobson(3) very artfully labelled it, it is perhaps the most
intriguing and demanding of all Pasternak's essays in a mode
that, for most of his creative life, was secondary to the writing of poetry, until 'Zhivago' and the creation of 'a novel in
prose'(4) assumed the character of a 'Lebenswerk'. But any
reader coming to 'Safe Conduct' expecting the drama of Tolstoy,
the spontaneity of Aksakov, the energy of Gorky, or the
sweep of Herzen - especially a Western reader for whom the
'Zhivago' affair transformed Pasternak into a special kind of
hero - cannot fail to be surprised by the structure and style
of the book, and the almost perfect self-effacement that Pasternak accomplishes from beginning to end of it. 'Safe Conduct'
is at the farthest remove from the Romantic self-dramatization
that the Western world thinks of as one of the hallmarks of
the Russian character, and is about as remote from the conventional self-portrait as it is possible to be.

There are a number of what we might call 'contingent'
reasons which help to explain why 'Safe Conduct' is so restrained and reticent. Pasternak's emotional life was in some
turmoil at this time, and his first marriage was breaking up.
His second 'autobiographical sketch' alludes to this, without
in fact acknowledging what the problem was:

> Soon after this [the visit of the Georgian poet Paolo Yashvili
> in the winter of 1930] there were painful upheavals, changes
> and complications which involved two families, my own and
> that of some friends of mine.(5)

More importantly, however, Pasternak was threatened at a
public level: in 1925 the Central Committee of the Communist
Party issued a literary manifesto that implicitly interfered with
the freedom of the writer to express himself as he wished, and
in a journal of about the same time Pasternak was caricatured

as a sphinx-like creature nervously pontificating from a podium
as elevated as an ivory tower. In 1929 - the year that Zhivago
dies - Stalin assumed complete control of the party machinery,
and began to put into practice the principles of 'socialist
realism' that became obligatory after 1934. On publication 'Safe
Conduct' was indeed widely denounced for its 'idealism' and
within two years Pasternak was effectively silenced. In this
respect, clearly, the book was far from being the 'safe conduct'
that the author may have hoped it might be, and for nearly
ten years thereafter Pasternak worked at the altogether safer
business of translation.

But it would be wrong to over-emphasize these 'contingent'
reasons for 'Safe Conduct' being as it is. And wrong, too,
to place excessive emphasis on the influence exerted on Pasternak by the writer to whom the book is dedicated. 'Safe Conduct'
is written 'to the memory of Rainer Maria Rilke' and begins with
a description of how the paths of Rilke and Pasternak once,
and once only, crossed. In the fifth section of the first part
of the book, Pasternak testifies to how important Rilke's
writing was to him as an adolescent, and much of Pasternak's
fascination with the way in which external things illustrate
or mirror internal feelings is obviously attributable to the
profound effect that Rilke's thinking on this subject had had
on him. But Rilke is not referred to beyond this point, and
the book is at no time a slavish imitation of Rilke.(6) Rilke
matters to the writer of 'Safe Conduct' not because of himself
and his theories, but because he is - like the Mayakovsky who
dominates the third part of the book - a poet of genius.
Pasternak hints as much when, at the end of the fifth section,(7)
he seems to contradict his own dedication: 'I do not present
my reminiscences to the memory of Rilke. On the contrary I
myself received them as a present from him.'(8) 'Safe Conduct'
is not so much an attempt at autobiography or 'autobiographical
sketch' as a history of how Pasternak became a poet, and what
'the life of a poet' actually means. Leading up to the climactic
sentences just quoted, Pasternak is quite explicit about this:

> I am not writing my autobiography. I turn to it when a
> stranger's so demands it. Together with its [i.e. 'Safe
> Conduct's'] principal character [i.e. himself] I think that
> only heroes deserve a real biography, but that the history
> of a poet is not to be presented in such a form. . . . The
> poet gives his whole life such a voluntarily steep incline
> that it is impossible for it to exist in the vertical line of
> biography where we expect to meet it.(9)

It is because of the poet's deep commitment to these ideas that
'Safe Conduct' deals with only a rigorously restricted selection
of the facts of Pasternak's life, and deals with them, moreover,
poetically. As the Russian title of the work, 'Okhrannaya
Gramota', very subtly hints, the book is not only an account
of how the author was conducted safely to the kingdom of
poetry, but also a protective or secret ('okhrannaya') record

or document ('gramota') that requires its reader to penetrate it poetically,(10) if he is to understand it in any meaningful way.

The oblique angle of vision that makes 'Safe Conduct' so strange is not, then, merely wilful perversity on Pasternak's part; it is part of the point that he is trying to make. And although the book may seem to be a perfect illustration of the 'ostranenie', the 'making strange' that the Russian Formalist critics (following Viktor Shklovsky's analysis of Tolstoy) made the cornerstone of their thinking, it is actually endemic to Pasternak, an extension of the technique he had adopted in the poetry that preceded it, most effectively in 'My Sister Life'.(11) For Pasternak only 'makes strange' in order to make familiar, and it is a feature of Pasternak's prose (as of his poetry) to use ordinary language as a counterpart to, and sometimes as a critique of, his attraction for more esoteric and cerebral analogies.(12) As Pasternak said to Alexander Gladkov in 1941:

> A genius is a quantitative extension of a mankind which is homogeneous in quality. . . . If a genius stands in contrast to anyone, it is not to the general public, but to the kind of set which so often, without waiting to be invited, forms a coterie around him. There is no ordinary man who is not potentially a genius.(13)

This is a useful gloss on part three of 'Safe Conduct', where Pasternak repeatedly refers to the hangers-on who accumulated around Mayakovsky. But it also helps to illuminate the crucially important passage at the end of part one, section five, where Pasternak says:

> [The biography of a poet] is not to be found under his own name and must be sought under those of others, in the biographical columns of his followers. The more self-contained the individuality from which the life derives, the more collective, without any figurative speaking, is its story. In a genius the domain of the sub-conscious does not submit to being measured. It is composed of all that is happening to his readers and which he does not know.(14)

This apparent paradox is fundamental to Pasternak's enterprise, in prose or poetry, and it is clear to any sensitive reader that his ostensible 'idealism'(15) is tempered by a thoroughgoing, if by no means orthodoxly Soviet, 'materialism'.(16) Pasternak's conversations with Gladkov in 1942 confirm this again and again, and only differ from 'Safe Conduct' in that Pasternak was at pains to emphasize his 'simplicity' after years of being considered a 'difficult' writer. 'On the sole condition', Pasternak told Gladkov, 'that there is a certain hidden balance and that a certain mysterious proportion is preserved, the greatest complexity in either style or composition may prove to be simplicity.'(17) Pasternak was obviously aware that a book like 'Safe Conduct' was difficult, and that an 'unobtrusive' style - 'a style almost as simple as

the prattling of a child'(18) - was to some extent unnatural
to him. But throughout his career, even in the early writings
that he was later disposed to reject,(19) Pasternak is committed
to life, his 'sister', in a way that is quite alien to exponents
and proponents of 'art for art's sake'. 'For me,' Pasternak
told Gladkov, 'the greatest boon is a life absorbed in the life
of everybody else around me . . . I dream of a form by virtue
of which the reader becomes, so to speak, one's co-author.'(20)
This is precisely what 'Safe Conduct' compels us to be, and
illustrates how astonishingly coherent and integrated Pasternak's
oeuvre is, despite his many changes of direction. For 'Safe
Conduct' is not, despite appearance, an unreadably impene-
trable book; it is, rather, 'one of those books you take along
with you in your suitcase, wherever you may be going, because you hate to be without it and can always open it at
random, at any page, and find something new.'(21) 'Safe
Conduct' is, indeed, the work in which Pasternak demonstrates
par excellence that, despite his critics, he is not self-centred,
but rather stands at the centre of life, where 'nothing is
so extraordinary as the ordinary.'(22)

So intense is Pasternak's awareness of the minutiae of life
that it is understandable that many critics have felt, with
Lezhnev, that 'he is a better colourist than draughtsman.'(23)
But 'Safe Conduct' is by no means so atomized a book as it
first appears. Without by any means sacrificing the sense that
each of the recorded events has no precedent,(24) Pasternak
is clearly intent on developing organically, as in a piece
of music, his 'theme and variations'.(25) Pasternak believes
that 'the world's best creations, those which tell of the most
diverse things, in reality describe their own birth,'(26) and
'Safe Conduct' is reflexive in precisely this way. There are
moments when Pasternak asks himself questions which give
the illusion that the book has been written spontaneously,(27)
and moments when he implicitly invites the reader to refer to
an earlier section for illumination.(28) But most of the time
Pasternak is content to present the reader with a succession
of apparently unconnected facts, periodically interspersed
with patches of more discursive writing - themselves often
highly charged and elusive - about the nature of art and
poetry. It is especially disconcerting to be told at one point
that the unfolding of the book is arbitrary: 'I am purposely
characterising the life I led during these years at random. I
could enlarge these symptoms or change them for others.
But those which have been cited are sufficient for my purpose.'(29) But in part two, in one of his most important
accounts of the creative process, Pasternak tries to show that
there is nothing gratuitous or wilful about his procedure:

Each detail can be replaced by another. Any one is
precious. Any one chosen at random serves as evidence of
the state which envelops the whole of transposed reality.
    When the features of this state are transferred to paper,

the characteristics of life become the characteristics of
creation. The latter strikes one more sharply than the
former. They have been studied better. . . . The interchangeability of images is an indication of the condition in
which the parts of reality are independent of each other.
The interchangeability of images, that is, art, is the
symbol of power. (30)

Pasternak explicitly dissociates himself here from the idea
that the artistic impulse can be 'directed at will where one
wants like a telescope'(31) because it is the impersonality of
art, and not its self-expressive power, that most impresses
him: 'In art the man is silent and the image speaks.'(32)
Pasternak is fairly obviously here erecting a personal preference into a general principle, for as he writes elsewhere: 'a
life without secrets and without privacy, a life brilliantly
reflected in the mirror of a show window is inconceivable for
me.'(33) But it is precisely the power of 'Safe Conduct' (the
power which is the very basis of art in Pasternak's poetics)
that makes the idea more than a merely temperamental inclination, and makes the book an exemplification of the strategies
it is so often discussing. The 'image' in 'Safe Conduct' does
more than merely 'speak'; it speaks volumes.

   The book is so full of passages of memorable but ephemeral
beauty, so full of images of real things substantial yet fleet-
ing, that it would be impossible to enumerate the variety of
devices that Pasternak employs. But Pasternak warns us,
as early as the second section, of the danger of becoming
'a slave to forms'(34) and much of the pleasure of the book
stems directly from the way shapes are allowed to crystallize
and then disperse. In part two, where poetry is seen as a
safeguard or 'safe conduct' protecting one from the blandish-
ments of philosophy, Pasternak opposes 'the mind which takes
one for a healthy constitutional' to 'the mind which leads
one to a given point.'(35) The latter he christens the causal
mind. Already, in the very first section of this second part,
he has warned us what happens to the mind which leads one
to a given point:

   This is all so far away that if imagination reaches back
   so far, at the point where it meets this scene a snowstorm
   rises of its own accord. It breaks out from extreme cold
   in obedience to the rule of the conquered unattainable. (36)

This apparently autonomous snowstorm is Pasternak's way of
indicating to us that the rational mind, the mind which proposes an artificial end in order to hypostatize the flux of
life as a sequence of fixed points, is certain to be defeated
by the quicksilver transformations that are the distinguishing
feature of reality. These only a poet can give voice to, and
only then when he has disburdened himself of the malady of
thinking his own personality is significant. Pasternak has a
particular penchant, as many commentators have noted, (37)
for snowstorms and downpours of rain, not because they are

the standard coefficients for poetic melancholy, but because
these are the moments when life is at its most fluid and mobile.
Pasternak is not, therefore, a trafficker in pathetic fallacies,(38)
but rather an exponent of the idea that man and nature interpenetrate. The 'rule of the conquered unattainable' permits
the poet to present an image of the real, but prevents him
from actually appropriating the real. Art is not, therefore,
a mimetic or straightforwardly reproductive mode; it is instead, in Jakobson's classic formulation, a metonymic
mode.(39)

Pasternak's sensitivity to climatic conditions is one of the
features that is bound to strike any reader of 'Safe Conduct',(40)
and it provides Pasternak with a means by which he can unify
the book. But before looking at this in more detail, there is
another, and related, image that needs to be recognized: the
image of the railway. Pasternak is one of the great (perhaps
the greatest) poets of the railway, as 'Doctor Zhivago' abun-
dantly proves.(41) 'Safe Conduct' begins with a railway
journey, and the first part ends with the author travelling
by rail to Germany. The most dramatic event in the whole
book, the author's trip from Marburg to Berlin and back again
in part two, is once again inseparably connected with the
idea of the railway. At the end of part two Pasternak travels
by train to Venice, and discovers 'the meaning of genius,
that is of the artist.'(42) In part three, with his vocation discovered but a new and much more difficult adversary
(Mayakovsky), the image disappears. Previous to part three
Pasternak has been exploring why he did not become a composer and why he did not become a philosopher; in part
three, despite the great impact that Mayakovsky has had on
him (an impact that has made him despair of being a poet),
he realizes that 'after all my metamorphoses I could not decide to alter course for the fourth time.'(43) The railway
journeys of parts one and two stand revealed as the experience of a personality that has yet to be fully formed, a
person who is forever in transit.

The image of the railway journey that dominates the first
two parts illustrates the paradox that, for Pasternak, all
things are at once unique and yet equivalent to one another.
Each railway journey teaches Pasternak something new, and
yet each is decisively different from the one that precedes it.
This helps Pasternak to dramatize the fact that each alteration in his course involves him in a total revaluation of his
position, and a complete reconstitution of himself from first
principles.(44) But the first principles involved are quite
different from the a prioris of philosophy, and thus preserve
the freshness which, for Pasternak, is the sine qua non of
'real life'. Each time Pasternak reorientates himself he crosses
'over the barriers' (as the title of his second volume of poetry
has it) into a world that is new to the point of incomprehens-
ibility. 'Every love', Pasternak writes, in a warning intended

not only for 'my fellow-travellers in the [train] compartment'
but also for any reader tempted to follow him in the journey
towards poetry, 'is a crossing over into a new faith.'(45)
The context - Pasternak has just come to terms with the
failure of a love affair - indicates that this 'new faith' is
not the faith that is the life-blood of established religion,(46)
but rather the faith that Pasternak has in the miraculous
benevolence of life. In a long and difficult passage in part
three of 'Safe Conduct' Pasternak points out that even death
can be viewed as a 'second birth',(47) and it is obvious that
the writing of 'Safe Conduct' gives a 'second birth' to the
facts of Pasternak's life. (Doubtless, for Pasternak, the fact
that he is about to begin his second marriage is also relevant
here.) Even the death of Mayakovsky, which is clearly part
of a disguised lament on Pasternak's part for what is rotten
in the state of Russia (although Mayakovsky's suicide was no
doubt as much due to emotional entanglements as to his dissatisfaction with the post-revolutionary period), is a kind of
'second birth'. For the death of the poet is the indispensable
preliminary to a balanced and judicious estimate of his achievement. Pasternak's whole aesthetic is committed to the idea
that the work outlives the man and that the object is more
enduring than the subject.

Pasternak's essentially optimistic attitude to life has often
been remarked on. But his optimism is of a distinctly fatalistic
kind. Life is continually presenting him with events that, like
the encounter with Rilke, are 'forgotten, presumably for
ever'(48) only to recur and reassert themselves in later life.
One of the most significant of this kind is his relationship with
his friend G—. Pasternak follows the advice of G— and leaves
Marburg: 'the dull ring of the nickel-plated cutlery died away
behind us, as it seemed to me then, for ever.'(49) Six years
later an 'untimely telephone bell'(50) - as 'untimely' in its own
way as that which signals a breach with Mayakovsky and that
which presumably brings the tidings of his suicide(51) -
announces the re-entry of his friend G— into his life.(52)
Pasternak presents this in a manner that will seem perverse
to a reader who has misunderstood his attitude to life. It is
not the fact that G— has rung up that is 'unexpected';(53)
it is what G— has become that surprises Pasternak. There is
a simple explanation for what seems at first like a miraculous
coincidence. But Pasternak's excitement derives not from the
fact of coincidence; it stems rather from the salutariness of
the reminder that Marburg and all it stands for are things of
the past:

> I had rushed to him as to a Marburger. Not of course so
> as to begin life afresh from that far-off misty dawn when
> we stood in the gloom like cattle at a watering-place. . . .
> O, of course not for that! But knowing in advance that to
> recapture this was unthinkable. I rushed to make certain
> why it was unthinkable in my life.(54)

'Safe Conduct' helps us, at moments like this, to see why Pasternak was so intent on denying the role of coincidence in 'Doctor Zhivago', or rather on making coincidence into something of a metaphysical principle. Life for him is never a static and stable medium, and its coincidences are never mere repetition. The same principle applies in Pasternak's account of how he sees an Italian in Venice whom he thinks he has seen before; it turns out that he reminds the author of a waiter in Marburg who has been one of the people suggesting that he ought to leave the medieval city.

Pasternak's attitude to coincidence - the fact that life only appears to repeat itself - is squarely bound up with his attitude to time, and the sequence of history. The first thing that strikes a reader of 'Safe Conduct' is that the linear chronology of the narrative is continually being fractured by unsequential inter-polations. This has the effect of making time seem like a continuum, and explains why, although the book seems to be (like most con-ventional autobiographies) orientated towards the past, it is actually quite as much (if not more) concerned with the future. A famous line from a poem in Pasternak's 'Themes and variations' brings this paradox into focus: 'It's past. You'll understand it later.' (55) 'Safe Conduct' is not a mere record of the past; it is the past understood. The climactic conclusion to part one, where Pasternak imagines himself in the posture of Lomonosov two hun-dred years before him, shows that the coincidence of past and present can bring the world into sudden focus:

As in the days of Lomonosov scattered at one's feet with the whole grey-blue swarm of its slate roofs, the town resembled a flock of doves enticed in a lively flight towards their cot at feeding time. I was in a flutter as I celebrated the second centenary of someone else's neck muscles. Coming to myself I noticed that the *décor* had become reality....(56)

It is typical of the 'impersonality' syndrome in Pasternak that he can only 'come to himself' with the help of an agency external to him. But what is even more important here is the way Pasternak can bring to life a moment two hundred years in the past and thus breathe life into his own present. His present has become, with the passage of time, his past: but 'Safe Conduct' gives it an eternal presentness. If Pasternak reminds us of Proust here,(57) it is with the important qualification that it is not so much 'time regained' as time collapsed. In conversation with Gladkov in 1941 Pasternak said: 'Everything that really exists does so only within the framework of the present. Even our feeling for the past comes to us from the present.' (58)

As early as 1916, in the essay The Black Goblet, Pasternak was groping towards this idiosyncratic theory of time. In this essay Pasternak distinguishes between 'time' as it turns into 'history' (which we are all a part of) and 'eternity' - which we can never truly know but which is the particular concern of the lyric poet. Since the poet is, in this formulation, at the farthest possible remove from those who 'make history' - a subject we have already seen Pasternak return to in 'Safe Conduct' (part one, section two) - it looks as if the poet is in danger of losing touch with 'time' altogether.(59) Pasternak counters this in 'Safe Conduct' by concentrating on the most important poet of his time, Mayakovsky,(60) and by at all times, even in the densest parts of his aesthetic meditations, trying to see how the lyric poet and his historical circumstances are related. It is no accident that Pasternak, at the end of the poem Variation No. 3, refers to Pushkin's poem 'The prophet' and also gives his autobiographical sketch a title derived (61) from the 'safe conduct' given by God to the prophet Isaiah who 'went unto the people.' The lyric poet is not, therefore, exclusively orientated towards the past; he is also, and more importantly, a prophet of the future. This explains a curious passage on Pushkin in section fourteen of part three:

who will understand and believe that it was suddenly given to the Pushkin of the year 1836 to recognize himself in the Pushkin of any year - in the Pushkin of the year 1936? That there comes a time, when echoes long flowing from others in response to the beats of that primary heart which is still alive, which pulsates, and thinks and wills to live, are suddenly united with a heart that has expanded and is resurrected. That these irregular heartbeats race on and on (62) until finally they are so multiplied that suddenly they become even and coinciding with the beat of the primary heart they begin to live one life with it in perfect harmony. That this is no metaphor....That it resembles death, but is not death, not death at all, and if only, if only people did not insist on an exact resemblance.(63)

As Jakobson was the first to point out 'Safe Conduct' dramatizes events against 'the deep horizon of remembrance'(64) and often the angle of vision is, as Pasternak admits, 'from a very long distance'.(65) But Pasternak knows that this is only a strategy designed to preserve a truth that will be more than transient:

What does an honest man do when he speaks the truth only? Time passes in the telling of truth and in this time life passes onward. His truth lags behind and is deceptive. Should a man speak in this manner everywhere and always?(66)

Precisely because he believes that it is the poet's task to collapse time, Pasternak is suspicious of the time-servers that cluster round Mayakovsky. But he is also suspicious of the extremism of Mayakovsky; for Pasternak 'a generation *preserves* a lyric truth rather than casts one off.'(67)

It may seem strange that a man with an attitude to time like Pasternak's should continually be referring, throughout 'Safe Conduct', to fate. In an important discursive passage at the end of the fourth section of part one Pasternak places the idea in a Greek context, as if to suggest that his ideas on the subject are analogous to the celebrated Greek conception of 'moira':

In her [i.e. Greece's] opinion some portion of risk and tragedy must be gathered sufficiently early in a handful which can be gazed upon and understood in a flash. Certain sections of the edifice must be laid once and for all and among

these the principal arch of fatalism must be laid from the
very outset in the interests of its future proportions.(68)
Previous to this Pasternak has been describing how he wanted
the composer Scriabin to decide for him whether or not 'music...
was my fate';(69) later, at the end of part one, he remembers
that Marburg was one of the stopping-points in the 'fatal journey'
(70) of Giordano Bruno. Later still, describing his abortive love
affair, he goes to V – (71) and 'beg[s] her to settle my fate',(72)
On returning to Marburg from Berlin, his love affair definitively
over, he sees 'my philosophy in its entirety and also its probable
fate'.(73) At the end of part two he acknowledges that his ideas
on the history of culture did not include 'the genius's fate'(74)
which he is about to witness in the career of Mayakovsky. At the
beginning of part three, describing the literary situation just
prior to Mayakovsky's tumultuous arrival, Pasternak indulges in a
justifiable exercise of hindsight – 'the fate of the conjectural poet-
elect was already hanging in the air'(75) – and an oblique predict-
ion of disaster – 'the fate of the movement was to remain a movement for ever.'(76) It is typical of 'Safe Conduct' that Pasternak
should concern himself with all these 'fates' and leave the most
important one of all – the fact that he was fated to become a poet –
for the reader to infer.

Pasternak's ideas on fate are bound up with his ideas about the
future: man cannot be the master of his fate because he cannot
know his future.(77) As he realizes on leaving Marburg, 'I had
to work out the morning's faith in me somewhere in the future.'
(78) Later, describing Mayakovsky in St Petersburg, he sees the
city 'covered with the haze of eternal conjectures about the
future' (79) and in the strangely off-hand conclusion to the elegy
for Mayakovsky which ends 'Safe Conduct', he decides that Mayakovsky was 'spoilt from childhood by the future, which he
mastered rather early and apparently without great difficulty.'(80)
The tone of this final comment is ambivalent: a mixture of admiration and wonderment at the way Mayakovsky strove to become
the master of his fate, and disappointment at the way Mayakovsky
failed to see that the future would always be resistant to his
mastery. Pasternak's own career, as described by 'Safe Conduct',
has been of a signally different kind,(81) and has involved 'great
difficulty'. But he is implying here, without complacency or self-
regard, that he has not been 'spoilt' by it; he is indeed no longer
a child, but an adult. He has, furthermore, managed to maintain
links with his childhood,(82) as Mayakovsky has not.

Pasternak's awareness of the 'palpable strangenesses'(83) of
nature derives from his ability to maintain a childlike angle of
vision even though he has reached adulthood. But he is not merely
regressive or nostalgic in this regard, as he indicates in the
important passage describing his reaction to Berlin when his love
affair has foundered:

I was surrounded by transformed objects. Something never
before experienced crept into the substance of reality....
Birds, houses, dogs, trees and horses, tulips and people

became shorter and more disconnected than when childhood
had known them. The laconic freshness of life was revealed
to me, it crossed the street, took me by the hand and led
me along the pavement.(84)

This is one of the great moments of clear-sightedness that stud
'Safe Conduct', comparable to the moment when the décor of Marburg becomes reality(85) and when the image of Venice is recognized as Venice proper.(86) It is, one infers, thanks to these
moments of clarity that the more discursive and philosophical
sections of the book can be written at all. But there are also
experiences that are at the furthest remove from clarity, moments
when 'we cease to recognize reality,'(87) and these are the moments in which art originates. It is striking how often Pasternak
finds himself driven to use the image of a fairy-tale (88) in 'Safe
Conduct', to apply to the 'fairy-tale holiday' of Marburg,(89) the
'fairy-tale' appearance of an old woman in Venice (90) and also
the 'fairy-tale' appearance of Venice itself.(91) The idea even
creeps in to his discussion of Greek culture, which I have already
referred to: the ancients possessed 'an art that was generalized,
ever unexpected, enthralling as a fairly-tale.'(92) But perhaps the
most powerful embodiment of the idea occurs, appropriately
enough, in one of the passages describing his childhood:

The street was not covered by the low kerchief of the winter
night as usually happened, and seemed to rise from under-
ground at the exit with some dry tale on her barely moving
lips. Along the strapping pavement the spring (93) breeze
shuffled. As if covered by a little live skin the outlines of
the mews shuddered in chill tremors grown cold in waiting
(94) for the first star, whose advent the insatiable sky post-
poned wearisomely, with the same leisureliness as the recital
of a fairy-tale.(95)

Pasternak dramatizes in a passage like this an idea that he has
warned us is of great importance to him: 'life opens for me only in
the place where [the reader] is inclined to balance accounts.'(96)
The moments of clarity, therefore, are at the same time the moments when he 'cease[s] to recognize reality',(97) as 'reality' is
usually understood. This brings us back, after what must seem
to have been an unjustifiably long digression, to the question of
Pasternak's sensitivity to climatic conditions, which I referred to
earlier. Time and again, especially in part one, Pasternak describes how reality is rendered magical and diaphanous by mist, or
rain, or snow, or smoke: these are usually moments when an
important revelation, and hence a clarification, is about to break
upon the writer's consciousness, the visit to Scriabin, for example,
(98) the evening of his attendance at the meeting of the Sirdards,
(99) the description of how 'the sensation of a town never answered to the place in it where my life passed,'(100) the description
of a visit to a flower-seller.(101) Despite his temperamental attraction for moments when all is flux, he is also intent on penetrating
the mist and seeing clearly. Once again Mayakovsky, who never
quite rids himself of flux, is an important education for him: 'He

had as much of the expressive and final about him as the majority
have little, issuing rarely as they do, and only in cases of exceptional upheavals, from the mists of unfathomable intentions...'
(102) The life and work (and indeed the death) of Mayakovsky
enables Pasternak to see through 'the mists of unfathomable
intentions' and to become 'expressive and final' as a poet ought
to be.

It is highly appropriate, therefore, that 'Safe Conduct' should
be a book that comes more and more into focus as we read it, a
book that, like all great art in Pasternak's opinion, describes its
own birth. Part two may end with the young poet in the same
'semi-wakeful state'(103) in which he confronted Marburg at the
end of part one,(104) but it also describes him looking up at the
sky (105) for the Constellation of the Lyre that will confirm that
he is to be a poet.(106) Part three, logically enough, begins with
a discussion of words, the poet's medium,(107) goes on to decry
the way Moscow 'hid behind phrases' of 'artifical brilliance',(108)
and ends with the heartrending words of an actual poem, Mayakovsky's 'I feel that my "I" is too small for me',(109) (Pasternak's
'I' is, of course, exceptionally 'small', which is what saves him
from the fate of Mayakovsky.) The seeds of Pasternak's later simplicity are sown here, in a conclusion that confirms the accuracy
of an earlier and apparently paradoxical, utterance: 'the direct
speech of feeling is allegorical.'(110) It is as if Mayakovsky's
doom has liberated Pasternak from the malady of pretentiousness,
which Pasternak associates with his early devotion to music: 'The
fifteen-year-old restraint from the word, as a sacrifice on the
altar of sound, doomed one to originality as any crippled limb may
doom to acrobatics.'(111) 'Safe Conduct' is not, of course, without its 'acrobatics', but they are the acrobatics of a man who is
temperamentally antipathetic to the medium he is enriching.
'Biography as spectacle' is anathema to Pasternak, but it is a
genre that virtually forces an author to make his life (and the
life of others) into a spectacle.(112) Pasternak was, ironically
enough, fond of comparing the poet to the great actor for whom
there is no gap between role and self,(113) and in the concluding
tableau, the death of Mayakovsky, he notes how 'death had ossi-
fied a mask which rarely falls into its clutches.'(114) This brings
to a perfect climax two images that have been spiralling round
one another throughout the book. In the first two parts Pasternak
has been, in the words of T. S. Eliot, 'preparing a face to meet
the faces that you meet';(115) here, he is confronted by a 'mask'
that is both impersonal and natural (just as Pasternak's own 'mask',
in writing the book, has been). For Pasternak only the person
who has not found his métier – like Pasternak the composer,(116)
or Pasternak the philosopher – is a poseur;(117) but the person
who has found a role that he can play – Pasternak the poet – has
achieved 'external integrity, the hardest of all [poses] for an
artist'.(118)

It is precisely this 'external integrity' that makes 'Safe Conduct'
so much more satisfying than a more confessional account would

have been. As Czeslaw Milosz has written, 'The paradox of Pasternak lies in his narcissistic art leading him beyond the confines of his ego.'(119) Writing of 'Doctor Zhivago', Pasternak told Stephen Spender that for him 'the top pleasure consist[ed]... in having succeeded in rendering the *atmosphere of being*, the surrounding whole, the total environment, the frame where the particular and depicted thing is... floating.' He went on to describe how he wanted the novel to seem 'as if reality itself had freedom and choice, and was composing itself out of numberless variants and versions.'(120) It lies beyond my brief to say whether or not Pasternak achieves this in 'Zhivago' (though it is fair to say that the novel was much less rapturously received by Russians than by the rest of Europe); but it seems to me incontrovertible that he achieved it in 'Safe Conduct', which is indeed, for all its difficulty, 'an honest and direct effort to understand... what constitutes culture and art - if not in general, at least in the destiny of an individual man.'(121)

5 MICHEL LEIRIS: 'L'Age d'homme' (1939)

Despite an international eminence in the field of ethnography and a growing celebrity among American literary critics of a structuralist persuasion, the writings of Michel Leiris remain little known outside his country of origin and have found almost no audience at all in England. Even in France he has had to wait until the 1970s to be accorded the status of a classic, despite a 1963 monograph by one of France's most respected critics in which his oeuvre is praised as 'the most original contribution to contemporary literature since Proust',(1) and despite a 'succès de scandale' with the book that will most concern me here.

'L'Age d'homme' was Leiris's first sustained attempt in the genre to which he has most richly contributed and in which he must be accounted one of the most outstanding innovators: autobiography. It was first published in 1939 and was forgotten in the aftermath of war. But on its second printing, in 1946, it achieved almost instant notoriety. Leiris had by then begun the composition of its much more lengthy and ambitious successor, the four-volume 'La Règle du jeu', in which the whole notion of autobiography is subjected to radical revision. But even without 'La Règle du jeu' Leiris's connection with his most famous book had grown more tenuous with the passing of time, for 'L'Age d'homme' was begun as early as 1931, two years after his secession from the ranks of the Surrealists (who had been the first to encourage him and to publish him), and completed in 1935. 'L'Age d'homme' is not without its Surrealist features, but the crucial influence on the book was a quite un-Surrealist ethnological expedition to Dakar and Djibouti in the years 1931 to 1933. Leiris has recorded how at the time he saw literature and ethnography as decisively different disciplines:

> Coming from an activity almost exclusively literary to the practice of ethnography, I intended to break with the intellectual habits that had been mine until then... and to break down the walls within which I was trapped and to enlarge my horizon to a truly human measure.(2)

'L'Age d'homme', as its title indicates, was clearly an attempt to achieve 'a truly human measure' in literary terms and was the first work in which Leiris explored the question of 'commitment' which his interest in two very different disciplines had obliged him to confront.

A background of this kind may strike the reader of 'L'Age d'homme' as more than a little eccentric, given that the 'human measure' of the book is, at least at first glance, almost exclusively erotic. But there are two conditioning factors that help to explain this. First, Leiris was at the time a close friend of the writer whose name is inseparably associated with eroticism in twentieth-century French literature, Georges Bataille, to whom 'L'Age d'homme' is dedicated. Regarding the role of Bataille, Leiris has said:

> I owe, so to speak, the core of the book to him. Bataille, who by this time had already written *Story of the Eye*, was planning to edit a collection of erotic books. He wanted something from me, but that didn't interest me in the least....Not wanting to do this kind of book, I proposed to Bataille that I should write an autobiographical piece touching on eroticism. I wrote the sections entitled 'Judith', 'Lucrece' and 'Holofernes'.(3)

Second, Leiris had suffered, at the time of his secession from the Surrealists, a kind of nervous breakdown as a consequence of which he began to take a committed interest in, and to seek a cure through, psychoanalysis. Leiris has said of this period

> I underwent psychoanalysis for approximately five years, and I can say that analysis taught me to see myself and to know myself better. Before, I had no sense of unity. I had the impression of doing certain things, of doing others and then not feeling there was any relation between them. I had the impression of totally disparate activities. Psychoanalysis showed me the connections between these varied behaviours. Freud seems of the utmost importance to me. I've remained a Surrealist in this respect... one of the great desires during the Surrealist era was to effect a synthesis, a conciliation, of Marx and Freud, the economic factor and the sexual factor. I continue to think that a true anthropology should be based on these.(4)

The erotic elements in 'L'Age d'homme' are much more clinically handled than anything in Bataille's oevre, not excluding his theoretical study 'Eroticism.' In one sense at least, 'L'Age d'homme' is much more of an auto-analysis than an auto-biography. Leiris has even gone so far as to say that the book was 'written under the influence of Freud whom I believed held the key to everything', although the specific use to which Freud was being put - 'to gather everything I could have in the way of properly Surrealist experiences'(5) - is obviously a long way removed from the life-long enterprise that Freud was engaged in.

It is precisely the presence in Leiris of a strong Surrealist tendency that poses problems for the English reader. Despite a flurry of interest in the years immediately preceding the Second World War, Surrealism, especially the literature of Surrealism, has been of little lasting importance in England, whereas for the French, despite periods of coolness and despite the auto-destructive crises of its leadership, the movement continues to be a seminal one. But although Leiris feels that 'in a certain sense...I am still part of [the movement]',(6) he has also been intimately associated with a movement that has proved more readily exportable: Existentialism.

Although Leiris sees himself as still 'pursuing....what Breton
called "the point at which life and death are indistinguishable",
the place where all contradictions are resolved,'(7) he has also
concerned himself, since the inception of 'L'Age d'homme' at least,
with the Existentialist question of 'engagement' or commitment.
But just as Leiris is only 'in a sense' a Surrealist, so he is only
in a sense an Existentialist: 'I am very fond of Sartre and Le
Castor [Simone de Beauvoir]; I appreciate them as philosophers,
as moralists, as guides; but I am obliged to admit that, personally,
this is not what I am looking for.'(8) This does not prevent Leiris
from feeling that Sartre's 'most beautiful book'(9) from a literary
point of view is his huge 'phenomenological essay on ontology',
'Being and Nothingness'. But it is symptomatic of Leiris's position
in relation to Sartre that he should see 'Being and Nothingness'
as first and foremost a work of literature, intent as he is on finding 'a properly literary form of "commitment" and not a "commitment" which would, in some way, be only a supplement.'(10)

The most important exposition of Leiris's attitude to commitment
is the essay – De la littérature considérée comme une tauromachie –
which was added as a preface to 'L'Age d'homme' on its re-pub-
lication in 1946, and which is almost unique as a theoretical contribution to the problems of formulating a distinctively autobiographical genre. The essay refers only obliquely to Sartre,
although in an interview Leiris summarized its contents in a manner that enabled him to define where he and Sartre part company:

> I have a conception of 'commitment' which differs from that
> of Sartre. I would like a 'commitment' which, of itself, rather
> than through its political consequences, is as dangerous as
> that of the bullfighter facing the bull. By 'dangerous commit-
> ment' I mean a commitment which can lead some to suicide, as
> in the case of Nerval, of Roussel, and of quite a few others,
> which can lead some to madness, and still others, like Rim-
> baud, to wreck their lives.(11)

'L'Age d'homme' has come to seem, by comparison with the cases
cited, 'a very limited risk'(12) as far as Leiris is concerned,
although he continues to see it as a 'commitment' he could not
have done without:

> what led me to make demands upon myself is the fact that I
> am married, that I love my wife a great deal, and because I
> know that this book could only upset her. I wanted this
> precisely for our own relationship, in order that it might be
> devoid of hypocrisy...'L'Age d'homme' represents a risk,
> and something quite difficult to swallow; it entailed displaying
> my own deficiencies. As a rule a man tries to puff himself up
> like a cock. This was a very meek attempt at introducing 'the
> bull's horn'. 'L'Age d'homme' was nevertheless a book designed
> to play a certain role in my life...I was completely escaping
> 'art for art's sake' by writing it.(13)

Escaping from 'art for art's sake' was the only way Leiris could
hope to achieve 'a properly literary form of "commitment" '.(14)
But, as the essay prefatory to 'L'Age d'homme' shows, the project

was not without a faint whiff of aestheticism. Leiris opens the
essay with the quotation of the preface he had intended to use on
the first publication of 'L'Age d'homme' in 1939, written 'on the
eve of the "phoney war" '(15) which, in the event, he decided to
omit, no doubt because it was as 'phoney' as the period it was
written in. The only element that is likely to strike the modern
reader of 'L'Age d'homme' as 'phoney' is the way Leiris, in pre-
facing a book that is dominated by the first-person pronoun and
given over to the analysis of a very distinct personality, abandons
the 'I' form in favour of a needlessly discreet third person 'he'
and a somewhat arch periphrasis, 'the author'. This is accompanied by an admission that the title of the book no longer represents an adequate description of its contents. The prospect of a
world war that could not be considered 'a long vacation' as (for
him) its predecessor had been, awakens an awareness in Leiris
that he has misconceived what the words 'l'age d'homme' really
mean:

> By 1935 when he completed his book, he no doubt supposed
> his existence had already sustained enough vicissitudes for
> him to pride himself on having attained the age of virility at
> last. Now in 1939, when the young men of the post-war
> period see the utter collapse of that structure of facility
> which they despaired of trying to invest with not only an
> authentic fervour but a terrible distinction as well, the
> author freely acknowledges that his true 'manhood' still
> remains to be written, when he will have suffered, in one
> form or another, the same bitter ordeal his elders faced.(16)

Leiris's only consolation, in the face of this recognition, is that at
least the title 'does not belie [his] ultimate intent: the search for
a vital fulfilment that cannot be realized without a catharsis, a
liquidation, for which literary activity - and particularly the so-
called literature of confession - appears to be one of the most
suitable instruments.'(17) The uncertainty here is immediately
made more poignant by an open acknowledgment that in his attempt
to introduce 'a bull's horn into a literary work'(18) he cannot consider himself to have been successful. Only the 'shadow' of the
bull's horn has been achieved, and this at the cost of Leiris being
reminded that, if he has not achieved an absolute equivalence
between the bull's horn and the work of art, 'what occurs in the
domain of style [is] valueless [because] it remains "aesthetic",
anodyne, insignificant.'(19)

The remainder of the prefatory essay is essentially an elaborate
gloss on the problem defined by this original preface, with Leiris
now, of course, having suffered 'the same bitter ordeal his elders
faced.'(20) The city of Le Havre becomes an emblem of this ordeal,
and an insistent reminder, much more powerful than his own pre-
publication awareness, that his book is an excrescence:

> Le Havre is now largely destroyed, as I can see from my
> balcony, which overlooks the harbour from a sufficient height
> and distance to give a true picture of the terrible *tabula rasa*
> the bombs made in the centre of the city....On this scale, the

personal problems with which *Manhood* is concerned are
obviously insignificant...the poet's inner agony, weighed
against the horrors of war, counts for no more than a tooth-
ache over which it would be graceless to groan; what is the
use, in the world's excruciating uproar, of this faint moan
over such narrowly limited and individual problems?(21)

But at this point Leiris realizes that the statement of the problem
contains its own solutions and that his sense of failure is not unconnected with the fact that his perspective is from too high up
and from too far away. Despite the devastation, life continues;
and despite his dissatisfaction with it, 'L'Age d'homme' is on the
point of finding an audience that, having survived the 'ordeal',
will not find it narrow and limited. Leiris's subliminal recognition
of this seems to liberate him from the constriction that he has
previously been feeling in trying to apologize for the book, and
the rest of the essay consists of an extended meditation on the
aims and achievements of the book. This is conducted with much
more fervour than would have been possible in the original preface, primarily because Leiris no longer conceives of himself in a
kind of solipsistic vicious circle but rather in relation to the world
at large. He does not suppress his inner needs, but he begins to
see that they may find an echo in his audience:

I intended to rid myself for good of certain agonizing images,
at the same time that I revealed my features with the maximum
of clarity and as much for my own use as to dissipate any
erroneous sense of myself which others might have. To effect
a *catharsis*, to achieve my definitive liberation, this autobiography would have to take the form most capable of rousing
my own enthusiasm and of being understood by other people
as well.(22)

It is, however, precisely this question of form that threatens his
achievement of a 'definitive liberation'. To pursue it further,
Leiris is forced to reconsider the 'art' of bullfighting:

What I did not realize was that at the source of all intro-
spection is a predilection for self-contemplation, and that
every confession contains a desire to be absolved. To
consider myself objectively was still to consider myself -
to keep my eyes fixed on myself instead of turning them
beyond and transcending myself in the direction of something more broadly human...if there has been a risk, a
bull's horn, it is not without a certain duplicity that I have
ventured to accept it: yielding on the one hand, once again
to my narcissistic tendency; trying on the other, to find in
my neighbour less a judge than an accomplice. Similarly, the
matador who seems to risk everything is concerned about his
'line' and relies, in order to overcome the danger, on his
technical sagacity.(23)

But even redefining the role of the matador proves of little consolation, and only when Leiris sees that there may be a sense in
which literature, like bullfighting, may be conceived of as an act
- in relation to the self, in relation to others and in relation to

one's whole previous literary production - is the analogy fully
reconstituted. In this context 'L'Age d'homme' ceases to bo otatio
and removed from life and begins to seem dynamically, indeed
retroactively, involved with life:
> [I was] expecting it to change me, to enlarge my conscious-
> ness, and to introduce, too, a new element into my relations
> with other people, beginning with my relations with those
> close to me, who could no longer be quite the same...(24)

Once Leiris had realized that the life/art dichotomy can only
be decisively dismantled by rejecting 'a fallacious compromise
between real facts and the pure products of the imagination', he
was bound to write something that was 'the negation of a novel'
and thus to create a positive, authentic realism which would be
'an extension of the moral order' and not merely a contribution to
the aesthetic order.(25) The analogy with the matador is once
again relevant here, as Leiris realizes that the code which the
matador cannot infringe actually helps, rather than hinders, his
authenticity: 'the tragedy he acts is a real tragedy.'(26) Leiris
extends this analogy by pointing out that the code 'far from being
a protection, contributes to [the matador's] danger' and that the
confessional writer is exposed to 'a danger directly proportional
to the rigour of the rule he has imposed on himself.'(27) The
analogy therefore involves Leiris, logically enough, in a recon-
sideration of how rigorous he has been, and in particular a revaluation of the respective claims of form and content:
> To use materials of which I was not the master and which I had
> to take as I found them (since my life was what it was and I
> could not alter, by so much as a comma, my past, a primary
> *datum* representing for me a fate as unchallengeable as for
> the *torero* the beast that runs into the ring), to say every-
> thing and to say it without 'doctoring', without leaving
> anything to the imagination and as though obeying a neces-
> sity - such was the risk I accepted and the law I had fixed
> for myself, such the ceremony with which I could make no
> compromise.(28)

Leiris sees this as a kind of classicism 'not excluding such excess
as one finds in even our most formalized tragedies,' a classicism
that by virtue of making no distinction between form and content
ensures 'a maximum of veracity'.(29) It is at this point that the
analogy of the bullfight undergoes a final transformation: 'the
order of the *corrida* (a rigid framework imposed on an action in
which, theatrically, chance must appear to be dominated) is a
technique of combat and at the same time a ritual.'(30) The life/
art dichotomy is here replaced by a combat/ritual dichotomy in
which Leiris the writer confronts, contains and finally kills Leiris
the man.

The preface reveals a profound desire on Leiris's part to synthesize his life into 'a single solid block (an object I can touch, as
though to insure myself against death...)', a desire which accounts
for his pleasure at the 'sculptural' character of 'that glorious
amalgamation in which man, material and the huge horned mass

seem united by a play of reciprocal influences.'(31) But alongside
his desire for synthesis, and in competition with it, is an equally
strong awareness that the image must not be a static one, that it
must form itself in its own organic way. This compels Leiris to
assert, without any false modesty, that his book is unlike any
other, although both Breton's 'Nadja' and Baudelaire's 'Mon Coeur
mis à nu' had encouraged him in his enterprise:
> It was therefore necessary that this method I had imposed on
> myself...should function simultaneously and effectively as a
> rule of composition. Identity, so to speak, of form and content,
> but, more precisely, a unique procedure revealing the content
> to me as I gave it form...it is precisely to the degree that one
> cannot see in a work any other rule of composition than the
> Ariadne's thread the author followed throughout the explan-
> ation he was making (by successive approaches or at point-
> blank range) to himself that works of this genre can be
> regarded, in literary terms, as 'authentic'.(32)

Leiris concludes his preface with an open admission that his meditation is an a posteriori one, and a troubled sense, on returning
to 'the authentic horn of the war' and its effects of Le Havre, that
he cannot be adjudged to have succeeded. With the benefit of an
extra thirty years of hindsight, Leiris not only saw the book as
'the kind of mosaic' that was 'ultimately a facile task'(33) but also
felt the need to 'reread' the preface in which he first reread
'L'Age d'homme':
> I am anxious to clarify the question of the 'bullfighter' in
> what I have called 'Of Literature considered as a Tauromachy'.
> Quite a few people have been mistaken about that...if I chose
> this title, it was for the purposes of irony...I reappropriated
> Thomas De Quincey's title: 'Of Murder considered as one of
> the Fine Arts'...I took this title to show that literature is not
> a tauromachy; I was being ironic.(34)

It is possible that Leiris, like other ironists, expected too much
of his audience, or perhaps he underestimated the way his book
of failure might become, for others, a book of success. 'L'Age
d'homme' has certainly proved to be 'of interest to others', allowing them 'to discover in themselves', in increasingly large numbers,
'something homophonous'.(35)

Although almost all of the available commentaries on 'L'Age d'homme'
begin with a consideration of the 1946 preface, it is important to
remember that it is more of an 'afterword' than a genuine foreword
and that its status is not far removed from the notes at the end of
the book (all but one of which date from 1946), which comprise
another attempt to 'reread' the self-portrait that has been so lab-
oriously constructed. As Alain-Michel Boyer shrewdly says, the
prefatory essay is 'at once a reflection on a finished book and a
clarification of the objectives in a current book,' the current book
being the first volume of 'La Règle du jeu', 'Biffures'.(36) But it
is perhaps misleading to speak of 'L'Age d'homme', with or without its preface, as a 'finished' book at all, for despite the

increasing rigour with which Leiris carries out his enterprise, it is throughout so multi-faceted that it is impossible to hold it in the mind as a single image. Like the Cranach painting which is its frontispiece, it is always dynamic and dialectical, and imbued with a sense of the incommensurability of even the most promising analogies. The book ends, indeed, even more in medias res than it has begun, and Leiris's penchant for mosaic is so strong throughout that even from a considerable distance the book seems to resemble a heap of fragments.

Leiris hardly ever provides his reader with explicit links between adjacent fragments, although increasingly, as the book unfolds, he harks back to crucial early experiences in his life to explain the significance of later occurrences. But even without Leiris's explicit acknowledgment of the fact, an intelligent reader would suspect that there is a more or less 'rigorous subterranean logic'(37) operating here, and that the experience of psychoanalysis has been a great influence in this regard. In the final chapter Leiris says of psychoanalytic therapy:

> The chief thing I have learned from it is that, even in what
> first appear to be the most heterogeneous manifestations,
> one always finds that one is oneself, that there is a unity in
> life, and that everything leads back, whatever one does, to
> a specific constellation of things which one tends to reproduce,
> under various forms, an unlimited number of times.(38)

It is in this belief that Leiris has felt justified in allowing his book to unfold without being subject to any apparent constraints, whether in regard to form or in regard to content. At the end of chapter 5 he confronts those who will be tempted to criticise him for this:

> My manner of presenting things may bring forth the charge
> of a certain arbitrariness in the choice of facts I am recording
> ...Admitting that there is something arbitrary about it, I do
> not see what the bias of such a choice can reveal if not,
> precisely, this predilection indicating the exceptionally dis-
> turbing value which sanguinary episodes have for me, and
> figures on a platform...or stuffed into grotesque masks.(39)

There is more than a little circularity and self-fulfilling prophecy here, and the syntax is more than usually tortuous, as if Leiris is on the one hand embarrassed by his defensiveness, and, on the other, genuinely unclear about the nature of his enterprise. It is Leiris at his driest, in a book much concerned with 'mineralization'. (40) And yet this passage is typical of the way Leiris oscillates between timidity and force majeure, allowing himself to become the passive medium through which events are recalled, and yet periodically asserting himself in a determined effort to articulate precisely the 'specific constellation' that constitutes his essential self.

This is by no means the only time in the book when, in the words of the first chapter after the prologue, Leiris 'face[s] the reef on which so many writers of confessions have foundered,' namely, 'attributing to these recollections a meaning they never

had, charging them after the fact with an affective value which
the real events they refer to utterly lacked – in short, resus-
citating this past in a misleading manner.'(41) But throughout
'L'Age d'homme' Leiris is not really intending to avoid this 'reef':
he is actually intent on shipwrecking himself on it. There is an
undeclared war going on within him between the automatic Surrealist writer who simply records whatever comes out of his pen
and the Freudian auto-analyst who must patiently reconstruct the
past if he is to liberate himself from his neurosis. As almost all
commentators on the book have observed, 'L'Age d'homme' is
heavily 'thematized' (as the titles to chapters 1 and 2 in the English translation, 'Tragic themes' and 'Classical themes', serve to
underline). This is a deliberate policy on Leiris's part designed
to enable him to comprehend – which, as a child he could not –
the motives, and hence the leitmotivs, of his behaviour patterns.
Just previous to the two dreams which end (though they do not
resolve) the book, Leiris says: 'I now understand quite clearly
my sense of guilt.'(42) If this is indeed the case, then he has
clearly achieved what the last paragraph of the prologue summarizes as the subject of the book: 'how the hero....leaves...the
miraculous chaos of childhood for the fierce order of virility.'(43)
But this 'thematization' is only one of the panels in Leiris's dip-
tych, and 'the goal of liquidating, by formulating them, certain
obsessions,'(44) is only partially achieved.

Leiris's 'thematizing' is the product of a very considerable
intelligence, an intelligence that threatens to turn parts of 'L'Age
d'homme' into a scientific monograph or inventory.(45) But the
intellectual side of Leiris coexists with, and is a product of, an
extremely turbulent emotional life which he clearly considers
irremediable. Although in one sense 'L'Age d'homme' does indeed
liquidate ('by formulating them')(46) certain obsessions, in another sense all it does is to present them in as unmediated a
manner as possible. Leiris's 'desperate need to express myself'
overrides his almost equally powerful desire 'to formulate in more
or less convincing phrases the always too little I experience, and
to fix it on paper.'(47) Because of this the reader is forced to
become as much a collaborator in the enterprise as Leiris himself
is. Leiris compares himself in the later text 'Biffures', with 'a
Narcissus who does not move, who takes snapshots...and watches
himself take snapshots,'(48) but this is certainly not the case in
'L'Age d'homme', where he is continually on the move and continually altering his angle of vision. This strategy derives
directly from his decision to 'treat literature at once as an end
and as a means'(49) and it gives the book its peculiar bifocal
character, 'midway', as Jeffrey Mehlman says, 'not only between
life and theatre but also between the pathological and the thera-
peutic'.(50)

There is an immense nostalgia on Leiris's part for 'the miraculous chaos of childhood'(51) which the book is supposed to be
leaving behind forever. Despite the narrow range of the recol-
lected material (which is both a cause and an effect of the desire

to 'thematize'), 'L'Age d'homme' recaptures as vividly as any comparable contemporary work a period of life in which everything is
enveloped in magic and mystery. The bizarre juxtapositions, the
disorganized time-scheme and the sheer inconsequentiality of many
of the events narrated, make the reading of 'L'Age d'homme'
something like riffling through an old photograph album or playing
with a child's kaleidoscope. Only the obsessive interest in erotic
(and erotogenic) material (another cause and another effect of the
'thematization') contaminates what is in essence as innocent and
ingenuous an account of childhood as one could well imagine, a
'simple confession'(52) indeed.

Concomitant, therefore, with Leiris's profound need to 'condense
my entire universe'(53) is an equally powerful regression towards
'the only happy period in my life, though already containing the
elements of its own disintegration and all the features which,
gradually deepening into wrinkles and lines, give my portrait its
likeness.'(54) There is a very strong strain of infantilism in the
adult Leiris, not least in his dealings with women, which are distinguished throughout by fantasy projections, trauma and a
tendency to impotence. But this infantile strain is not merely
self-indulgent: it is an important link in the chain that constitutes
Leiris's most individual contribution to the theory and practice of
literature. In the prologue Leiris elaborates on 'that chaos which
is the first stage of life' in a section which he justly sees as com-
prising the *'metaphysic of my childhood'*(55):
     the first stage of my life, that irreplaceable state when, as
     in legendary days, all things are still undifferentiated, when
     the rupture between microcosm and macrocosm has not yet
     occurred and the self is steeped in a kind of fluid universe,
     as at the heart of the absolute.(56)
Leiris laments the loss of this childhood world, and yet in a sense
'L'Age d'homme' belies its title by reconstituting it. It is precisely
because Leiris is for so much of the time 'at the heart of the
absolute' that the book is difficult to come to terms with; the
'self' of Leiris is 'steeped' in the 'fluid universe' of the book.
Despite (and to some extent because of) his intellectual attempts
to differentiate one thing from another, the book is all the time
synthesizing things back into a state of unity. If 'legendary days'
cannot be recaptured, legendary figures (Judith, Lucrece, Holofernes, Cleopatra, and all the other figures of Leiris's pantheon)
are timeless. And thus one's own life can be made - as in Genet's
'Journal du voleur' - into a kind of legend.(57)

Leiris leaves us to make these inferences for ourselves, as if
only half aware that such inferences can be made. His own interest lies in tracing 'the rupture between microcosm and macrocosm'
and proposing ways in which the rupture may be remedied. Three
ways, all of which interpenetrate to some degree, are of special
interest to Leiris: suicide, love and literature (or, as Leiris often
calls it, poetry). Leiris conceives of all three as acts: the act of
killing oneself, the sexual act, the act of writing. The primary
justification of Leiris's seemingly aberrant methods in 'L'Age

d'homme' is that he convinces the reader that these three ostensibly disparate activities are actually one and the same, so that
the following of any one of the threads (to adopt Leiris's own
Ariadne metaphor) leads inevitably to the other two and thus to
the heart of the matter. The act of writing 'L'Age d'homme' thus
becomes simultaneously an act of coitus and an act of self-
slaughter.

Leiris's first analysis of the suicide motif occurs in the prologue
under the rubric of Old Age and Death. The context is the
young Leiris's visits, in the company of his mother (who, by virtue of giving birth to him has obliged him to experience death at
some later time), to the graves of her family in the Père Lachaise
cemetery. But the stimulus towards suicide derives, as almost all
the deepest feelings of Leiris seem to do, not from a real experience, but from an illustration, in this case an illustration in a
newspaper. (Later Leiris describes illustrations in printed books -
albums, encyclopedias, literary works, bibles etc.) The particular suicide in question - the self-slaughter of a Malayan rajah
after he has ordered his wives to be killed - is of considerable
significance in relation to the rest of 'L'Age d'homme', which describes how Leiris 'kills off', figuratively if not literally, his
various mistresses either by failing to love them or (more often)
by failing to make love to them. And yet the main purpose of this
first approach to the subject is to establish the word 'suicide'
itself as a kind of talisman possessing magical properties. This is
the first and most explicit manifestation in 'L'Age d'homme' of the
fascination words have for Leiris, a fascination that dates back,
in terms of the corpus of his published work, at least as far as
'Glossaire j'y serre mes gloses' (1925) and points forward to the
'jeux de mots' in 'La Règle du jeu' (1946):

The only thing I perceived clearly was the word 'suicide'
itself, whose sonority I associated with the idea of fire and
the serpentine shape of the kris, and this association was
so deeply rooted in my mind that even today I cannot write
'suicide' without again seeing the rajah in his setting of
flames; there is the 's', whose shape as well as sound reminds
me not only of the torsion of the body about to fall, but of
the sinuosity of the blade; the 'ui', which echoes strangely
and insinuates itself, somehow, like the tongues of the fire
or the zigzags of a lightning flash; the 'cide', which concludes the word with an acid taste, implying something sharp
and incisive.(58)

Almost all the details of this passage recur later in 'L'Age d'homme':
the 'serpentine' shape, for example, recurs in the account of
Cleopatra's suicide, in the salamander design on the family stove,
and in the boy's visit to the Châtelet theatre;(59) the 'body about
to fall' recurs in the account of a young butcher-boy's accident,
in the description of Leiris's elder brother almost falling out of a
hotel window at Le Havre, in the fall of his eldest brother into a
chamber-pot, and in Leiris's own fall after a collision with a girl
in the school playground;(60) the fascination with the knife and

with the wound it makes recurs in a hundred or more details of
Leiris's real and fantasy life.

The theoretical gloss on this 'jeu de mots' – which the English
translation cannot hope to reproduce satisfactorily – is much less
extensive and compelling than the discussions of suicide later in
the book, of which the analysis of the bullfight at the beginning
of chapter 3 is one of the most important. Leiris only articulates
the suicidal aspects of the 'corrida' at the end of a description of
the bullfights he has seen, but the whole drift of the previous
paragraphs (the pleasure in 'watching something real' and finding
oneself in a 'terrain of truth' at last, the analogies with sexual
intercourse, and the awareness that 'between matador and bull...
there is a union along with the combat') prepares one for the
studied casualness of Leiris's conclusion:

> When I go to a bullfight, I tend to identify myself either with
> the bull at the moment the sword is plunged into its body, or
> with the matador who risks being killed [perhaps emasculated?]
> by a thrust of the horn at the very moment when he most
> clearly affirms his virility.(61)

The suicide impulse is clearly present here, however unprecipitated it may be. And even without the benefit of the 1946 preface
it might be intuited that in 'L'Age d'homme' Leiris is treating himself as both matador and bull, and thus committing, by an act of
writing - committing in the double sense of 'doing' and 'being
committed to' - a suicide that his inherent timidity will not permit
(or has not yet permitted) him to carry out in real life.

The suicide theme reaches its apogee at the beginning of chapter 6 (Lucrece and Judith) not, as might be expected, in the
context of the two titular heroines but rather in the figure of
Cleopatra, who operates for Leiris as a kind of synthesis of the
two. Here Leiris is at his clearest in identifying the reasons for
his attraction to suicide:

> this...corresponds to what for me is the profound meaning
> of suicide: to become at the same time *oneself and the other*,
> male and female, subject and object, killed and killer - the
> only possibility of communion with oneself....A punishment
> one inflicts on oneself in order to have the right to love
> oneself to excess - this, in the last analysis, is the meaning
> of suicide.(62)

The triangular relationship between death, love and literature is
reaffirmed here in a passage that only requires the slightest
alteration of focus to become an apologia for the kind of literature
with which Leiris is now inseparably associated. For the writing
of an autobiographical work of art requires the author to be at
once both subject and object of his enterprise and can never entirely escape the charge that almost every autobiography since
Rousseau has had to face: that it is an exercise in self-love. Despite the stress placed in the prefatory essay on the need for
objectivity and severity if the 'confession' is not to be written off
as inauthentic and gratuitous, there is also an awareness on
Leiris's part that one may be, in the words of the chapter entitled

Loves of Holofernes, 'a specialist in confession'(63) with the 'predilection for self-contemplation' of which the preface speaks (64) and which all of Leiris's prose oeuvre exhibits.

But it would be wrong to accuse Leiris of simple Narcissism 'tout court', wrong even to stress unduly the Freudian 'primary Narcissism' of the enterprise. A section at the end of chapter 4 entitled 'Narcissus' indicates why. It describes a visit made by Leiris to the Ballet Russe in which he is disappointed by the omission of a scene in which Narcissus immerses his body in the pool and - in this version - is decapitated by a witch-like woman. This disappointment, which seems intended to convey Leiris's oblique awareness that he is always postponing death and never fully acceding to it, is balanced by two indications that Leiris is not entirely self-orientated. The first is a retrospective aware- ness that there are men at the ballet who are homosexual; the second is a retrospective regret that his 'aunt' has not married his uncle.(65) Although the dramatis personae of 'L'Age d'homme' tend, as Robert Bréchon has said, to be reduced to essences,(66) it is striking how much of the book is concerned with Leiris's relationships with others.(67) It is not, despite appearances, a solipsistic book; it is a book that is oriented in the direction of other people. As Leiris says in his much more personal meditation 'L'Afrique fantôme': 'It is in pushing the particular to its end that one attains the general, and through the maximum of sub- jectivity that one attains objectivity.'(68) 'L'Age de'homme' is Leiris's first sustained attempt at constructing the 'tangential' states in which 'one feels tangential to the world and to oneself' of which he spoke in the 1937 essay, Miroir de la tauromachie (69)

As we have already seen, the suicide theme is almost always bound up with the theme of sexuality. 'L'Age d'homme' is indeed an overwhelmingly sexual book, although far too chilly to be in any sense pornographic. Leiris himself sees it as falling into the category of the 'erotic' that he and Georges Bataille were, in their different ways, concerned with,(70) and in chapter 7 discussing The Loves of Holofernes, he sets love and eroticism in explicit opposition to one another:

Love - the only possibility of a coincidence between subject and object, the only means of acceding to the sacred, as represented by the desired object in so far as it is exterior and alien to us - implies its own negation because to possess the sacred is at the same time to profane and finally to destroy it by gradually robbing it of its alien character....In mere eroticism, everything is clearer: for desire to remain aroused, it need only change its object. The trouble begins the moment man no longer wants to change objects....The only practical chance of salvation is in a love for a creature so self-centred that, despite an unceasing *rapprochement*, one never reaches the limit of one's possible knowledge of that being; or for someone so endowed with an instinctive coquetry that...it will seem that she is about to escape at every moment.(71)

This is an important but confusing passage, partly because Leiris overstates the case for love (when the previous discussions of suicide have shown that love is not the only possibility of coincidence between subject and object) and partly because Leiris's commitment to eroticism is no more final than his commitment to anything else. The innumerable femmes fatales that stud the pages of 'L'Age d'homme' might lead one to believe that Leiris is simply changing objects in order to remain aroused. But in fact they can almost all be classified as Lucreces or Judiths, suicides or homicides, and in this sense Leiris finds himself in the position of the man who 'no longer wants to change objects.' Furthermore, the love that Leiris describes as a possible salvation is not unlike a kind of self-love, since '[the being] one never reaches the limit of one's possible knowledge of' is par excellence oneself, as Leiris has shown by repeated returns to the subject.

The striking thing about the eroticism of 'L'Age d'homme' is that it is remorselessly, almost absurdly, thoroughgoing. Almost every incident of childhood, however small or accidental, is bathed in a heavily erotic light, a kind of Freudianism run wild. This overdetermination is at once authentic and fictitious. Like much else in the book it confirms the accuracy of Leiris's belief that 'by the play of contradictory forces, everything is always subject to a double movement.'(72) The primary 'double movement' of the erotic aspects of the book serves to establish Leiris as a kind of hermaphroditic figure,(73) not just in the sense that (since Freud) we have all become aware of our bisexual natures but, more importantly, in the sense that the differentiations of which Leiris speaks slightingly early in the book are rendered (in fantasy at least) inoperative. The book is full of vaginal images: wounds, orifices, chimneys and such like. But it is full of phallic images as well: horns, swords, statues etc. Leiris is revealed as at once heterosexual and homosexual, at one and the same time active and passive. The 'sexual spasm' impresses Leiris because of 'its character as a momentary return to chaos'.(74) But sexual penetration disturbs him profoundly, and the dominant image of the book is of a decapitated Orpheus-like head that, notwithstanding Leiris's disclaimer in the notes at the end, indicates an immensely powerful castration complex.(75) Only in the final chapter does Leiris reveal that his erotic attitudes are at the same time metaphysical attitudes and thus a response to the 'rupture between microcosm and macrocosm':

Always beneath or above concrete events, I remain a prisoner of this alternative: the world as a real object which dominates and devours me (like Judith) in suffering and in fear, or else the world as a pure fantasy which dissolves in my hands, which I destroy (like Lucrece thrusting home the dagger) without ever succeeding in possessing it. Perhaps, above all, the question for me is to escape this dilemma by finding a way in which the world and myself - object and subject - confront each other on an equal footing, as the matador stands before the bull.(76)

The privileged status of the bullfight in the Leiris of the 'L'Age d'homme' period derives from the 'corrida's' qualities of ritual and magic. For Leiris it preserves what organized religion has lost: a sense of the sacred. Leiris discusses this in the 1938 essay Le sacré dans la vie quotidienne(77), and it is clear that the eminently quotidian events recounted in 'L'Age d'homme' are an attempt on his part to find something sacred in the facts of his life.(78) Unlike the adult who, in Leiris's opinion, lives in a homogeneous and profane world, the child lives in a 'cosmos sacralisé'. (79) 'L'Age d'homme' shows that the child's earliest awareness of this cosmos is stimulated by visits to the opera and the theatre, so much so that the 'pronounced taste for the tragic'(80) that he acquired there has never left him. The theatre is conceived of as

a world apart...where all things, mysteriously arranged in
the space which begins beyond the footlights, are transposed
to the level of the sublime and occur in a realm so superior to
that of ordinary reality that the drama developed and unrav-
elled there must be regarded as a kind of oracle or model.(81)

Concomitant with this fascination is an abiding and profound affection for the actor who makes the space come alive, whether it be the circus acrobat (like his uncle) at one end of the spectrum, or the diva (like his 'aunt') at the other. Later the child finds that it can carry out transformations analogous to those previously confined to the world of the theatre by making up stories, either on its own or with a willing contemporary (in this case, Leiris's elder brother).(82) The vividness of these stories is much more important than their more or less secure basis in fact. Leiris's description of his first return by boat from England illustrates this aspect particularly well:

Shortly after the ship had left Dover, a 'dry storm' came up,
with long rolls of thunder and an almost uninterrupted series
of lightning flashes at all points of the horizon; it was extremely dark, and the effect was all the more striking since
there was not a breath of wind and despite the stormy light
the sea remained absolutely calm. I have often told people -
and I am quite incapable of saying today if it was altogether
false - that at the height of the storm St. Elmo's fire broke
out on top of one of the masts.(83)

On the occasion of another boat trip, a day excursion from Trou-ville to Le Havre, the young Leiris fabricates a much more elaborate fiction involving jockeys and adultery and with a pronounced Oedipal component. The fiction in this case seems to operate as a kind of talisman; at any rate reality contrives to confirm and, as it were, to ratify what might otherwise have been seen as the transgression of a taboo:

The night was passed one way or another; I had plenty of
time to ponder my little adultery with the trainer's wife, and
the next day on the boat, I was very proud to see my father
flattened by seasickness which I myself did not suffer from
or at least gave no evidence of, except perhaps for a certain
pallor.(84)

Leiris's real fascination is with stories that do not yield up their
secrets readily, that retain their enigmatic quality. This is one
reason why he is so often content to transcribe, either in the body
of a chapter or more strikingly as an epigraph to it, the content
of his dreams. At the beginning of the second chapter - immediately after having recorded, for the first time in the book, a
dream-narrative in the epigraph - Leiris confronts his fondness for
'enigmatic lessons in images'.(85) 'Allegories' as he calls them -
the etymology of the word reminds us that it means 'speaking
otherwise than one seems to speak' - possess the same transfor-
mational power as the theatre, the opera, the circus and the bullfight. As in the case of the word 'suicide', the word itself seems
to stimulate Leiris to feats of transfiguration:

the word 'allegory' was enough to transfigure everything....
To a large degree my taste for hermeticism proceeds from
the same impulse as this early love of 'allegories', and I am
convinced that it must also be related to my later habit of
thinking in formulas, analogies, images - a mental technique
of which, whether I like it or not, the present account is
only an application.(86)

The reflexive quality of 'L'Age d'homme' is very clearly signalled
here; it, too, is hermetic and allegorical, inducing in even the
most sensitive reader the kind of vertiginous dizziness of which
Leiris so often speaks. It is clearly Leiris's intention that the book
should induce in the reader a desire to penetrate the mysteries, in
order that the self-revelation should at least approximate to the
penetrative force of the bull's horn or the matador's sword in the
'corrida'. Leiris himself is a good deal less naked than the figures
of Lucrece and Judith in his frontispiece. And in the very last
words of the book proper, it is not just his mistress whom he is
telling 'how necessary it is to construct a wall round oneself by
means of clothing':(87) it is the reader also. But by virtue of ex-
plaining from time to time what he is up to, and thus encouraging
the reader to suspect that he is 'speaking otherwise' than he
seems to be speaking, Leiris is effectively dismantling the wall at
the same time as he is building it.

In this typically Leirisian 'oscillation' one cannot help but be
struck by the manner in which, especially in the epigraphs to each
chapter, ingenuity and ingenuousness turn out to be one and the
same. For instance, in the citation from the 'Nouveau Larousse
Illustré' that heads the last chapter, we are faced with a kind of
literary equivalent to the 'objet trouvé' so much prized by the Surrealist painters. The description of a famous Géricault painting is
on the face of it neutral and circumstantial, but certain details
have a peculiar resonance in the context of the book we are reading. Géricault, in 'The Raft of the "Medusa" ', is not the only
artist who has 'chosen the moment which precedes the rescue';
Leiris has also done this, although the 'rescue' of psychoanalysis
leaves him in a 'void...which...is all the more apparent.'(88) Nor
is Corréard the only person to have published 'a narrative of the
shipwreck'; this is what Leiris has done in writing 'L'Age d'homme'.

There is even a prefiguration of the initial fate of Leiris's book in
the account of the reception of Géricault's painting: 'This work,
remarkable for its skilful composition, the realism of its expression, the scale of its drawing and finally the brilliance of its
colouring, was not understood when it was first shown.'(89) Similarly, in the epigraph to the penultimate chapter, Leiris - this
time using a different kind of 'objet trouvé', an entry in a diary -
undercuts the narrative proper (in which, as he gets closer to
'manhood', things inevitably get slightly clearer) by anticipating
the very last words of the book and implying that the clarity is
illusory: 'I bear in my hands the disguise by which I conceal my
life. A web of meaningless events, I dye it with the magic of my
point of view.'(90) The 'hermetic' technique actually reaches a
kind of high-water mark here in a prophecy that is true in one
sense and false in another: 'when I'm drunk, I'll make my confession, omitting, of course, to say how, in order to ignore the
banality of my life, I make myself examine it only through the
lenses of the sublime.'(91) In fact, of course, as Robert Bréchon
has shown, no reader of the last half of 'L'Age d'homme' could be
unaware that Leiris's 'drama...is to be incapable of establishing
himself in the domain of tragedy and to be continually thrown back
into mediocrity.'(92)

As all this goes to show, literature cannot hope to be the 'terrain of truth' that the bullfight is. It is much more like the
'expedient form of error' of which Nietzsche spoke.(93) In Leirisian terms it represents an 'adventure' that staves off the inherent ennui that afflicts him and, like all his other adventures -
especially perhaps the trip to Africa that killed for ever the myth
of travel as an escape - it cannot be sustained. 'I have never been
able to work except discontinuously, in flashes', Leiris tells us;
(94) and the very form of 'L'Age d'homme' confirms this. Like the
powder that Leiris puts on his face, literature represents 'a
defence-reaction against my inner weakness and the collapse by
which I felt myself threatened.'(95) But it does not enable him, as
he has for a long time hoped it would, to 'conquer my destiny as a
man with the help of words.'(96) Most of the last third of the book
is concerned with Leiris's attempt to demystify a medium that is
still something of a mystery to him. The irony here is that, for all
his timidity, Leiris is actually too aggressive to succeed in this
aim. As Jeffrey Mehlman has very acutely pointed out:

In thematizing his obsessions, Leiris seems to consecrate them.
...It is only when Leiris yields the initiative to words, risks
and affirms his alienation in language, that the obsessive
images yield their secret - and their grip on him. If 'L'Age
d'homme' is the record of Leiris possessed, 'La Règle du jeu'
reveals Leiris expropriated.(97)

It would be wrong, however, to minimize the manner in which
Leiris shows himself aware of the need to 'yield the initiative'. One
of the most moving passages in 'L'Age d'homme', towards the end of
the chapter entitled The Head of Hologernes, describes a morning
walk on Pentecost Monday after a night of debauch in Le Havre.

(Many of the crucial episodes in the book take place in Le Havre, which gives an extra aptness to the locale of the prologue.) The explicit opposition here is between the scientific work ('which I consider paltry') on which bourgeois comfort depends, and the passionate cry 'at the heart of the world' which emanates from a clanging buoy, and which recalls to Leiris's mind the words of a prostitute he has spoken to the day before. But it is also quite clear that the scientific work of which Leiris is speaking includes 'L'Age d'homme' itself, for Leiris not only identifies himself with the mineralogist that he sees working on the cliff, but also he himself is engaged, metaphorically speaking, in 'occasionally... [chipping] off a sample piece of rock from the cliff'.(98) The clanging buoy is more immediate, more passionate and altogether more important:

at the heart of the world, as out to sea, beyond this bay, there was something so passionate, raving, crying all alone, asking only to be heard, asking you to have enough courage to dedicate yourself to it utterly.(99)

Leiris makes no attempt to elucidate what this clanging buoy means, and it is possible to see it as representing the kind of literature he would like to write. But it is more likely, I think, that he intends it to represent - along with all the other dramatic noises of the book (100) - that which is beyond literature, the unmediated cry that is the most basic verbal performance of humankind. In the second of the three dreams which end the book, Leiris wakes up with a shriek that is equally irreducible to literature, a shriek which yields even less certainty about its origins. The 'most terrible agony' and 'a shattering pleasure'(101) are finally indistinguishable. But the syntheses of literature, as almost all commentators on 'L'Age d'homme' have more or less strongly suggested, are rather more ambivalent than the sexual spasm and the suicidal thrust.

Although it is much more highly charged than Leiris's professional ethnological writings 'L'Age d'homme' may ultimately be seen as an ethnological work. In 'Cinq Etudes d'ethnologie' (1969), Leiris says that the true ethnologist 'does not content himself with a humanism of pure reason but rather seeks to take a total view of man through his double existence as a product of culture and a particle of nature.'(102) Leiris's attempt at such a total view is predicated on the belief that there can be such a thing as a total man, 'for whom the real and the imaginary are one and the same, who has recognized that he belongs to nature and no longer sees natural productions and his own creation in separate planes.'(103) This is what he is trying to achieve in the 'totalized' form of 'L'Age d'homme' and what, with the active collaboration of the reader, he may be said to have come surprisingly close to, whatever the book's ultimate shortcomings.

6 JEAN-PAUL SARTRE: 'Les Mots' (1964)

In the 'cri de coeur' at the conclusion of Sartre's first and most famous novel, 'Nausea', the diarist Roquentin records his final reflections on the jazz tune that has haunted him throughout the book:

I too have wanted to be. Indeed I have never wanted anything else. That's what lay at the bottom of my life: behind all these attempts which seemed unconnected, I find the same desire: to drive existence out of me, to empty the moments of their fat, to wring them, to dry them, to purify myself, to harden myself, to produce in short the sharp, precise sound of a saxophone note. That could even serve as a fable....(1)

Of all Sartre's subsequent works - in philosophy, drama, fiction and biography - it is 'Les Mots' that comes closest to making a reality of Roquentin's desire. This brief and unique attempt on Sartre's part at a sustained autobiographical work was begun in 1954 but not published until a decade later, Sartre having, in the interim, substantially completed it only to lay it aside and to return to it, for revision purposes, prior to its publication.(2) The warm reception that 'Les Mots' received, together with (and no doubt on account of), its comparative clarity and brevity beside Sartre's other writings, suggest that, together with 'Nausea', 'Les Mots' is assured of permanent survival among the writings of the most celebrated of post-war intellectuals. In its purity of style, clarity of vision and relative equanimity of mood, 'Les Mots' may seem, at first glance, far removed from the anxious turbulence of 'Being and Nothingness' and 'Huis-Clos', and the elephantiasis of 'Saint Genet' and 'L'Idiot de la famille'. In some respects, it is indeed the least characteristic and most anomalous of all Sartre's many books. But despite its apparent isolation, 'Les Mots' in fact confirms what Roquentin could only dimly grasp, and demonstrates that behind all Sartre's seemingly disparate activities as a writer, there is actually a unifying principle.

Sartre's achievement has been so exceptionally varied that it is only natural for commentators to have been intent on what a recent critic has called the 'internal contestation'(3) in Sartre's works. Certainly, beneath the rubric 'Existentialist' there lurked a multiplicity of attitudes not always consistent one with another. For the literary critic in particular, it is difficult to understand how the 'sharp, precise sound' of 'Les Mots' could emanate from the same instrument that gave us the arid and discursive 'Critique of Dialectical Reason', and the brilliant but head-spinning 'tourniquets' of 'Being and Nothingness'. Michel Leiris has written of the

latter in a manner that implicitly acknowledges its unevenness as
a book, although his reaction is otherwise best seen as the exception that proves the rule:

> I feel that, even from a literary point of view, *'L' Etre et
> le néant'* is Sartre's most beautiful book. It is precisely there
> that we find sensational descriptions: the 'Garçon de Café'
> and the 'Trou de la Serrure' are prodigious. (4)

Prodigious indeed; none the less the book seems to grow out of
Sartre's control. In 'Les Mots' Sartre seems to be the master
rather than the slave of his immensely fertile mind, and to have
become the writer that 'Les Mots' suggests he has always been.
Leiris's remark has the virtue of reminding us that even in books
orientated towards areas of intellectual discourse in which aesthetic values are not normally relevant - the 'phenomenological
essay on ontology', the 'Sketch for a Theory of the Emotions', the
study of 'the intentional structure of the image' - Sartre could be
a writer as well as, and at the same time as, being a philisopher.
Sartre himself became more and more aware that it was the fact of
his being a writer that distinguished him from those engaged in
other pursuits. In an interview of 1957, during the writing of
'Les Mots', Sartre said:

> I am a writer: the first thing I must try to explain is why
> I write. I could have chosen another job: I could have been
> a painter or a business man. Why did I in fact prefer that
> activity to all others?
>
> I have been able to find out only in the last three or five
> years. Why? Because I was so concerned with this writing
> purpose that anything I could say to myself about it pro-
> ceeded from it. (5)

Sartre's admission that it was only in the early 1950s that he
discovered the answer to this question should not be allowed to
obscure the fact that as far back as 'Nausea' he was obsessively
concerned with it. The 'undated sheet' that begins Roquentin's
diary opens with a resolution that asserts the importance of writing and closes with the diarist hesitating and ambivalent:

> The best thing would be to write down everything that
> happens from day to day. To keep a diary in order to
> understand.
>
> I'm going to bed. I'm cured, and I'm going to give up
> writing down my impression, like a little girl in a nice new
> notebook.
>
> There's only one case in which it might be interesting to
> keep a diary: that would be if.... (6)

After this false start - which Dominick La Capra compares to the
much more substantial 'false start' of 'Being and Nothingness'(7) -
Roquentin, throughout the diary proper, never loses sight of the
fact that, although he is writing only a history book, his anguish
and his sense of abnormality derive directly from his being a
writer. Roquentin's desire to cease being a writer stems from his
initial polarization of life and literature:

a man is always a teller of tales, he lives surrounded by his
stories and the stories of others, he sees everything that
happens to him through them; and he tries to live his life as
if he were recounting it.
But you have to choose: to live or to recount.(8)
But even at the end of 'Nausea', Roquentin is haunted by the
possibility of combining the two, of 'being' a writer:
Couldn't I try?....It would have to be a book: I don't know
how to do anything else. But not a history book....Another
kind of book. I don't quite know which kind - but you would
have to guess, behind the printed words, behind the pages,
something which didn't exist, which was above existence.
The sort of story, for example, that could never happen, an
adventure. It would have to be beautiful and hard as steel
and make people ashamed of their existence.(9)
There has been an understandable tendency, partly no doubt
because of the reflexive character of the 'nouveau roman', to
apply Roquentin's remarks to the novel 'Nausea'. Sartre has even
acknowledged, Flaubert fashion, that 'Roquentin - c'est moi.'
But it is difficult to see Roquentin's remark as an accurate
forecast of Sartre's subsequent career: his next book was
'L'Imaginaire' (1940) and after 'Being and Nothingness' he in fact
wrote a kind of history book, the unfinished trilogy 'Roads to
Freedom'. Sartre had not, however, forgotten the ideas of Roquentin. In a public lecture of 1945, he strove to prove, against those
who had found 'Being and Nothingness' dehumanized, that Existentialism was a kind of humanism(10) and for a decade thereafter
- in 'What is literature?' (1947), the first of his Existential biographies, 'Baudelaire' (1947), and the massive study of Genet
(1952) - Sartre was primarily occupied with the eminently human-
istic discipline of literature. At the end of this period comes 'Les
Mots', as 'beautiful and hard as steel' as anything Roquentin could
require, 'an adventure' in its way, 'another kind of book' certainly.
No doubt it would be very instructive to regard 'Les Mots' as a
substantially accurate transcription of the facts of Sartre's life and
then to read all his writings in the light of it. But this would be
quite false to the profile of Sartre's thinking and would hypostatize the book in a manner that Sartre himself would have found
quite unacceptable. In so far as it is a terminus at all, it is a
'terminus ad quem' not a 'terminus a quo'. Sartre, as befits the
'traveller without ticket' that in 'Les Mots' he finds himself to be,
was never a man for terminal utterances, not even in a book dominated by the realization that death could not be far away, a book
which therefore inevitably bears the marks of being a final testament. The 'unfinished' nature of Sartre's whole enterprise is
epitomized by the non-appearance of the promised successor to
'Being and Nothingness', his inability to complete the third volume
of 'Roads to Freedom', and his decision to halt the autobiography
long before the years of adulthood.(11) Questioned in 1970 about
why no second volume had appeared, Sartre made one of the typically helpful, and at the same time slightly puzzling, replies that

interviewers always seemed to get from him:
>'I do not think that a sequel to 'Les Mots' would be of much
>interest.(12) The reason why I produced 'Les Mots' is the
>reason why I have studied Genet and Flaubert; how does a
>man become someone who writes, who wants to speak of the
>imaginary....It is the birth of the decision to write that is
>of interest. Thereafter, what is equally interesting are the
>reasons why I was to write exactly the contrary of what I
>wanted to write. But that is another subject altogether - the
>relationship of a man to the history of his time.(13)

A sequel, Sartre continued (implicitly identifying 'Les Mots' as a
personal testament) would have to be 'a political testament' and
this he was unable, or unwilling, to produce, at least in a form
that would invite comparison with 'Les Mots'.(14)

It is helpful to know that Sartre saw 'Les Mots' as a kind of
companion to his studies of Genet and Flaubert, although most of
the really sensitive reviewers (15) of the first translation into
English had made the connection with the Genet volume for themselves. Sartre's failure to include the study of Baudelaire is
slightly more puzzling. Sartre did, it is true, repudiate the book
as 'very unsatisfactory, extremely bad, even';(16) but no less a
Sartre expert than J. P. Thody has said that 'the basic principles
of..."existential psychoanalysis"...seem to have been put into
practice with most consistency in his essay on Baudelaire.'(17) So
much of the Baudelaire book is relevant to 'Les Mots' that Sartre's
rather extreme self-criticism - which does not extend to the work
in which the idea of an 'existential psychology' was first promul-
gated (18) - begins to look faintly protective or, rather more
damagingly, raises questions as to whether Sartre really understood the relationship between his books. One's puzzlement is only
exacerbated by Sartre's suggestion that 'the relationship of a man
to the history of his time' is 'another subject altogether.'(19)
Interviewed in 1957, Sartre took a diametrically opposed view of
'Les Mots':

>My experiences are significant inasmuch as they may be
>similar to those of many people like myself, French intel-
>lectuals of the Third and Fourth Republics among others...
>   While writing this biography [sic], I am not only con-
>cerned with the particular meaning of one life. I want to
>recall the rather curious evolution of a generation.(20)

One explanation for this apparent contradiction is that the events
of 1968 in France reawakened in Sartre a sense of the potentiality
of practical politics after more than a decade of doubts about the
viability of a 'third force' in politics.(21) But it is less important
for my present purposes to mediate these two opposed views than
to demonstrate that Sartre's understanding of his own achievement
was in fact subject to an 'incompleteness' similar to that which
characterized and, in part no doubt, promoted it.

Like any honest writer, Sartre's view of what he wrote was mod-
ified by his most recent book (and even by what he intended to
publish in the future).(22) But there are certain constants in

Sartre's vision that enable us to see what kind of book we are
confronted by in the case of 'Les Mots'. The most important of
these is the spectre of the 'true fiction' that is present as early
as 'Nausea' and recurs as late as an interview given in 1970:
> A writer is always a man who has more or less chosen the
> imaginary: he needs a certain dosage of fiction. For my part,
> I find it in my work on Flaubert which one can, moreover,
> consider a novel. I even wish people to say that it is a *true*
> novel.(23)

In this perspective (echoed in 'L'Idiot de la famille' itself - 'I confess that it's a fable. Nothing proves it happened this way')(24)
Sartre's secession from writing novels in 1947 - usually put down
to the growth in his political consciousness (25) - comes to seem
only a strategy within his lifelong concern for 'l'imaginaire'. And
yet it is a striking feature that whereas, after 'Nausea', most of
Sartre's important literary essays were studies of novels and
novelists, after 'Baudelaire' - intended, significantly enough, as
an introduction to Baudelaire's 'Journaux intimes' - most of Sartre's important essays concern themselves with unclassifiable
prose works with a pronounced autobiographical colouring. The
distinction is clearest if we set the famous reviews of Mauriac's
'La Fin de la nuit' (1939) and Camus's 'L'Etranger' (1943) against
the long introductions to André Gorz's 'le Traître' (1958) and
Paul Nizan's 'Aden-Arabie' (1960). It is also important to notice
that the two lengthy semi-biographical essays on Tintoretto (1957)
and Merleau-Ponty (1961) would have been quite out of character
for the essayist of the war years.(26)

Sartre's uneasiness at the falsity of fiction when it manifests
itself as a novel is especially well exemplified by the final paragraph of his review of Camus's first novel:
> How are we to classify this clear, dry work?...M. Camus calls
> it a 'novel'...I would hesitate somewhat to use the term 'novel'
> for this succession of inert present moments which allows us
> to see, from underneath, the mechanical economy of something
> deliberately staged. Or, if it is a novel, it is so in the sense
> that *Zadig* and *Candide* are novels.(27)

This invites comparison with the similar conclusion to Sartre's
notorious essay on Mauriac, except that there Mauriac's book is
'not a novel'(28) in the pejorative sense of the phrase. Again in a
1939 essay on John Dos Passos - who very clearly influenced
Sartre's novelistic practice in 'Le Sursis' - Sartre notes approv-
ingly that 'Dos Passos's time is neither fictional nor narrative'(29)
and that he is truer to life because of it. Interestingly enough,
Sartre's sensitivity to 'false fictions' manifests itself in the very
first paragraph of his first published essay of literary criticism,
on Faulkner's 'Sartoris':
> With a little perspective, good novels come almost to resemble
> natural phenomena. We forget that they have authors....It
> is true that all art is false. Paintings lie about perspective.
> There are, however, two kinds of picture: real pictures and
> the illusionist kind.(30)

Sartre takes 'Sartoris' to task because in this novel 'Faulkner
betrays himself in it: we catch him red-handed all the way
through.'(31) But by the time of the 1952 book on Genet, Faulkner's vice has clearly become a virtue, and in a 1964 interview
Sartre goes so far as to criticize his own 'Nausea' because he has
not embedded himself more completely in it.(32) It is, of course,
typical of Sartre's dialectical thinking that in an interview four
years previously we should also find him expressing regret at
the way an author's own personality intrudes into a work of art.
The stimulus for this view, interestingly, was a question as to
whether he still believed that Mauriac was not a novelist:

> I think that I would be more flexible nowadays, by thinking
> that the essential quality of the novel must be to arouse
> passion and interest, and I would be much less punctilious
> about methods. This is because I have come to see that all
> methods involve trickery,(33) even the methods of the Amer-
> icans. One always arranges things in order to say what one
> thinks to the reader, and the author is always present.
> American trickery is more subtle, but it is there. Having
> said this, I think that the best method of constructing a good
> novel is not to show oneself too obviously. If I had to re-
> write 'Roads to Freedom', I would try to present each char-
> acter without a commentary, without showing my feelings.(34)

Sartre was always impressed by the way art-objects, whether in
prose or paint, can come 'to resemble natural phenomena'(35) and
was much concerned with the business of perspective that allows
this to happen. In a 1959 essay on the paintings of Giacometti, he
stresses the importance of distance in the Swiss sculptor's art:
'For him, distance is not voluntary isolation, nor even a moment
of withdrawal. It is a requirement, a ceremony, a sense of difficulty, the product...of powers of attraction and forces of
repulsion.'(36) In another important essay two years previously,
The Prisoner of Venice, Sartre discussed the Florentine Ren-
aissance's conquest of perspective in connection with Mantegna's
'Christ' and Piero della Francesca's 'Annunciation': 'Perspective
is profane, sometimes even a profanation....Perspective was the
violence which human weakness inflicted upon God's little world.'
(37) In The Prisoner of Venice Sartre is particularly antagon-
istic to the way Titian vanquished 'the logic of the eye' with 'the
logic of the heart', made a 'compromise with Heaven' and allowed
his paintings to become 'realizations'.(38) Tintoretto, by contrast,
is praised for the kind of dishonest honesty that Sartre also finds
commendable in Genet and Giacometti.

One does these remarkable essays scant justice if one so much
as suggests that they are mere pendants to 'Les Mots'. But they
do provide insights that are relevant to understanding why 'Les
Mots' is as it is. In writing his autobiographical essay Sartre was
faced with a severe problem of perspective;(39) standing back too
far from himself would turn the book into a novel like 'Nausea'
which, in one of his moods at least, he considered to contain an
insufficient amount of self; standing too near would be to make

the same mistake as Titian and to give people the illusion that he
had created the 'thing itself'. Sartre's reaction to the critical
reception of 'Les Mots' shows him especially intent on establishing
the proper perspective for reading it:

The critics have reproached me with being too severe on the
child that I was. They find it pleasant that memories should
be penetrated by indulgence towards oneself, that the writer,
being moved, moves the reader. I am neither severe nor
tender, I do not make the child responsible, but rather the
epoch that has made him. And above all I detest the worn-
out myth of childhood put about by adults. I'd prefer them to
read this book for what it is: at attempt at destroying a
myth.(40)

This is an important statement, not least in the way it shows
that Sartre sees his autobiographical essay as a contribution to
the 'engagée' literature that he was always intent on promoting.
One of his many explanations of how and why he came to write
the book actually situates it in relation to his political activities in
the 1950s:

Thrown into the atmosphere of action, I suddenly saw clearly
the kind of neurosis that had dominated my life previously:
I was inside it....It is the property of every neurosis to
offer itself as natural. I calmly considered that I was made to
write. Needing to justify my existence, I had made an absolute
of literature. It had taken me thirty years to destroy this
spiritual condition.

When my relations with the communist party gave me the
necessary room, I decided to write my autobiography. I wanted
to show how a man can pass from literature as a sacrament to
an act which still remains the act of an intellectual.(41)

The literary act of 'Les Mots' was clearly not conceived, therefore
(as a 'journal intime' might be), as a medium for self-education,
but rather as an education for others. Sartre even claimed that he
did not publish the book in 1954 because its educational value was
diminished by personal feelings:

In 'Les Mots', I explain the origin of my madness, my neurosis.(42) This analysis can be of help to young people who
dream of being writers....In 1954 I was very close to
regretting [having chosen literature]. I was a neophyte in
another world [sc. the world of politics]...there are two
tones in 'Les Mots': the echo of this condemnation [of lit-
erature] and an attentuation of this severity. If I didn't
publish it earlier and in its most radical form, this was
because I thought it excessive. There is no sense in drag-
ging an unfortunate through the mud just because he writes.
Moreover, in the interim I had realized that action also has
its difficulties and can lead one into neurosis.(43)

Sartre's prolonged and assiduous work on 'Les Mots' helps to
account for one of the features that must immediately strike any
reader of it: the extremely elusive, and even confused time-
scheme of the book. The point of reference is sometimes 1954 and

sometimes 1963.(44) It would be wrong to see this as a merely
contingent aspect of 'Les Mots', a result of carelessness on Sartre's part. The formal aspects of the work, without being immediately obvious, are clearly the result of considerable deliberation
and, as Sartre himself admitted, 'For me, the two - form and
meaning - are always related.'(45) Sartre's primary formal problem was 'to avoid the novelistic, and even the anecdotal insofar as
the anecdote was not important,'(46) and in trying 'to define myself in relation to the historical situation'(47) he used a method
similar to that which he had used in his studies of Baudelaire and
Genet.(48) This method is adumbrated in the final section of
'Being and Nothingness'. But in 'Being and Nothingness' Sartre
is intent on denying the validity of Freud's concept of the Unconscious. By the time he came to write 'Les Mots', Sartre's attitude
to Freud had changed considerably.(49) In interviews of 1957 and
1964 Sartre asserted that Freud was as important as Marx in this
kind of investigation and that, contrary to what most Marxists
believed, it was not impossible to synthesize the systems of the
two men.(50) This radical change of heart stems from Sartre's
ceasing to regard himself as merely an existential phenomenologist
and beginning to see himself as a kind of anthropologist.(51) It is
symptomatic of Sartre's change of direction that in the conclusion
to the preface of Questions of Method (first published in 1957
and later placed at the head of the 'Critique of Dialectical Reason')
Sartre should ask whether it is possible to create a structural and
historical anthropology, and should confront, towards the end of
the essay, the question of how a man's life is structured: 'A life
unfolds in spirals; it always passes through the same stages, but
at different levels of integration and complexity.'(52)

'Les Mots' is the clearest exemplification of the truth of this in-
sight, concluding as it does with the eminently anthropological
postulate of 'a whole man, made of all men, worth all of them, and
any one of them worth him.'(53) Every person, Sartre is suggesting in Questions of Method, passes through the same 'stages'
as everyone else; the stages that Sartre passes through in 'Les
Mots' are representative of a whole society's development or, as it
turns out, non-development. But there is a problem here, which
stems directly from Sartre's conviction that form and meaning
should be inseparable. For 'Les Mots' not only describes a life
unfolding 'in spirals'; as a literary artefact it has a spiral form,
passing 'through the same stages, but at different levels of integration and complexity'.(54) Criticism of 'Les Mots' has been much
concerned with the book's repetitiveness and the virtual absence
of temporal specifications, and has suggested that, whilst Sartre
(as almost all his remarks in interviews confirm) is intending to
present his neurosis as a neurosis conquered, the book is as much
a product of neurosis as an account of how that neurosis came to
be cured.(55) Barish, for instance, suggests that because the
adult Sartre, like the child Sartre, persists in seeing the self as an
artefact, 'Les Mots' 'reflects the persistence of the same complaint'
(56) that it is describing. Conor Cruise O'Brien, without reaching

precisely the same conclusion, confesses to finding 'something wrong' with 'the smiling irony...[It is] all a little too jaunty; one is reminded rather often that this autobiographer is after all a writer of fiction.'(57) Another writer to stress the 'bad faith' of the enterprise - although still considering it 'one of the finest pieces of writing Sartre has produced' - is Zimmerman:

Sartre cannot keep himself from performing 'tours de passe-passe' [a term taken from 'Saint Genet'] even when he ostensibly condemns them in 'Les Mots'...where notions are repudiated and recreated simultaneously, the existence and form of the essay belying certain of its statements.(58)

This is also the view of almost all the critics who rely on structuralist or semi-structuralist techniques: Jeffrey Mehlman, Dominick La Capra, Philippe Lejeune, J. Arnold and J.-P. Piriou. Indeed almost all the accounts of the book of any substance, and even some of the more or less ephemeral reviews,(59) are united in regarding 'Les Mots' as a book that requires considerable reading between the lines.(60)

Much the most sustained attempt to read between the lines of 'Les Mots' is that of Philippe Lejeune, who experiences little of the difficulty in 'establishing a chronology in this highly repetitive text'(61) that La Capra, like many others, has testified to. Lejeune demonstrates that the book covers the period from 1909 (when Sartre was four) to 1916 (in the autumn of which year his mother remarried and the family moved to La Rochelle).(62) But, as Lejeune goes on to show,(63) Sartre has tried to freeze the time-structure of his book so as to signal to the reader that this is by no means a conventional (auto)biography, nor even a narrative in any ordinary sense of the word.(64) By concentrating almost exclusively on his behaviour up to the age of eleven, Sartre is trying to demonstrate to the reader how dominant his 'neurosis' was, and how much his growth as a human being was stunted by the pernicious interaction of heredity, environment and his own peculiar fictions. Only at the end of 'Les Mots' does Sartre significantly widen his focus in order to show that 'Nausea' (begun in 1935) and 'Being and Nothingness' (which originates in his thinking of the 1930s) can also be seen, from the vantage-point of 1964, as products of neurosis. 'Les Mots' is not, therefore, despite appearances, a contribution to the literature of childhood autobiography, an especially strong tradition - almost a recognizable genre - in French literature; rather, it is a contribution to the literature of neurosis and hence, in the words of Arnold and Piriou, 'a research into the origins of his own imagination'.(65) Paul de Man has called it 'a full-fledged clinical essay on the experience of alienation'.(66) Lejeune, without apparently recognizing that his description invites comparison with the famous words of Roquentin with which I began, calls it 'a dialectical fable' and concludes by saying that it is 'the most totalized book he has written.'(67)

The dialectics of 'Les Mots' are much more complex than its simple division into two roughly equal parts, 'Reading' and 'Writing', would suggest; in this respect the book is typical of the tourniquets into which Sartre's mind seems naturally to lead him. The 'fabular' aspects are, by contrast, relatively straightforward, since it is clear from the start that this is a story with a moral, and that the moral content is always more important to Sartre than the merely anecdotal. As befits a fable, it begins and ends with an apophthegm, 'Glissez, mortels, n'appuyez pas,' that Sartre's maternal grandmother (68) has purloined, doubtless without knowing it, from a minor eighteenth-century poet; and, again as in a fable, a distinctly 'narrative' tone, detached and witty,(69) is present from the beginning. The opening section even seems to have the simplicity of a fable, with its apparently casual account of the two strains, maternal and paternal, Schweitzer and Sartre, that have come together in the young Jean-Paul. But this section is actually far less casual than it appears. To begin with, it is important to notice that the maternal side of the family takes precedence over the paternal, on which Sartre spends only a paragraph. Particularly dominant is the figure of Sartre's maternal grandfather who, in one way or another, dominates the book. But the Schweitzer and Sartre families are not unlike each other: both are bourgeois and provincial, and both are riddled with dissatisfaction and conflict. The Schweitzer strain is characterized by 'shabby vulgarity and theatricality';(70) the Sartre strain is distinguished by silence, gloom and a longing for death. Both families are committed to the continuation of the species but without any transcendent sense of why the species should be continued and without taking much pleasure in ensuring that it is. Of Charles Schweitzer Sartre writes: 'He sprang four children on [his wife]; a daughter who died in infancy, two sons and another daughter';(71) of Doctor Sartre that he 'did not speak to his wife for forty years....Yet he shared her bed and, from time to time, without a word, got her with child...two sons and a daughter.'(72) Sartre reinforces the obvious parallels by indicating that the two marriages were roughly contemporaneous, and by showing that the two sets of offspring led similarly desultory lives of loneliness, distress and even madness. This section, without being strident, is as 'engagée' as anything Sartre wrote, with the reader almost obliged to draw the inference that the bourgeoisie is deeply, and irremediably, divided against itself.

But Sartre wants to do more than simply show a decaying bourgeoisie; he also wants to demonstrate the active harm it can do, and has done, specifically to him. This section is not, therefore, to be seen as the kind of background information, the obligatory genealogy, that is virtually de rigueur in an autobiography. Instead it shows precisely why the young Jean-Paul Sartre should later be burdened with a greatness that the family, impressed by his precociousness, were intent on investing him with. It also shows how deterministic, not to say fatalistic, a bourgeois existence must be, in which no one explores the possibility of an existential 'choice' (73) without being disappointed by it. Charles Schweitzer cannot catch up with the bareback rider he has gone in pursuit of, and is forced to adopt the role that his father has long had in mind for him: to 'form souls',(74) and in particular the soul of the young Jean-Paul. Jean-Baptiste Sartre, who 'wanted to study for the Navy and see the sea', is undermined in health by his travels and dies, leaving his son not only fatherless but also, by poisoning his wife's milk, effectively motherless:

On my father's death, Anne-Marie [his mother] and I woke from a common nightmare: I was cured. But we were the victims of a misunderstanding: she lovingly rejoined a son whom she had never really left; I regained consciousness on the lap of a stranger.(75)

Sartre takes a typically bifocal view of this event, the event that conditions all subsequent traumas of his life: juxtaposed with his sense of being a victim is the concomitant awareness that consciousness has been conferred on him (76) by his father's death: 'Jean-Baptiste's death was the great event of my life: it returned my mother to her chains and it gave me my freedom.'(77)

Sartre begins the second section of 'Les Mots' by recreating a partial portrait of his absent father in order to show the benign effects of the event, but shifts almost at once to the more malign influences which inevitably filled the gap. The primary problem is that a role is conferred on him, together with a set of assumptions that he will later have to cast off or, as it turns out, in the event transmogrify. In particular the 'fatherless' family is stiflingly and bogusly religious:

It was conveyed to me that I was the child of a miracle rather than a dead man's son...I was shown a young giantess, and I was told that she was my mother. On my own, I should more likely have taken her for an elder sister. This virgin...would sketch in a few light words the future which she praised me for wanting to achieve....I allowed myself to be trapped by these soft prophecies.
   That left the Patriarch: he looked so much like God the Father that he was often taken for him.(78)

Thus begins what Lejeune has aptly called the 'comédie familiale' which is mirrored in the 'comédie littéraire' which follows it. Both these sections exploit the double meaning of the word 'comédie', for both are not only theatrical but also funny. Family life is revealed as 'one long succession of ceremonies'(79) epitomized by the grandfather's penchant for sublimity (already adumbrated in the first section), the sentimental melodramas of the mother and grandmother, and the wholehearted embrace of 'causa sui' fantasies on the part of the young boy. Sartre's description of this period is, appropriately enough, very dramatic, with the form and meaning reinforcing one another in the reciprocal manner that Sartre believes important.(80) Charles Schweitzer is both grandfather in fact and grandfather in act:

I see this handsome man with his flowing beard, for ever
between two melodramatic effects, like an alcoholic between
two drinks, as the victim of two recently discovered techniques: the art of photography and 'the art of being a
grandfather'. [A reference, as Sartre's footnote tells us, to
a book by Victor Hugo.] He had the good and ill fortune to
be photogenic; photographs of him filled the house; since
there was no such thing as rapid exposure, he had acquired
a taste for posing and holding his poses; everything was an
excuse to freeze a gesture, to adopt a noble stance or to
turn to stone; he relished those brief moments of eternity
when he became his own statue. Because of this love of his
for taking up a pose, my memories of him are like stiff magic-
lantern pictures.(81)

The young Jean-Paul naturally enough imitates these paternal-
istic fictions, but imitates them so fervently and so imaginatively
that he reverses the normal relationship between adult and child,
becoming a kind of self-generated deity to be worshipped. The
child finds the best arena for his own statuesqueness to be the
Catholic Mass, and the Christian idea that 'out of the mouths of
babes and sucklings' comes wisdom is hilariously transformed
into an absurdly self-congratulatory egotism. The more the family require him to 'put on the disguise of childhood', the more
Jean-Paul sees himself as repeating 'the favour of being born'
without any external agency. Not surprisingly, the third section
begins with the ironic acknowledgment that 'It was Paradise'(82)
and continues with the boy, unruffled by the 'cheerful inconsis-
tency' of reality, separating humanity into sheep and goats,(83)
thus making it a kind of Last Judgment also. But at this point the
complexities of the pre-First World War Franco-German situation -
epitomized by the unstable status of Alsace-Lorraine - are less
important to the boy than the creation of a talismanic word of his
mother's invention ('Karlémami'), which enables him to 'maintain
the flawless unity of the family'(84) when all around is disunity
and disagreement.

Sartre's mother is at this point scarcely a member of the family
at all, and in the long fourth section, which is an elaborate gloss
on Sartre's recognition in the previous one that he was a 'cultural
possession',(85) the mother's role remains subservient to the
grandfather's. The boy is indoctrinated here (or indoctrinated
himself) with the idea that literature is a kind of religion: 'I was
the grandson of a craftsman who specialized in the manufacture
of holy objects.'(86) The primary contrast here is between the
sublime and intellectual books of the grandfather and the 'trashy
works' that the grandmother (as the first section has strongly
hinted) prefers. Sartre returns to this contrast at the end of the
section with the disarming information that 'even today, I would
rather read "thrillers" than Wittgenstein',(87) and occupies the
interim with an account of how he tried to appropriate and cere-
monialize the act of reading just as previously he had done in the
matter of acting as a child.

Books pose another problem for the child. They pre-exist the child and yet they appear to be self-supporting and autotelic, as he imagines himself to be:

Anne-Marie made me sit down in front of her, on my little chair; she leant over, lowered her eyelids and went to sleep. From this mask-like face issued a plaster voice. I grew bewildered: who was talking? about what? and to whom? My mother had disappeared: not a smile or trace of complicity. I was an exile. And then I did not recognize the language.... After a moment, I realized it was the book that was talking ....I felt I was turning into someone else. Anne-Marie, too, with her blind soothsayer's look, was someone else: it was as if I were every mother's child and she were every child's mother.(88)

It is after this initial shock that Jean-Paul learns 'to enjoy this release which tore me out of myself' and 'to prefer prefabricated tales'.(89) But as in the earlier case of reversing the roles, so here: the child is determined to make himself the 'causa sui'. Sartre represents this in what has already become a characteristic paradox: books offer a splendidly satisfying refuge from the 'boring cemetery'(90) of everyday life, but they also engender a fondness for fiction that diminishes everyday life to virtual non-existence. As in the third section, Sartre's language becomes very highly charged with a wealth of metaphoric and metonymic transformations, so that form and meaning are once again united: 'books were my birds and my nests, my pets, my stable and my countryside; the library was the world trapped in a mirror; it had its infinite breadth, its variety and its unpredictability.'(91) At this point the vivid recapture of these childhood details is tempered by the drier wisdom of the ageing adult:

A Platonist by condition, I moved from knowledge to its object; I found ideas more real than things, because they were the first to give themselves to me and because they gave themselves like things. I met the universe in books: assimilated, classified, labelled and studied, but still impressive; and I confused the chaos of my experiences through books with the hazardous course of real events. Hence my idealism which it took me thirty years to undo.(92)

But the child and the adult are recognizably the same person: the 'ivory tower' attitudes of the child are reflected in the adult Sartre's choice of a tenth-floor apartment overlooking Paris,(93) and the child's tendency to interpret dead authors as 'other children ...who had managed to remain my age all their lives'(94) survives in the way the adult Sartre treats the 'famous dead like school-friends'(95) in his studies of Baudelaire and Flaubert. The Sartre of 'Les Mots' is, indeed, no more convinced that he has cured his neurosis than critics of the book have been:

I got rid of Karl's humanism, that prelate's humanism, the day I realized that every man is all men. How sad it is to be cured: language loses its magic, the heroes of the pen, once my equals, stripped of their privileges, have returned to the ranks: I wear mourning for thom twice over.

What I have just written is false. True. Neither true nor
false, like all that is written about madmen or about men.(96)
This is one of the most dramatic moments in 'Les Mots', and one
of the most crucial for a proper understanding of the book. Sartre
confronts here the objection that any reader of autobiography
feels compelled to raise: how authentic is the image of the past
that is being constructed in the present? At this point Sartre is
at once subjecting his enterprise to a critique of his own and protecting it from anyone else's critique. What he is seeking to create
is a 'true fiction' of the kind he has spoken of in interviews. Sartre illustrates the point by finishing this section with a contrast
between reading as 'play-acting' and '*genuine* reading',(97) and
then abandoning this in favour of a more straightforward contrast
between the fantasies of the child and the reality of the 'common
laws' of the school. But in the paradoxical contradiction that lies
at the centre of this section Sartre is effectively playing the game
of 'loser wins all'(98) which he admits to at the end of part two,
and which the Genet book would suggest that he sees as an inseparable part of the writing process. This helps to explain why
it is precisely at this moment that Sartre chooses to remind us of
the book as book, by referring to the precise day on which he is
'correcting this manuscript'.(99) With words,(100) Sartre is saying, and in particular with these words (the French title is
ambiguous, meaning both 'words' and 'the words'), the author is
building a personality for himself that is at one and the same
time true and false, which the reader cannot but half-believe in
and yet which he cannot repose any faith in. Sartre's description
of his rereading is intended, in other words, to make us sceptical
about our own habits of reading.

Having reminded us of how deceptive 'Les Mots' can be, it seems
only natural that the next section should underline this by dealing with Sartre's first experience of school and concentrating our
attention on the way he habitually misspelt words.(101) But it is
the misuse of words in graffiti that really intrigues him:

I went over and read it: '*Le père Barrault est un con*'. My
heart pounded, I was rooted to the spot with astonishment,
and I was afraid....It was too much even to have to read it.
...I did not want this cockroach on the wall to jump into my
mouth and be changed deep down in my throat into a clarion
call. If I pretended that I had not noticed it, perhaps it
would go back into a hole in the wall. But when I looked
away, I kept seeing the hateful name *Le père Barrault,* which
upset me still more.(102)

The graffiti is both repulsive and attractive to the child: it expresses something that he has been subconsciously feeling and
yet at the same time is evidence of the 'intolerable disorders' that
are normally masked by the 'order of the world'.(103) The insult
extends from Barrault to Charles Schweitzer his effective 'père'
and beyond him to his real father who has died. But the real
insult is to his mother, as the oral and vaginal fantasies obliquely

indicate. The unified role that up till now the boy has been playing is here threatened with a schizophrenic split and will later,
in part two, be recognized as 'madness': 'it seemed to me as if
some cruel madman were sneering at my politeness, my respect,
my eagerness, and the pleasure I took each morning in raising
my cap and saying "Good morning, Sir" and that I myself was
that madman....'(104)
    The demolition of the role that the child has been playing con-
tinues in the next two sections as 'one transparent certainty'
spoils everything: 'I was an impostor....Those bright, sunlit
appearances which composed my personality gave themselves away
through a defect of being which I could neither quite understand
nor stop feeling.'(105) But the first casualty of this recognition
is not so much the child as the adults who have made him what he
is (or, as the Sartre of 'Being and Nothingness' would say, is
not):(106) he begins to suspect them of play-acting. At this
point the absence of a father - dramatically and poignantly rendered in the conclusion to the previous section where Sartre sees
himself as 'alone between one old man and two women' - is subsumed into a more metaphysical 'defect of being' which is the
immediate cause of the child falling ill and experiencing something
like 'La nausée';(107)

    Breathing, digesting, defecating listlessly, I went on living
    because I had begun to live...I felt myself become an
    object,(108) a potted plant...I confused my body with its
    sickness: I no longer knew which of the two was undesir-
    able.(109)   ·

It is not, however, until an innocent remark made by his grandfather in the next section that the condition really worsens. The
child misinterprets the remark to mean that his grandfather's
statuesque (110) friend and collaborator, Monsieur Simmonnot, is
the kind of person who makes good a 'defect of being' by making
the party up to its proper numbers. All the child can do is to take
'refuge in the family comedy' in the hope that he is fulfilling a
similar role.
    The 'nausea' experience is dominated by an awareness of death,
which is imaged in terms of the mouths and madness that first
surfaced in the experience of the word 'con', the organ which
condemns one to life and therefore also to death. The experience
of disgust is so strong here that one can see why Sartre should
be keen to mention two saints whose lives (though 'tall stories' to
the adult Sartre) show them conquering initial feelings of disgust.
(111) Sartre himself cannot emulate these stories, but he can tell
'the story of a missed vocation'(112) instead. At this point he
reveals how his adopted vocation of play-actor suffered two dis-
astrous set-backs, the first in the context of a patriotic play
written by his grandfather, the second in the context of a quest-
ionnaire given to him by a Madame Picard. In both instances the
child learns that there are 'others' as well as 'self', and both
events culminate in him standing in front of a mirror that is showing him his true self: 'The mirror had told me what I had already

known: I was horribly ordinary. I have never got over it.'(113)

The young Sartre's reaction to this shock is to revert to the 'causa sui' project of earlier days, but at the same time to translate it from religious terms into literary ones; in short, to become a writer: 'to escape the desolation of created things, I prepared for myself the middle-class solitude for which there is no cure: that of the creator.'(114) Previously he had given birth to himself anew to satisfy the family; now he is doing the same thing to satisfy himself:

> When I recall my life from six to nine, I am struck by the continuity of my spiritual exercise. They often altered in content but the programme did not vary; I had made a false entrance, so I retired behind a screen and started my birth over again at a selected point, at the very moment when the universe was silently crying out for me.(115)

The first period of writing is dominated by 'rakehell fantasies' of a thoroughly conventional and compensatory kind, which are essentially plagiarisms of the trashy literature previously associated with his maternal grandmother. In these stories the young Sartre plays God with all the fervour that he will later accuse Mauriac of, so as to fill up the 'defect of being' that he has still not successfully remedied. It is noticeable, however, that at the point of maximum disaster in the stories he is telling himself, the child suspends the whole activity, half-aware that the business of fiction-making is preventing him from attaining the fulness of being that would be the only real consolation: 'it was obvious the building was about to crumble. At this point, I would say aloud the prophetic words: "To be continued". "What do you say?" my mother would ask. I would reply, prudently, "I'm holding myself in suspense." '(116)

In the last section of part one of 'Les Mots' Sartre describes the transition from writing as a false imposture to writing as a true one. This transformation is only achieved by virtue of two important intermediate events: going to the cinema (117) and listening to his mother playing the piano. These two events are linked by the motif of the piano: the cinema piano that makes up for the absence of words and the piano at home that stimulates a multiplicity of fantastic associations. The cinema experience points forward to the truism with which Sartre ends the book, although here the overtones of defeat as the defining feature of human life are more explicit:

> the very mixed audience seemed to have been united by a disaster rather than by a show; once dead, etiquette finally unmasked the true link between men, their adhesion. I came to loathe ceremonies, but I adored crowds; I have seen all kinds, but I never recovered that naked awareness without recoil of each until 1940.(118)

Sartre acknowledges that his love was a dubious and even perverse phenomenon predicated on 'what it still lacked' (i.e. words), but this 'absence' is more positive than any previous 'absence' has been.(119) Previously absence had been synonymous with vacuum;

now, thanks to the piano accompaniment, it becomes almost a plenum: 'I had found the world in which I wanted to live - I was in touch with the absolute....Out in the street, I was a supernumerary once more.'(120) The piano operates here not only as a bridge between the subjective situation of the boy and the perception of an object outside himself, but also as an index of the predestination that has been lacking in the child's previous experience:

> that was not me, that young widow crying on the screen,
> and yet she and I had but one soul: Chopin's Funeral March
> ....I felt that I was a prophet unable to foretell anything....
> How lucky those cowboys, musketeers and policemen were:
> their future was there, in that foreboding music, and it
> determined the present.(121)

Sartre's own future remains uncertain right up until the moment when his grandfather 'saves' him, which forms the dramatic and abrupt conclusion to the first part of the book. But his salvation is preceded by the last of his fantasy roles in which, under the stimulus of his mother's piano-playing, he 'impersonate[s] all the characters'(122) who are thronging his hypersensitive imagination. Sartre links this with a retelling of the story of patient Griselda, but gives the story a sado-masochistic colouring that is a fairly obvious reflection of the unprecipitated Oedipus complex from which, even as an adult, he is suffering:(123)

> What I liked about this hardly commendable tale was the
> victim's sadism and that inflexible virtue which, in the
> end, brought the cruel husband to his knees. That was
> what I wanted for myself: to force the magistrates to their
> knees, and make them do reverence to me, as punishment.
> But each day I postponed the acquittal to the next: always
> a future hero, I longed already for a consecration which I
> was forever thrusting away.(124)

This fantasy, as Sartre shows, can be infinitely repeated, but it cannot be transformed into the destiny (125) that the cinema has given him a transient glimpse of. It is a novel by Jules Verne, 'Michel Strogoff', which offers him the first real opportunity to liberate himself: 'No repetition: everything changed and must keep changing. Saintliness repelled me: in Michel Strogoff it fascinated me because it wore the trappings of heroism.'(126)

The assumption of the role of writer does not follow immediately; as befits a text whose oscillations are mimetic of a real-life struggle, there is a sudden reversion to abject misery. The loneliness of the child reaches a new low as he sees himself in the context of other children, his contemporaries and equals, and the animal imagery reaches a kind of climax, with the young Sartre now 'a shrimp that interested no one' and now 'a bird on the heights where my mind could breathe, among my dreams.'(127) This opposition is clearly an intractable and irresolvable one, and could continue forever in a vicious circle. But at this point the circle is broken, and by the very agency that has been most instrumental in bringing it into being: Charles Schweitzer.

Part two of 'Les Mots', 'Writing', is of almost equal length with
part one, but has only five sections rather than nine. It is simpler in character, as if in confirmation of Sartre's claim at the end
of the first of the five sections that he has begun to understand
himself. Sartre's new orientation towards reality is still, however,
bedevilled by a lingering attachment to previous impostures:

I was trying to tear ideas from my mind and bring them to
life outside myself, amidst real furniture and real walls, as
bright and clear as the ones which flowed on the screen. In
vain; I could no longer ignore my twofold imposture: I was
pretending to be an actor pretending to be a hero.(128)

Chronologically, this period is roughly contemporaneous with the
final section of part one; but here there is a new commitment to
the outside world which indicates a development in the child's
psychology. No longer does Sartre feel compelled to confuse himself with the objects of his perception and thus preserve unitary
relationships that will compensate for the disunited family his
father's death has brought into being: 'As an author, I was still
the hero: I projected my epic dreams though him. Yet there were
two of us: he did not bear my name and I referred to him only in
the third person.'(129) Although the child has been stimulated to
write by the silent films he has seen - he describes his writing to
his mother as 'making films' and overhears her saying 'He's not
making a noise'(130) - the new activity is a lot less passive. Sartre stresses that it involves active confrontation with the real
rather than with the unreal world: 'it was nothing to do with
imagination: I did not invent these horrors: I discovered them,
like everything else, in my memory.'(131) At the same time, despite the increased strength of the reality principle (and in part
because of it), the threat of madness - previously confronted in
the 'nausea' section of part one - is increased. Sartre at this
point recounts a newspaper story in which he read of a madman
escaping from an asylum and frightening a young bride to death.
Sartre is here, as previously, for example when faced by the
graffito, the madman. But he is also rewriting his origins. Hard
upon this account of the death of a potential mother comes Sartre's
admission: 'I was born from writing.'(132) This is a kind of active
parallel to the passive birth(s) he has described in part one. In
part one, the casualty is his father; in part two, the casualty is
a surrogate version of his mother.

The second section of part two consolidates this parellelism by
presenting the same elements as part one in a different configuration: the mystical theology, the sense of 'lack', the 'epic cast of
mind', the 'imperative mandate', the anxiety dreams. No other
section of the book so well exemplifies the view that Sartre put
forward in Questions of Method that life 'passes through the
same stages, but at different levels of integration and complexity.'
At the same time Sartre is once again showing that form and meaning are inseparable. For now that Sartre has attained the status
of Writer (which he admitted to being ever thereafter), what could
be more natural than for him to reassemble, and in effect rewrite,

the elements held in suspension in part one?

The role of writer is uniquely adapted, in Sartre's formulation, to filling up the 'lack' that he had first found epitomized by the absence of the statuesque Monsieur Simmonnot in an important incident in part one. But writing transforms the writer into something almost as statuesque as the world he has escaped. Sartre shows this by talking about himself in the third person, a strategy previously reserved for his first childish attempts at fiction:

An imaginary child, I was becoming a real knight-errant. I was sought after!....Round about 1930, people began to get impatient [for my works] and to say to each other: 'He's taking his time! We've been feeding him for twenty-five years and he's done nothing! Shall we die without reading him?' I answered them in my 1913 voice: 'Hey, give me time to work!'(133)

Once again his grandfather unconsciously suggests to him a temporary escape, and the 'writer-knight' is transformed into the 'writer-martyr'. But this is only reversing the narrative order of part one, where the 'missed vocation' of the priesthood preceded the 'epic cast of mind'.(134) Sartre's sudden discovery of his future 'determine[s] the present' for him just as it has done for the characters in the films he has seen. And in appropriating the present, it begins to appropriate the past also: 'I chose for a future the part of a famous dead man, and I tried to live backwards.(135) Between the ages of nine and ten, I became entirely posthumous.'(136)

This perverse and yet brilliant formulation is the first and type of many in a journey towards madness that is minutely and memorably charted. And as further preparation for the 'real' madness of the last three sections, Sartre plants any number of clues that even a bewildered reader will recognize as relevant to the writing of 'Les Mots' itself. The clearest clue is when Sartre, who has already quoted twice, apparently casually, from Chateaubriand, begins to make his own book seem like a version of 'Mémoires d'outre-tombe'. By identifying himself with other writers (a much more restrictive strategy than the identification with all others that occurs at the very end of the book), Sartre immures himself in a kind of grave:

I found myself on the other side of the page, *in the book*: Jean-Paul's childhood was like those of Jean-Jacques and Johann Sebastian, and nothing happened to him that was not for the most part a foreshadowing. Only this time the author was winking at my great-nephews. I was being looked at, from death to birth, by these children to come whom I could not imagine and to whom I kept sending messages which I could not myself decipher...dispossessed of myself, I tried to recross the page in the opposite direction and rejoin the reader's side....There was no way out of the book: I had finished reading it long since, but I remained one of its characters.(137)

Just as previously, in the description of travelling to Dijon, Sartre

has imagined himself as at once the culprit, the ticket-inspector
and the train,(138) so here he is once again playing all the roles.
The effect is to collapse the time between when he allegedly felt
all these things (in the years immediately preceding the First
World War), the time of writing the book we are reading and the
time of reading 'Les Mots' in perpetuity. Not surprisingly, he
immediately shifts the discussion to questions of sincerity which
have already been effectively silenced by the 'true-false' dichotomy of part one and which have now been rendered almost
unanswerable by the unstable interfaces of this extraordinary
passage.

Sartre's experience of finding himself 'on the other side of the
page' is analogous to his experience with the mirror in part one,
with the important difference that he has, as it were, become the
mirror: 'I was being looked at...' This is a stage on the road to
madness, but not madness proper. The two events that finally
propel Sartre over the edge are the declaration of war on 2 August 1914 and his entry as a day-boy to the Lycée Henri IV. The
first is a public event, the second a private one, although, like
almost all the events in part two, it involves the outer world.
The public event drives the boy into an embattled privacy in
which 'I discovered the imagination. For the first time in my life
I re-read myself.'(139) This private orientation is exacerbated by
a change in the relationship with his mother which is here more
openly Oedipal than at any time previously. Even here, however,
we encounter the tendency to objectivize, partially in order to
deflect the real emotions that are being felt, and partially as a
result of the previous experience of being unable to escape from
the book: 'We acquired the habit of recounting to each other in
epic form the details of our life as they occurred; we referred to
ourselves in the third person plural.'(140) The viability of this
strategy as a defence-mechanism is shattered by one of the most
dramatic moments in the whole of 'Les Mots' when a mad young
man (an alter ego of Sartre himself, no doubt) takes a fancy to
Sartre's mother and accuses the boy of being spoilt.(141) This
acts as a kind of corrective to the child's growing Oedipal feelings,
although Sartre implicitly acknowledges that he has never fully
thrown them off in the conclusion to the incident. As Phillipe
Lejeune has very shrewdly remarked, the book not only describes
the act of 'looking away' but actually embodies it in the book by
changing the subject.(142)

Sartre's experience at the lycée offers more appropriate and
collective gratifications. At the lycée he becomes what he has
wanted to be ever since the discovery that Simmonnot was lacking:
'I was indispensable: *the right man in the right place.*'(143) It is
at the lycée that he meets Bénard and Nizan, who have certain
physical features in common, Nizan being the 'satanic double'(144)
of Bénard and also, by virtue of his squint, another of Sartre's
alter egos. The squint is an important motif, because Sartre has
been stressing how, in order to become a writer, he has had to
learn to use his eyes. In the period of lucid 'madness' that follows,

Sartre for the first time loses sight of himself and 'blindly *realized*
everything.'(145) The last two sections of 'Les Mots' explore the
consequences of this, with Sartre for the first time employing the
present tense more frequently than the past.

These two sections are largely made up of 'those rare lightning-
flashes which reveal to its lovers that the earth was not created
for them,'(146) and are the closest that Sartre comes to offering
any kind of general assessment of his career. The business of
being a writer which, in part one, had seemed a thoroughly im-
penetrable mystery, is here subjected to a thoroughgoing demystification. But the myth of the 'vast collective power' that is
lodged in the figure of the Writer resists total demystification,
and it is quite understandable that so many commentators should
have experienced difficulty in explicating the two concluding
sections of 'Les Mots'. The unstable chronology which has been
one of the strengths of the rest of the book here becomes, as La
Capra points out,(147) something of a weakness, and the 'internal
contestation' begins to look a little like a defensive vicious circle.
The tone, whilst predominantly melancholy, is not quite grave
enough to be construed unironically; the fantasies of rebirth, re-
newal and salvation are only just held in check by Sartre's endemic
habit of thinking 'systematically against myself'.(148) The dazzling
speed of utterance and sudden changes of direction leave the
reader without any really secure foothold. Perhaps the most important admission by Sartre in these final pages is the one immediately subsequent to his rereading of the 'conversion' crises in his
more obviously fictional works: 'I became a traitor and I have
remained one.'(149) It would be difficult, indeed, for any reader
of 'Les Mots' to resist the temptation to apply Sartre's description
of the relationship between himself and his fictional characters a
fortiori to his attempt at self-portraiture, and to say of 'Les Mots'
that it presents him not as he is, but as he has wanted to be.

The net result of what Sartre aptly calls, at one point, 'truquage'
is to make the book less a matter of Sartre looking in his own mirror and more a matter of him turning the mirror round to face the
reader. One of the few resonantly positive things that Sartre can
find to say in conclusion indicates his tacit awareness that this is
what he is up to: 'Culture saves nothing and nobody, nor does it
justify. But it is a product of man: he projects himself through it
and recognizes himself in it; this critical mirror alone shows him
his image.'(150) The guarded humanism of this belief, however
attenuated, prepares the way for the aggressively humble egal-
itarianism of the final words, in which Sartre suddenly diminishes
the gap between his reader and himself and postulates a 'whole man,
made of all men, worth all of them, and any one of them worth him.'
(151) But the book does not tell us whether such a totalized man is
a possibility or an impossibility, and still less does it tell us
whether this final paradox is intended to transform the paradoxical material that has preceded it and to render it more precise.

In so far as Sartre's whole writing project was a matter of continual redefinition, it would be futile to expect 'Les Mots' to

conclude in any final and definitive way. In much the most sensitive account of 'Les Mots', Dominick La Capra has pointed out how

> the myth of self-genesis, closely related to the myth of
> literature, is not as fully and as critically scrutinized as the
> latter, and the superabundant attention paid to the latter
> may even function to obscure the role of the myth of self-
> genesis...As Sartre writes, he is implicated in the text that
> simultaneously writes him as it repeats the problems that are
> seemingly under control.(152)

'Les Mots' ends, like the majority of rigorous self-scrutinies, with the genesis of the self arrested but not permanently halted, with the reader left to piece the puzzle together as best he may, and the only certainty being that the 'critical mirror' will show him his image.

7 VLADIMIR NABOKOV:
'Speak, Memory'
(1966)

The first publication in England of Nabokov's 'Speak, Memory' (1951) carried the subtitle 'a memoir' and a brief 'author's note' - the first and least characteristic of all the 'forewords' that Nabokov later developed into almost a mini-genre of his own invention - to the effect that the book is 'as truthful as he could possibly make it' and that any lapses from the truth are 'due to the frailty of memory, not to the trickery of art.'(1) Even the title of the original American edition, 'Conclusive Evidence' (later glossed by Nabokov as meaning 'conclusive evidence of my having existed'),(2) suggests that Nabokov's concern is with offering as veridical an account of his life as he is capable of.(3) But even a cursory reader of the book in those pre-'Lolita' days, one who knew nothing of Nabokov's two English and nine Russian novels (only two of which had then been translated), could not fail to have been struck by how artful Nabokov had been in reconstructing his European past. Certainly it would be impossible now, with the oeuvre of Nabokov in front of us, to swallow without demur Nabokov's disclaimer regarding the 'trickery of art', and it is not surprising that Nabokov omitted the phrase in the very much longer foreword to the 1966 edition of 'Speak, Memory', subtitled 'an autobiography revisited'. In the interim Nabokov had translated his 1951 text into Russian 'Drugie Berega' ('Other Shores', 1954)(4) and 'tried to do something about the amnesic defects of the original ',(5) and in retranslating his Russian version he created what is, in detail if not in overall shape, a different work, and as definitive a version as we can now hope for, a 'final edition'(6) in fact.

Nabokov's 1966 foreword is both informative and elusive, clear and yet out of focus, like 'Speak, Memory' itself. The almost manic scholarly accuracy of the bibliographic information is both disorientating and seductive, much like the thousand-page commentary that Nabokov appended to his notorious translation of Pushkin's 'Eugene Onegin'. It is not, however, mere window-dressing, any more than the 'Onegin' commentary is; it is fun, certainly, but it is serious fun. If it seems, at first glance, to court disaster, this is only in order to, in the author's own words, 'annoy the vulgar' and 'please the discerning'.(7) In this respect indeed, it is precisely designed to educate the reader and to prepare him for what the author has in store for him. In the third section of chapter 14 of 'Speak, Memory' proper, Nabokov reminds us that 'competition in chess problems is not really between White and Black but between the composer and the hypothetical solver

(Just as in a first rate work of fiction the real clash is not between the characters but between the author and the world).'(8)
This may not be an adequate account of a 'first-rate work of
fiction' but it is a more than adequate account of a first-rate work
of autobiography like 'Speak, Memory'. For the reader (and hence
the critic) of this work finds himself, from beginning to end, in
the role of problem-solver, and the first problem he has to solve
is Nabokov's foreword.(9)

The first thing in the foreword that might 'annoy the vulgar' is
Nabokov's claim that the book is 'a systematically correlated
assemblage of personal recollections'.(10) It irritates, first, because 'assemblage' sounds precious: second, because it sounds
alien to 'systematically' and 'correlated'; and third, because the
subsequent details suggest a genesis more heterogeneous than
systematic. The seemingly irrelevant details of the photograph in
which Nabokov is 'wrongly identified'(11) is important here, a
reminder that printed matter is inherently less accurate than it
appears to be. This is a subject to which Nabokov returns at the
end of the foreword when he speaks of 'those blessed libraries
where old newspapers are microfilmed, as all our memories should
be.'(12) The sheer diversity of publication dates, titles and magazines, followed by Nabokov's implicit admission that the book
could have been called by any one of five different titles, is
intended to make us marvel that the book actually exists as a book
at all, rather than as a lot of fragments immured in French and
American magazines. And it is precisely at this point that Nabokov chooses to tell us that he 'had no trouble...in assembling a
volume' because since 1936 the chapters had 'been neatly filling
numbered gaps in my mind which followed the present order of
chapters.'(13) It hardly seems to matter to Nabokov that even the
'discerning' reader will be tempted to dismiss this as a patent
fabrication with a liberal sprinkling of hindsight, because he has
bombarded the reader with so many facts of a provable kind, and
sees no reason why the reader should not grant him the one un-
provable 'fact'. Nabokov intends us to marvel at the sheer labour
of hammering these fragments into a unity, just as he later intends us to marvel at the 'diabolical task' of ' "re-Englishing"...
a Russian re-version of what had been an English re-telling of
Russian memories in the first place.'(14) He also intends us to
share his wonderment at the difficulty of establishing, through
the medium of memory, 'conclusive evidence' of any kind; hence
the excursus that corrects the chronological blunders of the 1951
version, and describes Mnemosyne as 'a very careless girl'.(15)

The foreword is only uncharacteristic of the book that follows
in that it elects to confine itself primarily to facts that have not
been filtered through the distorting (and yet focusing) prism of
the imagination. But even here there are moments when Nabokov
cannot forbear from colouring the facts in an imaginative and distinctive way. Speaking of the 'cornerstone' of his edifice - the
fifth chapter that began the 'erratic sequence' - Nabokov suggests
that it

already held in its hidden hollow various maps, timetables,
a collection of matchboxes, a chip of ruby glass, and even -
as I now realize - the view from my balcony of Geneva lake,
of its ripples and glades of light, black-dotted today, at
teatime, with coots and tufted ducks.(16)

This is not so much self-regarding applause at his own prophetic
powers as an illustration of how time, at privileged moments,
effectively ceases to exist as a stable entity. It links a real 1966
Montreux to a piece of writing originally published as a short
story. Later in the foreword Nabokov relates how prolonged
attention to a single object 'which had been a mere dummy' elicited
that the object was an 'oystershell-shaped cigarette case, gleam-
ing in the wet grass at the foot of an aspen...where I found on
that June day in 1917 a hawkmoth rarely met with so far west, and
where a quarter of a century earlier, my father had netted a Peacock butterfly.'(17) Both these instances, the one linking the past
with the present, the other relating the past to the remote past,
are illustrations of a principle most memorably expressed in Nabokov's introduction to his Pushkin translation: 'In art as in
science there is no delight without the detail, and it is on details
that I have tried to fix the reader's attention.'(18) The foreword
to 'Speak, Memory' is full of details designed to 'fix the reader's
attention' in preparation for what will follow, details so physically
present that the reader stumbles over them and has to reorientate
himself. Later, in section six of chapter 6, Nabokov unveils the
suppressed principle of his devious foreword: 'I confess I do not
believe in time. I like to fold my magic carpet, after use, in such
a way as to superimpose one part of the pattern upon another. Let
visitors trip.' (19) This may smack of arrogance, but it is not quite
so devil-may-care as it sounds. For it is only at the beginning of
'Speak, Memory' that the reader is a mere 'visitor'; by the end of
chapter 6 the reader has become aware of the folds in the magic
carpet and has effectively become, under the spell of the artist,
'one of those creatures that [are] not oneself but that [are] joined
to one by time's common flow.'(20) 'Speak, Memory' is not so much
a Proustian quest, a 'recherche du temps perdu', but a 'recovery'
of lost time,(21) a monument designed to withstand time and to
bring time to a halt.(22) The atomized time of the foreword prefigures the disregard for chronology in the body of the book. But
despite this disregard the book begins with a cradle rocking above
an abyss, and ends with the Nabokovs' departure for America
However much of a 'chronophobiac'(23) - Nabokov's own coinage
for himself as a small boy,(24) but equally applicable to the adult
who does not want to 'believe in time' - the author is, he also
knows that 'the prison of time is spherical and without exits.'(25)
From his 'present ridge of remote, isolated, almost uninhabited
time', Nabokov looks back to 'a radiant and mobile medium that
was none other than the pure element of time'(26) and aims, in
this connection, to make his book 'Speak, Memory' as 'radiant' and
'mobile' a medium as possible.

The foreword, then, is only apparently confined to the 'multiple

metamorphosis'(27) of a book; what it is really alerting us to is
the 'multiple metamorphosis' of a life now being relived and narrated in its own 'space-time'. Nabokov's nostalgia is, by his own
admission, 'a hypertrophied sense of lost childhood',(28) and the
writing of 'Speak, Memory' obviously exacerbated the nostalgia· to
a point that was barely endurable. It is no surprise to learn that
several of the chapters were written 'at a time of great mental and
physical stress'.(29) But the confident arrogance of the foreword
is predicated upon a hypertrophied sense of recovered childhood,
of time relived rather than simply regained, a memorialization
rather than a mere memoir.

There are beauties enough in 'Speak, Memory' proper not to
want to dwell unduly on the book's foreword,(30) and I have done
so only because it enables us more easily to unravel the threads
of the 'magic carpet' Nabokov is weaving. But even after taking
cognizance of its foreword, 'Speak, Memory' is by no means a
straightforward book. Although the title suggests that the author
has only to command his mnemonic apparatus, or Muse, for recollection to come flooding back, the process is inevitably attended
with 'blank spots, blurry areas, domains of dimness' that only
'come into beautiful focus' for a reader prepared to emulate, however vainly, the 'intense concentration' Nabokov himself has tried
to achieve when confronted by a 'neutral smudge'.(31) 'Speak,
Memory' is full of the 'elaborate interlacements and expanding
clusters' that made Nabokov want to call the book 'The Anthemion'.
(32) This is because, as in a chess problem, it is the themes that
matter most to the author. 'The following of...thematic designs,
through one's life,' Nabokov states in the third section of the first
chapter, 'should be, I think, the true purpose of autobiography.'
(33) But Nabokov does not intend these 'thematic designs' to be
immediately apprehensible, being sceptical in any case as to the
possibility of life surviving 'captivity in the zoo of words'.(34)
In the very last paragraph of the book, where the 'fall' (i.e.
autumn) of 1939 is linked to the 'fall' (i.e. collapse) of Paris in
1940 (and thus linked further to the suggestion that 'everything
has fallen through'(35) in section three of chapter 1), Nabokov
describes a garden which he and his wife and child are walking
through on their way to catch the boat to America:

> Laid out on the last limit of the past and on the verge of the
> present, it remains in my memory merely as a geometrical
> design which no doubt I could easily fill in with the colours
> of plausible flowers, if I were careless enough to break the
> hush of pure memory that (except, perhaps, for some chance
> tinnitus due to the pressure of my own tired blood) I have
> left undisturbed, and humbly listened to, from the beginning.
> (36)

This is Nabokov at his most elegantly deceptive and ironic. For
the 'tinnitus', the ringing in the ears, that has coloured his memories throughout is by no means random and haphazard, and the
construction of the book has been much more than simply listening
to a memory that has been ordered to 'Speak!'(37) The clue to the

construction of the book is, in a sense, embedded in the final
sentence of all,(38) where Nabokov contrives to describe not only
the reactions of himself and his family at a particular point in
time, but also, and more importantly, the ideal attitude to be
taken up by anyone who has read his book this far:
> There, in front of us,...where the eye encountered all
> sorts of stratagems...it was most satisfying to make out
> among the jumbled angles...something in a scrambled
> picture - Find What The Sailor Has Hidden - that the
> finder cannot unsee once it has been seen.(39)

This serpentine concluding sentence, from which I have extracted the essential utterance, makes a satisfying conclusion to
the book precisely because it does not identify what the finder (or
reader) should be looking for. And the allusion to a child's game
is not quite as innocent as it looks, for the sailor in this case is
none other than Nabokov himself, who appears in one of the photographs (40) in the sailor-suit to which he often refers in the
narrative, and who has, of course, deceived and dazzled our eyes
throughout with 'all sorts of stratagems' designed to send us up
blind alleys. In this respect, the end of the fifteenth and final
chapter is very like the end of the penultimate chapter, which
describes Nabokov's composition of a particularly cunning chess
problem. (This is itself a gloss on the beginning of chapter 14
where Nabokov indulges in a prolonged speculation about spirals
and circles, and how they may be subsumed under Hegel's triad
of thesis, antithesis and synthesis.)(41) The chess problem is too
long to quote, but involves a typically Nabokovian exploitation of
a 'false scent'.(42) The passage concludes with an account of a
document stamped with a violet imprint and lettering, together
with an ostensibly helpful comment from Nabokov himself: 'it is
only now, many years later, that the information concealed in my
chess symbols, which that [passport] control permitted to pass,
may be, and in fact is, divulged.'(43) Now, in terms of 'Speak, Memory' itself, it is clear that only Nabokov himself is in control of
the information; in this respect, it is never a fair contest between
author and reader, for the author cannot fail to win, either by
disclosing irrelevancies or by covering up relevancies, or even
(as to some extent happens here) changing the game altogether -
in this instance, from chess to ciphers. It is easy to imagine even
a sophisticated reader getting irritated with Nabokov here, and
accusing him (as indeed many critics have done) of being absurdly
ivory-tower and mystagogic. But Nabokov has, in a way, divulged
information here, and the actual clue to the solution of the chess
problem is embedded in a passage three paragraphs back.(44)
What Nabokov is doing here is pretending to observe the golden
rule that a magician never explains how a trick is done,(45) and
at the same time offering, to those who can 'find what the sailor
has hidden', a key to unlock the mystery. There is another passage, from the end of the second section of section one, that
seems relevant here:
> the individual mystery remains to tantalize the memoirist.

Neither in environment nor in heredity can I find the exact
instrument that fashioned me, the anonymous roller that
pressed upon my life a certain intricate watermark whose
unique design becomes visible when the lamp of art is made
to shine through life's foolscap.(46)

If the individual mystery (which is also the mystery of being an
individual) cannot be solved by the memoirist, what chance does
the reader or critic have of unlocking it? The solution to the chess
problem can be found if one looks hard enough (either at the
board or at the book). But the key that will unlock life has very
obviously yet to be invented, so that even if 'the following of...
thematic designs' is, as Nabokov claims, 'the true purpose of
autobiography', it is not to be supposed that the critic's articu-
lation of those designs will reveal the whole mystery of a personality. It is ironically appropriate that Nabokov should tell us, in
the foreword, that he was disappointed at the way the title 'Conclusive Evidence' 'suggested a mystery story',(47) for in a sense
'Speak, Memory' is nothing less than a mystery story in which the
puzzle is never solved.(48)

This does not, of course, absolve us from entering the mystery
and attempting to demystify those parts of it that are open to
interpretation; it is, indeed, clear that Nabokov expects the
'discerning reader' to do so, and to derive delight from the activity. Strangely, it is only when we stand too far back from the
book that it seems shapeless and indecipherable. When we look at
it close to, each facet seems to possess a logic and charm of its
own. There is a moment in chapter 4 when Nabokov obliquely
indicates that this is the only way to read it:

In an English fairy tale my mother had once read to me, a
small boy stepped out of his bed into a picture and rode his
hobbyhorse along a painted path between silent trees. While
I knelt on my pillow in a mist of drowsiness and talc-powdered
well-being, half-sitting on my calves and rapidly going
through my prayers, I imagined the motion of climbing into
the picture above my bed and plunging into that enchanted
beechwood - which I did visit in due time.(49)

Charming as this is as a description on a realistic level of the
magical transformations of childhood, it seems to me that it also
describes what Nabokov is doing in 'Speak, Memory', stepping as
he is into a picture of pre-Revolutionary Russia and plunging
into a time that the power of art has filled with fairy-tale enchant-
ment. But above and beyond that, it invites the reader to climb
into the picture and ride his own hobbyhorses, under the personal
supervision (Nabokov, in a sense, as mother) of an artist who can,
seemingly, carry out metamorphoses at will. Nabokov claims in
chapter 1 that the harmonious world of a perfect childhood possesses 'a naturally plastic form in one's memory, which can be set
down with hardly any effort,'(50) whereas the recollections of
adolescence make Mnemosyne 'choosy and crabbed'. But it must be
clear to any reader - as Nabokov half admits in the foreword -
that a very considerable amount of imaginative effort is required

on the part of both author and reader, if the full effect of this
harmony is to be perceived.

The great attraction of 'Speak, Memory' is that, whilst Nabokov
is always pointing out how this connects with that, there are any
amount of important connections that the author leaves the reader
to work out for himself. At the end of chapter 1, for instance,
Nabokov recounts 'a marvellous case of levitation' involving his
father being rewarded by grateful peasants tossing him in the air.
(51) The explicit comparison is with an angel, although (like the
map at the beginning of the work) it inevitably reminds one of
the butterflies that the young (and the old) Nabokov relentlessly
pursued.(52) The passage ends by referring to 'funeral lilies
conceal[ing] the face of whoever lies there...in the open coffin'
(53) which prefigures his father's death described later in the
book, and confirms the wisdom of an old governess who has pre-
dicted that one day he will fall.(54) (Chapter 2 ends similarly,
with an account of how Nabokov sees the dead in dreams;(55)
chapter 3 ends with a dream-world in which 'nothing will ever
change, nobody will ever die';(56) thereafter each chapter ends
more optimistically, although chapter 9 concludes with a duel that
does not take place, and a real death - once again his father's
assassination - several years later.)(57)

Again, in chapter 7, after describing in the previous chapter
his first expedition into 'the vast marshland beyond the Oredezh'
(58) (which makes him think of America and leads up, by a process of inner logic, to the passage in which he declares his
disbelief in time), Nabokov recounts his first experience of puppy-
love, with a girl called Colette whom he used to play with by the
sea at Biarritz. Three chapters later he describes his fruitless
affection for a servant-girl called Polenka, whom he used to ride
past on his bicycle.(59) Later still, in chapter 12, with his bicycle again much in evidence, he devotes most of a chapter to his
passionate affair with a girl he calls Tamara, during which he is
reminded of Biarritz and the (now, we must suppose) inappositely
named Rocher de la Vierge.(60) Between these two chapters, in
chapter 11, Nabokov describes the composition of his first poem.
This helps to explain two apparently casual references to the poet
Blok in the twelfth chapter,(61) but relates more centrally to the
failure of the affair, as Nabokov explains: the 'banal hollow note,
and glib suggestion that our love was doomed since it could never
recapture the miracle of its initial moments.'(62) The 'love' and
'literature' motifs (63) have been circling round one another previous to this, for example in chapter 10, where the account of
Polenka grows out of a discussion of the effect on the young Nabokov of the Wild West fiction of Mayne Reid (itself developing
naturally out of the previous chapter's description of Nabokov's
love for his father before an abortive duel, and a reference to the
famous love duel in which Pushkin died). But it is only in chapter
12 that Nabokov combines the themes openly or, to use his own
terminology, 'blends' the 'lines' of 'a difficult composition'.(64)

These are only two, albeit the most important, of the 'combin-

ations' that Nabokov has left for the 'discerning reader' to discover for himself.(65) Chapters 10,11 and 12 of 'Speak, Memory'
are indeed particularly rich in 'elaborate interlacements and expanding clusters',(66) and Nabokov seems actively to be encouraging the reader to collaborate with him in making his memories
coherent.(67) There is so much detail in the foreground that it
becomes exceptionally difficult to 'find what the sailor has hidden.'
But the sailor is always implicitly prompting us, as for instance at
the end of chapter 11, when Nabokov's mother is deeply moved by
his recitation of his first poem: 'she passed me a mirror so that I
might see the smear of blood on my cheekbone where at some
indeterminable time I had crushed a gorged mosquito by the unconscious act of propping my cheek on my fist.'(68) We are not
encouraged to make anything overly-symbolic out of this, although
it is difficult not to feel that the incident has something to do
with the death of Nabokov senior which dominates the end of several of the preceding chapters.(69) If, however, like Nabokov
himself, we concentrate simply on the details, this squashed
mosquito begins to connect with other dead lepidoptera mentioned
in the text. In chapter 11, for example, describing the girl who
preceded Colette in his youthful affections, Nabokov recalls how
he arrived one morning to be given 'a dead hummingbird moth
found by the cat.'(70) In the following chapter, before the affair
gets under way, Tamara kills a horsefly, which is clearly intended
to relate back to the 'dead horsefly...on its back near the brown
remains of a birch ament' that Nabokov sees at the beginning of
chapter 11, when he is sitting in a pavilion composing poetry.(71)
Each of these details seems quite innocent on first reading, but on
rereading (72) they become ominously charged with meaning. The
effort of the first poem runs aground on a squashed mosquito;
the great hopes of the first love affair come to nothing.(73)
'Etymologically,' Nabokov casually notes, ' "pavilion" and "papilio"
[butterfly] are closely related,'(74) but they are also very closely
related emotionally. Life has a nasty habit of up-staging art; the
butterfly is even more elusive than the poem. At the end of chapter 4 Nabokov speaks of 'a queer shock...as if life had impinged
upon my creative rights by wriggling on beyond the subjective
limits so elegantly and economically set by childhood memories
that I thought I had signed and sealed,'(75) and 'Speak, Memory'
is shot through with the realization that, however much Nabokov
may 'picket nature', nature will have the last word. This is why,
to return to the end of chapter 11, there is such drama (76) in
the perfectly ordinary act of a mother handing a mirror to her
child:

> I saw more than that [i.e. the smear of blood]. Looking into
> my own eyes, I had the shocking sensation of finding the
> mere dregs of my usual self, odds and ends of an evaporated
> identity which it took my reason quite an effort to gather
> again in the glass.(77)

The drama here is more subtle than it seems, because Nabokov is
also trying to tell us about his difficulties with the autobiographical

genre. The book has begun by stressing how unusual the young
Nabokov is; now, on the brink of first love, a conventional
enough subject, he is confronting his 'usual' self. The raw material of 'Speak, Memory' is, in a sense, little more than 'odds and
ends of an evaporated identity' and the considered composition of
the book obviously cost Nabokov a considerable 'effort' of reason
before the glass was recomposed.

Nabokov is attempting in 'Speak, Memory' to recompose (to *re*-
compose also) a lost identity by means of an effort of reason. But
it cannot be achieved by reason only; the forces of the imagination,
described by Nabokov in the foreword to the novella 'The Eye' as
'ultimately the forces for good', must have some part in it.(78)
Not just the author's imagination, but the reader's also. The
figure of Nabokov looking into the glass at the end of chapter 11
links up with the hypothesized image of the reader looking into
the puzzle at the end of chapter 15. 'Speak, Memory' is an attempt
to merge the real estate of Nabokov's youth with 'the beauty of
intangible property, unreal estate',(79) the estate of the imagination. It is a book of great sadness, and yet it ends on an optimistic note,(80) as Nabokov realizes that the fragments have at last
added up to something:

I do not doubt that among these slightly convex chips of
majolica ware found by our child there was one whose border
of scroll-work fitted exactly, and continued, the pattern of
a fragment I had found in 1903 on the same shore, and that
the two tallied with a third my mother had found on that
Mentone beach in 1882, and with a fourth piece of the same
pottery that had been found by *her* mother a hundred years
ago - and so on, until this assortment of parts, if all had
been preserved, might have been put together to make the
complete, the absolutely complete, bowl....(81)

Like James, whose 'golden bowl' this may remind us of, Nabokov
has reached the conclusion that 'it is art which makes life.' But
he has not so much set the two in opposition as tried to see how
they relate reciprocally. It is no accident that, in describing the
birth of his son in the last chapter,(82) Nabokov discusses
theoretically the 'stab of wonder' that he has all along been dramatically recording:

It occurs to me that the closest reproduction of the mind's
birth obtainable is the stab of wonder that accompanies the
precise moment when, gazing at a tangle of twigs and leaves,
one suddenly realizes that what had seemed a natural component of that tangle is a marvellously disguised insect or
bird.(83)

This not only prefigures the last words of the book, the 'find
what the sailor has hidden' puzzle, but also sends us back to the
beginning where 'the mind's birth' of the 4-year-old Vladimir
Nabokov is rendered with great economy and power. It is easy to
forget what Nabokov has 'planted' there, and thus to over-
emphasize the sadder aspects of the book: 'To a joke, then, I owe
my first gleam of complete consciousness - which again has

recapitulatory implications, since the first creatures on earth to
become aware of time were also the first creatures to smile.'(84)

It is rare for Nabokov to make us laugh out loud, because his
humour is almost always tinged with melancholy (as in the splendidly circular account of his two visits to his Cambridge tutor,
both of which end with him trampling on the teacups,(85) or the
equally circular account of 'Mademoiselle O' which begins the
ostensibly 'erratic sequence' in 1936).(86) But his melancholy is
almost never cloying, because the 'stab of wonder' heals as well
as wounds. Nabokov obliges his reader to become fascinated, as
he is, by puzzles, because life discloses itself to him as a puzzle
to which human beings can only find a temporary solution. This
is why he describes his life (and implicitly his book), as 'a coloured spiral in a small ball of glass',(87) for it is both fragile and
strong, simple and complex, precious and yet as ordinary as a
marble.

There is a moment in chapter 2 of 'Speak, Memory' where Nabokov speaks of inheriting from his mother 'an exquisite simulacrum, the beauty of intangible property, unreal estate' which
'proved a splendid training for the endurance of later losses'.(88)
This is an important remark because it helps to explain why Nabokov is finally not, despite his passion for puzzles and ciphers,
an exponent of 'art for art's sake'. He is ultimately, like any great
writer, a moralist, which is why the remark in the foreword to the
novella 'The Eye' needs to be stressed: 'The forces of the imagination are in the long run the forces for good.' This is why he tells
the absurd story of 'the giant polygonal Faber pencil' that his
mother bought for him, 'far too big for use and, indeed,...not
meant to be used.'(89) The pencil is extraordinary and wonderful,
but unreal. Nabokov concludes the story by saying: 'All one could
do was to glimpse, amid the haze and the chimeras, something real
ahead...somewhere beyond the throes of an entangled and inept
nightmare, the ordered reality of the waking hour.'(90)

In order to see clearly, it is imperative for Nabokov to lift himself above 'the haze and the chimeras'. Otherwise he will become
like the waxwing slain by the false azure of the windowpane in the
first line of John Shade's poem 'Pale Fire'. There is an implicit
gloss on the conclusion to the story of the pencil at the end of
chapter 2:

> It is certainly not then - not in dreams - but when one is
> wide awake, at moments of robust joy and achievement, on
> the highest terrace of consciousness, that mortality has a
> chance to peer beyond its own limits, from the mast, from
> the past and from its castle tower.(91) And although nothing
> much can be seen through the mist, there is somehow the
> blissful feeling that one is looking in the right direction.(92)

The mixed metaphors here, of land and sea (and inevitably, if
only implicitly, chess), are very clearly not the products of an
inept littérateur, but rather the product of a mind that is trying
to bring experience together. Nabokov repeatedly images himself
as a sailor (93) adrift on a sea of phenomena, or as a balloonist

drifting vaguely through the air.(94) But he also sees himself
on terra firma, as the goalkeeper, 'the lone eagle, the man of
mystery, the last defender'.(95) Much of the poignancy of the
love affair with Tamara - and indeed the composition of his first
poem - stems directly from the fact that he has been flying and
has been brought down to earth with a bump. In the end Tamara,
or her letters, become, like almost all Nabokov's memories, butterflies beating their wings in vain;

> letters from Tamara would be still coming, miraculously and
> needlessly, to southern Crimea, and would search there for
> a fugitive addressee, and weakly flap about like bewildered
> butterflies set loose in an alien zone, at the wrong altitude,
> among an unfamiliar flora.(96)

If there is a fear here on Nabokov's part, as I think there is,
that we who read his book will be bewildered - for all readers of
autobiography are by definition in an alien zone, among an unfamiliar flora - it is a needless fear. For though we can only respond
to his book vicariously, and must always to some extent be 'fugi-
tive addressees', it is precisely what Nabokov calls the 'almost
pathological keenness of the retrospective faculty'(97) that keeps
us in touch with the author. The 'robust reality' of Nabokov's
obsessively detailed evocations do indeed make 'a ghost of the
present'.(98) For, however much 'trickery of art' is employed in
'Speak, Memory', Nabokov's orientation is indeed, as he claimed
in the 1951 foreword, towards the truth. 'The man in me', he
writes, 'revolts against the fictionist,'(99) and it cannot be accidental that whereas he entitled an early novel 'Camera Obscura'
(later 'Laughter in the Dark'), we find him talking, in 'Speak,
Memory' of 'certain camera-lucida needs of literary composition'.
(100) There is a great moment in chapter 5 where Nabokov catches
himself idling in a 'stereoscopic dreamland' where 'All is still,
spellbound, enthralled by the moon, fancy's rear-vision mirror',
and then suddenly awakens: 'The snow is real, though, and as I
bend to it and scoop up a handful, sixty years crumble to glit-
tering frost-dust between my fingers.'(101) Something similar
occurs at the end of chapter 8 which Nabokov has begun with the
apparently casual and gratuitous aim to 'show a few slides',(102)
and ends with a reality that is enduring and permanent:

> I witness with pleasure the supreme achievement of memory,
> which is the masterly use it makes of innate harmonies when
> gathering to its fold [cf. the fold of the magic carpet](103)
> the suspended and wandering tonalities of the past....
> Through a tremulous prism, I distinguish the features of
> relatives and familiars, mute lips serenely moving in for-
> gotten speech.(104)

The prism here is not so much the glass of the cinema projector
upon which Nabokov's slides are to be run: it is the prism of
'Speak, Memory' itself.(105) The cinematic image is habitual to
Nabokov (as Alfred Appel has very ably shown)(106) but the
natural image (the sunset at the end of chapter 10, for instance,
(107) or the water-lilies he touches when coming out of a poetic

trance),(108) is even more powerful in 'Speak, Memory'. It is not
only with Tamara that Nabokov parts 'the fabric of fancy' and
tastes 'reality';(109) the whole book is committed to doing precisely that.

Notwithstanding his devotion to imaginative processes, then,
Nabokov very obviously sees his task in 'Speak, Memory' as
decisively different from, and in some ways more complex than,
his enterprises in fiction.(110) Nabokov hints as much in chapter
12: 'That twisted quest for Sebastian Knight [1940] with its
gloriettes and self-mate combinations, is really nothing in comparison to the task I balked in the first version of this memoir
and am faced with now.'(111)

The task is also more complex than biography, a genre to which
Nabokov has also contributed with his 'rather frivolous little book'
(112) 'Nikolai Gogol' (1944). Nabokov believes that the temptation
to blend biography and fiction must be resisted at all costs because it gives rise to those ' "*biographies romancées*" which are
by far the worst kind of literature yet invented,' and requires
instead 'a delicate meeting place between imagination and knowledge'.(113) The only analogy he can find is the composition of
chess problems,(114) which is precisely why he deals with the
subject in so much detail. In 'Speak, Memory', as in the chess
problem, he has been prepared to 'sacrifice purity of form to the
exigencies of fantastic content, causing form to bulge and burst
like a sponge-bag containing a small furious devil.'(115) But he
has gone further, for although 'beautiful' and 'complex',(116)
'Speak, Memory' is at no time 'sterile'(117) like a chess problem.
(118) It is more like an actual game of chess, full of 'simple and
elegant' moves.(119) The 'circle...has ceased to be vicious,'(120)
and has become a 'spiritualized' circle, a spiral.(121) If 'defocal-
ization'(122) periodically occurs, unlike in the crystalline world
of the chess problem, this is because it is endemic to the genre,
however 'carefully wiped' the 'lenses of time'(123) may be. The
moments when Nabokov feels, as he did in childhood, 'a sense of
drowsy well-being' when he has 'everything neatly arranged'(124)
are counterbalanced by those in which he is left holding a 'wisp
of iridescence, not knowing exactly where to fit it'.(125) In this
respect the book, like most autobiographies, seems to require the
reader's 'collaboration' and 'corroboration'.(126) Just as there
must be 'perfect co-operation between headsman and victim',(127)
so there must also be co-operation between the artist and the
world. Even the dedication, as usual to his wife, Véra, has a part
to play in this minutely considered book, for it is of course Véra
who is the 'you' that Nabokov refers to with increasing frequency.
(128) This device, which is so surprising on its first occurrence
that it seems not only to buttonhole the reader but also to bundle
him into the book (just as the child in the fairy-tale stepped into
the picture), indicates that the book is by no means a self-
contained artefact, but rather a retroactive gift,(129) from art to
life. In the end, our experience of 'Speak, Memory' is qualitatively
different from the 'best novels' of V. Sirin (130) (Nabokov, of

course) in which Sirin 'condemns his people to the solitary con-
finement of their souls,'(131) and more complex than the philosopher Vivian Bloodmark (Nabokov again, as the incident of the
squashed mosquito and, most helpfully, the index remind us)
would have it. For if the poet 'feels everything that happens in
one point of time,'(132) the memoirist,(133) however 'chronophobiac' he may be, cannot defeat time definitively. 'Speak,
Memory' has the 'yielding diaphanous texture of time'(134) that
Nabokov experienced in Cambridge, so that ultimately 'Nothing
one look[s] at [is] shut off in terms of time, everything [is] a
natural opening into it.'(135)

CONCLUSION

I want in conclusion to rehearse some theoretical considerations that may help to add to our understanding of a kind of literature that will no doubt always, by virtue of its close relationship to the individual and unrepeatable life, elude the constraints and categories that we are pleased to place on it. For if it is clear that the genre is indeed as 'lawless' as all commentators seem to assume, then it is peculiarly important for the nearest thing to laws to be confronted and explored. It may be, as in the quotation from Herbert Read with which I began, that the genre is inherently less rich than others. Irving Horowitz, for example, has written recently: 'if the vocabulary of motives for preparing an autobiography are infinite, the capacity to carry it off as a literary device are severely finite.'(1) But even if this is the case, the genre has had much to do with the distinctively modern development of the notion of 'the author', as Michel Foucault has reminded us.(2) This notion has recently been very much under threat, and a good deal of ultra-modern criticism has concerned itself with the 'death' of the author and the 'birth' of the reader. (3) One would not expect autobiographical literature to be popular in an ambience of this kind, and yet this is precisely what it has become, partly because it offers a stern test to those who subscribe to a belief in the relative impersonality of structures, and partly because - as I hope to have shown - it is very much a literature in which the reader has a collaborative role.

The dominant recognition on the part of commentators after Roy Pascal is that, in the words of Pasternak in 'Safe Conduct', the greatest works of art are those which describe their own birth.(4) This idea has virtually hardened into an orthodoxy with critics who are interested in the phenomenology of reading, in which every moment sees the death of what has gone before and the birth of what will come after. It is no surprise therefore to find a critic like John Sturrock discussing autobiography not, as common sense might want to do, in terms of the past, but in terms of the present:

> if autobiography is to progress...it requires a revaluation
> less of the past than of the present, of the moment of
> writing....The autobiographical contract between writer
> and reader surely has a clause which says that the writer
> is addressing us from the moment of writing, not from the
> moments he is remembering.(5)

Sturrock's ideas are essentially an extension of Jean Starobinski's stress on style as 'a particular mode of speaking' and are obviously conditioned to some extent by Starobinski's belief that 'one would

hardly have sufficient motive to write an autobiography had not
some radical change occurred in his life.'(6) They are part, in
other words, of what I would want to call the 'autobiography-as-
crisis' school, exemplified by a remark in an essay of Stephen
Shapiro's: 'Men who had always felt at peace with themselves and
the world around them would have no need to write autobiographies.'(7)

It seems to me that the logical (some would say illogical) terminus of this kind of thinking is to consider autobiography not so
much as a literature of being as a literature of non-being, and
this strain of thought is well represented by one of the respond-
ents to Starobinski's paper:

> every *I* necessarily implies a *you*; the *you* is the image which
> one supposes the other to have of himself. As for the 'I' of
> autobiography, there is no other definition of 'I' than 'the
> one who calls himself "I" '...the autobiographical 'I'...is the
> exorcising substitute for the linguistic tautology that ' "I" is
> the one who says "I".' It tries to exorcise the tautology, to
> divert it, to substantivize and deformalize it....The auto-
> biography is something which fills that which is unfillable
> at the level of language.(8)

Starobinski, whose paper is mercifully free of entanglements of
this kind, 'found himself in substantial agreement' with this unnamed speaker,(9) whose development of Starobinski's position
transforms the ostensibly straightforward 'I' into a major critical
problem. Subsequent writers on the subject have reminded us -
largely, one suspects, under the influence of Emile Benveniste(10) -
that 'the first person...always conceals a hidden third person,'
an idea which consolidates the notion that the author is an 'absent'
figure. But it has also been claimed that autobiography is 'a
unique, self-defining mode of self-referential expression',(11)
which has the opposite effect of making the reader into an 'absent'
figure. With critics who are less troubled by the absence of the
two crucial figures, there has been concern at the way an autobiographer 'loses clarity and authority...as he multiplies himself,'
(12) which has had the effect of making the addressee into the
dominant partner in the relationship: 'the hero of [the autobiographer's] book is its reader, who alone can master its final
form.' (13) But clearly, in so far as one believes that 'in all
autobiographies...subject and object are one,' (14) someone will
soon be tempted to go further and to propose that author and
reader are also one,(15) even if the existence and roles of each
have become a matter of uncertainty.

Parallel with this paradox runs another, which is that the 'art
of life' is actually much possessed by death, not only in celebrated
cases like Chateaubriand's 'Memoires d'outre-tombe' (where the
author 'blunts his terror of the perishable by making the perishable seem less conclusive')(16) but also in much less obvious cases
as well. Robert F. Sayre, for example, who gives no evidence of
being influenced by the modish intellectual leanings I have been
presenting, writes thus of the conclusion to Henry James's 'Notes

of a Son and Brother':
> [James] may have altered [Minnie's] letters the way he did
> William's and his father's, not to falsify them but to prevent
> them from impairing the image of her he wished to present.
> He was deeply proud of the last chapter of 'Notes of a Son
> and Brother' and very complimented when old friends con-
> gratulated him on it. She clung to consciousness just as he
> himself might have and just as he was doing at the time he
> wrote about her....[James's autobiographical volumes are]
> elegiac books *written* to defy [death]. To give up the inward
> life was in effect to die, die in the only sense death had any
> real meaning to James.(17)

These ideas are taken much further, and made more abstract, by
a more recent writer:
> the death-wish that informs Narcissus's experience informs
> as well the experience of the autobiographer, for the wish to
> return to an inorganic state is, in Freud's terms, the ultimate
> expression of the repetition compulsion. Moreover, in trans-
> forming life into destiny - in resurrecting the past as
> necessary - autobiographers in effect anticipate death,
> because they deny their continuing historical natures in
> order to repeat the past. Anticipating death, however, is a
> strategy for overcoming it...(18)

There is a third and related paradox that forms another important platform in the current critical orthodoxy. This third
paradox is that, whilst, as Paul Nash suggested, autobiographies
(especially those telling the story of an artist's development) tend
to be 'fated' narratives, they cannot, like other 'fated' narratives,
be considered 'tragic'. Stephen Shapiro has proposed that autobiography be considered a comic genre in that it 'asserts the ego's
transcendence of circumstances,'(19) and M.K. Blasing has, without referring to Shapiro's article, consolidated this idea:
> since the self is both the narrative and the creator of the
> narrative, the very creation of the self in autobiography
> constitutes its transcendence...[autobiography] is an
> essentially comic genre, because the authors consider their
> historical selves - indeed, history itself - from a comic per-
> spective outside history.(20)

This latter notion is obviously not tenable if one takes Sturrock's
line and places one's emphasis on 'the moment of writing', a stance
that must lead one to the same conclusion as Sturrock, that autobiography is an 'unrepeatable event'.(21) But this is itself obviously
not meant literally or, if it is, must needs be tested against the compulsion to compose autobiography that is basic to many of the
authors studied here. James wrote two volumes of autobiography
and an unfinished third; Yeats wrote four (some critics would say
three or two):(22) Pasternak rejected his first attempt at the
genre and tried to substitute a second; Nabokov's autobiography
was 'revisited' at least twice; and so on. Nor is this an exclusively
modern phenomenon: Franklin, Thoreau and Whitman (among
American writers) and Stendhal and Tolstoy (among Europeans)

were always going back to their self-portraits and retouching
them. These examples, together with those considered in the bulk
of this study, remind us that autobiography is always a transfor-
mational or metaphorical act, in which a version of the self, rather
than the self per se, is being attempted.(23)

But none of this demolishes the point Sturrock is making; indeed it may almost be said to confirm it. For the final effect of
this compulsion towards autobiography is inevitably to threaten
the notion of the substantiality of the self, at least as a literary
artefact.(24) And the natural tendency, for us as readers, is to
take refuge in the substantiality of the text, 'the mirror itself' in
Machado's phrase, which then becomes, as Christine Vance has
said, 'the only modality of self-awareness'.(25) Despite this, most
modern criticism is extremely suspicious of the text's substantiality. Louis Renza has recently reminded us of the genre's
inherent inability to 'totalize' itself: 'though we are bound to lend
narrative totality to autobiographical significations, they intent-
ionally reside...beyond the narrative they are set in and as a
consequence tend to detotalize - make contingent - the narrative.'
(26)

The language in which these ideas are couched makes them sound
extremely new. But it seems to me that this may be only another
way of talking about the 'large ease of autobiography' and the
'terrible fluidity of self-revelation' of which Henry James spoke in
the preface to 'The Ambassadors'.(27) What Renza has called the
'pull toward anarchic privacy'(28) is not very different from what
Henry Adams regarded as an essential feature of the 'esoteric'
literary art which would survive him. But it is no part of my
intention to disparage Renza; what I am seeking to show is that the
idea of autobiography as a 'lawless' genre is extremely tenacious.
And of course, in so far as an 'art of life' must be presumed to be
reciprocally related to life,(29) it is unlikely and undesirable that this
notion will ever be completely dispelled. But this does not commit
one to the idea that, unlike other literary art forms, autobiography
has no masterpieces, or to the supposition that the qualities which
make for distinction in the other genres are not to be found in this
one. And it seems to me incontrovertible that, with the texts discussed in this study, we are dealing with works of the most sensitive and rigorous artistry.

Just as the authors in question have transformed themselves as
subjects into themselves as objects, so - however much these
works may pull us towards their private lives - our primary commitment must be to the works as artistic objects in their own right,
not just supportive background evidence for a consideration of
their better-known works. This enables the author and the reader
to coexist in a peculiar allegiance; for both of them the object (and
the objectification) transcends the subject. This is, it seems to me,
one of the special satisfactions to be derived from this particular
branch of 'post-Romantic' literature, and one of the most interesting evidences of the twentieth century's continuing struggle
with the legacy of Romanticism. Just as many of the great figures

of twentieth-century literature in the traditional forms (Joyce, Eliot, Wyndham Lewis, Ezra Pound, Paul Valéry, Rilke) have sought to go beyond the self and proposed a modern version of 'classicism', so - and precisely where one might least expect it - these modern 'Preludes' are orientated outwards, in what Henry James very aptly called an 'act of life'.(30)

APPENDICES

There is a reluctance in England to acknowledge the major status of autobiographical writing which is reflected in the way that works as diverse as Ruskin's 'Praeterita', Edmund Gosse's 'Father and Son' and John Cowper Powys's 'Autobiography' have had to wait, and to some extent still are waiting, to be recognized as classics of their kind. The traditions of personal literature in England are decisively orientated towards the diary, or the personal journal or the autobiographical novel,(1) and it would be difficult, if not impossible, to trace a living line of development, of a vigour comparable to that manifest in France, or Russia, or America, in the special area of autobiographical art I am concerned with here. There are perhaps no works in the modern English literature written by Englishmen that could survive comparison with Pasternak's 'Safe Conduct' or Jean-Paul Sartre's 'Les Mots', and the absence of an achievement of distinction has led to the neglect of several works which, though isolated and easily considered marginal, may yet in the long run prove more seminal and central.

In so far as this study concerns itself not so much with the national differences that prompt a given writer's autobiographical impulse, but rather with the private and, as it were, ideological origins of such utterance, no reasons will be offered here for the comparative dearth of achievement, on the part of the English, in the mode of 'autobiography as art'. But if, as is often assumed, there is an endemic taboo against self-display in the English temperament, it has to be said that a similar suspicion on the part of foreign writers with a more active tradition behind them has not inhibited or throttled the impulse to the point of preventing the enterprise from achieving success. And it is one of my contentions that, in the two English examples I elect to deal with, it is precisely the manner in which each writer confronts an intrinsic 'pudeur' and yet contrives to create an artistic work of sustained, if reticent, candour that makes the English venture into such a seemingly alien mode so engaging and so revealing. In each case, we shall find similar subtleties of organization and similar ends in view to those elaborated in the main bulk of the book, although it has seemed advisable to treat them separately, in acknowledgment of the fact that they may with some justice be considered as eccentric, or even minor, in relation to the other authors I have been concerned with.

A HENRY GREEN: 'PACK MY BAG'

In so far as the quality of Henry Green's novelistic achievement
has still to be widely appreciated, it is no surprise that his 'self-
portrait', 'Pack My Bag', first published in 1940 and reprinted
twelve years later, should be even less well-known. It is not a
work that sets out to shock, as Powys's autobiography partly did;
nor is it, like Gosse's 'study of two temperaments', a work intended to pay off old scores and to relieve the mind of a burden
of guilt, or at least not obviously so. It makes no pretension to
completeness, in the manner of Rousseau, discusses none of the
author's distinguished acquaintances by name, and is throughout
scrupulously considered and written in a style of impassioned
restraint. But 'Pack My Bag' should not be thought of, as it has
tended to be in the very few monographs devoted to Green, as
merely a useful source-book for critics of the rest of his oeuvre,
nor as a secondary pleasure in comparison with any one of his
nine novels.(2) Precisely because of Green's refusal to play the
accepted autobiographical game that those more famous than he
are all too often encouraged into, 'Pack My Bag' emerges as among
the most intimate and compelling portraits of a personality within
a particular milieu, and the damage the one can inflict upon the
other, in twentieth-century English literature.

What is at first glance curious about 'Pack My Bag' is the way it
seems to court instant neglect by enshrining a world of bourgeois
privilege which had already, by 1940, been very largely eroded
and which, within a few years, as a result of a major war, had
become virtually fossilized. The preponderance of hunting, shoot-
ing and fishing scenes in 'Pack My Bag' would put even the most
egregious eighteenth-century Tory memoirist to shame. Worse
still, from our present perspective, Green writes at a time (1938-9)
of resurgent nationalism in the face of the foe in a manner that
suggests he is not unduly concerned about the saving of his own
skin but perhaps surreptitiously seeking to galvanize national
feeling at a time of emergency. Further, his concentration on
childhood experience at a time when civilization seems to be
threatened by destruction looks culturally regressive and danger-
ously immature. If we are to appreciate the virtues of 'Pack My
Bag', it is important to disinfect it of these misconceived ways of
looking at it; but it is also important if we are to understand why
the book has such a strange flavour, to see how close Green has
come to writing something that, even at the time, would have been
regarded as eminently disposable.
   Green's opening remarks are an index of how difficult it is to
judge the tone of 'Pack My Bag':

   I was born a mouthbreather with a silver spoon in 1905,
   three years after one war and nine before another, too
   late for both. But not too late for the war which seems to
   be coming upon us now and that is a reason for putting
   down what comes to mind before one is killed, and surely

it would be asking much to pretend one had a chance to
live.(3)

Perhaps the first thing that strikes one about this is its awkward-
ness, which is never really conquered by the energetic rhythm.
If it is artless, it is studiedly so; the style is idiosyncratic to the
point of wilfulness and the mood gloomy without apparent justification. The second paragraph continues in much the same mode:

> That is my excuse, that we who may not have time to write
> anything else must do what we now can. If we have no time
> to chew another book over we must turn to what comes first
> to mind and that must be how one changed from boy to man,
> how one lived, things and people and one's attitude. All of
> these otherwise would be used in novels, material is better
> in that form or in any other that is not directly personal,
> but we I feel no longer have the time. We should be taking
> stock.(4)

The combative, peremptory tone is unchanged; the reason for
writing, now slightly embellished, remains the same. But a number of new and slightly disturbing features are to be observed
here: the distaste for self-display that lies behind the word 'excuse' (later rationalized into an aesthetic principle), balanced by
the distaste for any kind of writing at all in 'to chew another book
over'; the strange pressure of the phrase beginning 'and that
must be...' (as though what really 'comes first to mind' is, as the
first paragraph suggests, one's own death) balanced by the
equally curious flatness at the end of the same sentence, as
though it has expired from being overlong; the attempt to pass
off the book we are reading as a piece of spontaneous overflow
without premeditation, balanced by the careful attention to rhet-
orical effects which leaves the last sentence ringing in our ears as
the only thing to do under the circumstances. Surely few self-
portraits begin so bewilderingly as 'Pack My Bag'?

It is, perhaps mercifully, nowhere quite so odd again: it does
not take Green long to conquer his obvious embarrassment at contributing to a genre he is deeply suspicious of, and getting on,
with more or less of a good grace, with the task in hand. But we
ought not therefore to disregard this beginning, for it is in many
ways representative of Green's prose at its best, and it prepares
us admirably for the self-portrait that follows. Green's sentences,
short or long, simple or complex, apparently clumsy or exagger-
atedly artful, are always alive. Within two paragraphs, for example, Green employs three different types of short declarative
sentence, modulating from the aggressive 'We should be taking
stock' to the delicately ironic 'I suppose he had not much use for
children' (of the family gardener) and, within four pages from
this, to the nakedly honest 'I remember he did not call me sir and
that I blamed him for it' (of the family butler encountered after he
had left the Yorke employ).(5) Throughout the book Green uses
this device to administer a subtle ironic corrective to a perspective that has threatened to become static, preserving the life of
the book by giving the impression that he has just that minute

thought of it. But he is also a master of the long and complex
sentence, as when the prose quickens to protect the idea of nostalgia from being too sentimental:

Where from the cottage we could only hear [Tewkesbury
Abbey's] bells when the wind was right, here they were
much nearer, only over the river, and always at any time
the pealing bells would throw their tumbling drifting noise
under thick steaming August hours and over meadows
between, laying up a nostalgia in after years for evenings
at home.(6)

This is obviously the other side of the aggressive and barely
restrained energy of the opening, a languid and almost overblown
preciosity. Green seems unable to conjure up anything that might
stand between the two types of utterance, and uninterested in
establishing any norms that we might take comfort from. It is not
surprising that Green finds himself, seven paragraphs into his
self-portrait, obliged to stop and to reaffirm that, although his
account may lack cinematic verisimilitude, it will none the less
give an impression of 'what seems to have gone on' and 'what one
thinks has gone to make one up.'(7)

The impression 'Pack My Bag' gives, for all Green's scrupulous
restraint, is of a small boy exceptionally sensitive, lonely to an
almost pathological degree, and tougher than he was ever aware
of. The young Green, like the young Stephen Dedalus, possesses
an especially powerful sense of smell, which leads the mature
Green to record, irrespective of their importance to his narrative,
the smell of 'wet exhausted tea leaves' in dustbins, the smell of
the heavily waxed wooden panel in the boarding-school chapel,
the smell of the fives-courts at his public school, and the smell of
snobbery in later life. The feelings of loneliness are, as we shall
see later, primarily sexual in origin, but they are also part and
parcel of being at a school that makes him think of 'a humane concentration camp'.(8) And yet Green obviously believes that most
of the inmates are rightfully imprisoned there, and he pursues
images of crime and punishment with a certain relish as he relates
the thefts which dominated the life of the school. Green concentrates on theft not because he is a devout materialist, but because
a sense of loss remains his abiding impression of childhood: 'Being
a child', he concludes with a heaviness that is obviously the result of mature deliberation, 'is having things taken away from you
all the time.'(9) Although the loss of possessions can now be seen
às trivial, it is the irreplaceable losses, the losses that have
marked him, that haunt Green most - the deaths of those close to
him and the erosion of ideals. Green's childhood years seem un-
usually death-orientated, partly perhaps because he is so convinced that he will not survive the impending conflict, although
it would be possible to argue that the latter attitude is very much
a product of the former. Green certainly finds it difficult not to
revert to the present:

they let us cut laurel up to mix with water in jamjars and
this let off fumes to gas any butterfly we caught. It was

thought less cruel to use gas than to stick them on pins.
Our difference is, now we are older, we may die both ways
at once.(10)

The almost childish petulance of this typically blunt conclusion is
not especially attractive, despite its power. But the immediately
subsequent description of the staff and schoolboys listening to
the sound of someone suffering corporal punishment is both powerful and subtle:

when it was over a mistress asked the beaten one, 'Was it on
the bare?' It was she who told us later when her young man
died of wounds how he screamed when these were dressed.

But then one remembers only the horrible of such times.(11)

Here, behind the discriminating gloss, it is the exacerbated childhood sensibility which shows through. And yet at moments like
this Green has a toughness which (as in his novels) is likely to
make his reader feel suddenly chill and unprotected. The entranced
fascination of those who are unconscious of their own sadism is
balanced against Green's own fascination with pain as something
abnormal and wrong. And yet there is nothing self-congratulatory
or finger-wagging about this moment; only later, when a gallery
of more or less sadistic women has passed before our eyes, does
this schoolteacher take on a representative status which has ensured her persistence in Green's memory over so many years.

The mature Green, like the child, is obviously more fascinated
than repelled by death. He admits as much when he returns to the
subject a few pages later:

as our school was on the south coast, some formation of the
hills round about brought no louder than as seashells echo the
blood pounding on one's ears noise of gunfire through our
windows all the way from France so that we looked out and
thought of death in the sound and this was sweeter to us
than rollers tumbling on a beach.(12)

The unpunctuated, but turbid, flow of this (like the example I
quote later (p.130) which says so much about Green's attitude to
women) is very ambivalent, at once immensely literary (and therefore calculated) and at the same time extremely awkward (and
therefore spontaneous). Green's aim seems to be not so much to
record the 'Schadenfreude' of youth (of which there are any number of equally succulent examples) as to show that one must be
able to write about death without it necessarily causing one pain.
Perhaps this prefigures Green's later ability, despite his avowed
reasons for writing, to quite forget the agonizing aspects of death,
and to uncover those things in life which will endure. But it is
also part of an elaborate strategy gradually allowing him to deal
with the deaths that matter most to most children, which betoken
the break-up of the family unit, for which Green prepares us with
quite extraordinary care.

Green begins with the stridently asserted prospective death of
himself (prophetic of some universal holocaust), moves on to the
death of someone not totally remote (the schoolmistress's lover)
and on from there to the collective death that could actually be

enjoyed because of its remoteness. In discussing how the Yorke household was turned, during the First World War, into an officer's convalescent home, Green retells a story he has heard, which he can enjoy because of its ridiculous features (and perhaps subconsciously because it is a German, an enemy, who dies):

> One [story] in particular I shall not forget of the middle aged German who each morning went to do his duty behind a stump instead of going to the latrines. The stump was some distance off and modesty made him put it between him and his own lines. He was out of rifle range but the artillery officer could see him through glasses and the problem was how to get the range to blow him up without frightening him away. They spent days in working it all out and with the first shell they sent over they got him.(13)

It is difficult to imagine a more disturbing mixture of human ingenuity and pig-headedness in the midst of the futility of war, and the incident is retold as the child would hear it, with no moral filter to mediate or otherwise interfere with the shock. Later, when Green speaks of the absurdity of the 'circus world'(14) he inhabits in London, it is this story that is likely to come to mind, with its appallingly vivid and yet curiously anaesthetized trenchancy.

The mature mind cannot resist an implicit moral gloss on the story, and Green immediately recounts another story in which this time he himself figures, making friends with a shell-shocked Australian who ultimately commits suicide. In telling this story, Green modulates from the unsparingly acute childlike vision that he has already experimented with ('He was no longer human when he came to us....Unattractive in every way, small, ugly, with no interests that one could find') to a more philosophical attitude to death and the absurdity of being human. After a cycling accident which the Australian has largely brought on himself, Green discovers for perhaps the first time that there is no correlation between cause and effect and that true morality consists in getting above such facile mathematical considerations:

> He was up again in four days and it did not do him any harm but it damaged me and somehow, because he was ill he was acute, although he never spoke of it again I think he knew because it was not until then I realised by sharing it with him, how hopelessly far gone he was. We grow up by sharing situations, what we share of another person's increases us, and my memorial to all of them at that time in my heart now is my anguish remembered as I saw him stagger in disclosed, wondering whether perhaps it were not my fault.(15)

The problem of sharing surfaces again in Green's accounts of his sexual development, and the idea of memorial is present in the first paragraph of the book. It is one of the strengths of 'Pack My Bag', even at moments of serpentine obliquity like this, that each experience recalled contributes to our understanding of all the others, in 'a gathering web of insinuations'.(16)

Green obliges us to see the death of his brother Philip and the reported death of his parents against this background of absurdity

and guilt. In the case of his brother, it was, Green notes, 'the
first death'(17) (after so many more remote ones), and yet no
more personal than any of the others. Nor is this Green's fault
alone; it has much to do with his upbringing and his environment.
Green's critique of the elaborately protective devices of the
school-headmaster contrive to be both horrifying and amusing,
because the 'right' feelings are suddenly exposed as not the right
ones after all:

> He told me Philip had been ill with great cheerfulness as if
> he were better, but that night I dreamed he was dead or
> rather that we had both of us died and were being received
> for some kind of judgment into a presence. Some days later
> I was called into the old devil's study to be told my brother
> was dead. It meant absolutely nothing to me at all.(18)

Against this childhood inability to know what was the correct role
to play Green balances his quite categorical mature belief that the
idea of grief is to 'raise a feeling of pity which will in turn become self-pity';(19) pity is not something that leads to the sharing of emotions upon which the whole book is predicated. Green
is nevertheless very impressive here, as he conjures up a real
unhappiness by recording a spurious one:

> when the old man told me to sit on in his room alone I cried
> because I thought I had to cry, because there had been a
> disaster and because here I was sitting unfeeling in this
> school holy of holies, all alone.(20)

The structurally parallel account of his parents' misreported
'death' brings Green's study of the subject of death to a climax.
But the climax is an exceptionally muted one, quite unlike most
autobiographers' treatment of the subject, and it tells us perhaps
as much about the incipient novelist in Green as it does about the
structure of his family relationships. We also begin to see at this
point why Green should have retold so many stories of death,
stories which had touched him precisely because they had had
nothing personal about them. Fiction-making becomes a kind of
refuge from the horrifying emptiness that he had also experienced
on hearing of his brother Philip's death:

> Again, as before, when my housemaster read out the tele-
> gram he had received I felt absolutely nothing at all.
>   In my life I have had no similar experience....I walked
> up and down a long time as I had done when I had earache
> at home while still at my first school. But whereas the
> physical pain had then made thought impossible in this
> case the shock made the sensation of grief, which I am not
> sure I have ever felt, altogether out of the question. In-
> stead, and I fear this is horrible, I began to dramatize
> the shock I knew I had had into what I thought it ought to
> feel like.(21)

Green suggests that this is the only thing he could do because he
had been placed in a public situation and all his education had
taught him that one's real feelings should always be kept hidden.
But whereas the Stoic tradition presupposes the repression of real

feelings, what complicates the issue here is that Green has no real feelings at all. Green is therefore doubly cut off from human experience, and having tried to tell a fellow pupil how he really feels, and been totally misunderstood, he is left in an isolation more extreme than any he has previously had to face:

It was not that he could be afraid I should burst out into the simple desperate crying of those parents. If I had he would have forgotten. No, what I told him separated us because it was outside his experience and so was awkward, no longer creepy but something to be dodged. It was all this for me as well, I felt even more apart than ever but I could not escape the event. It had happened to me and as I lay in bed that night I whipped myself up to more than meet it in what I more than ever felt in my self-pity to be a society entirely hostile.(22)

The whole episode of Green's parents' death is suddenly and disturbingly distanced by the admission that his personality crisis was predicated on an event that had not taken place; it all ends in the 'comedy'(23) of finding out that they were alive after all. But the comic aspects obviously do not interest Green at all. He passes over this major discovery in a paragraph. It is his self-accusation that really interests him, a self-accusation none the less real for having no roots in anything real. Green concludes this section of his self-portrait with an account of accidental violence done by him to a girl-cousin which is obviously meant to be seen in the context of his tangled feelings at his parents' 'death'. It is also the climax of his discussion of sexual issues, which I shall turn to next. But it is clear that, as well as wanting to make connections between death (whether fake or real) and sex (whether overt or covert), Green is also using this event to stiffen the imaginary guilt at his parents' 'death' with a dose of real and justifiable guilt that will strike us as comparatively normal. The carefully composed cadences of this coda are to be seen as not only artful but truthful, not just carefully juxtaposed one with another, but how he really feels or felt. 'Real life', Green states later, 'is an inextricable tangle,'(24) whereas art offers consoling patterns. By leaving out the vital connections between the manifold areas of his experience at this climactic point, Green is able to offer us a simulacrum of the 'inextricable tangle' while at the same time surreptitiously insinuating a pattern, causing – through his 'gathering web of insinuations' - a pattern to emerge. And it is no surprise to find Green describing to us, within a page or two, his first serious fictional efforts. Art is seen at last to be not just the completion of life, but the necessary accompaniment to it.

The predominantly melancholy tone of 'Pack My Bag' derives not only from Green's fascination with death, but also from his ambivalent attitude to sex and love. 'Any account of adolescence', says Green, 'is necessarily a study of the fatuous', but, in so far as it is also necessarily a study of the sexual, 'it would be wrong to

treat it on the lines of comedy as could so easily be done.'(25)
There is indeed little of the comic in Green's sexual memories:
they are annals of the most acute disappointment. The dominant
note is struck early on in an extraordinary non sequitur to being
caught smoking: 'some maids teach little boys to kiss they say but
not in my experience.'(26) Despite (or perhaps because of) its
compression, this conveys that Green is both terribly disappointed
(as a mature man) that this should be so, and terribly relieved
(as a child). Green finds the sexual impulse difficult to understand because it seems to require a giving of oneself in an act of
selflessness that runs counter to the reserve and self-interest that
have been inculcated in him by his privileged background and his
predatory environment. But sexuality remains (as those of us who
have read his novels would expect) what he most wants to understand, especially in the matter of how it relates to love. It is no
accident that 'love' should be the last word of 'Pack My Bag', and
that it should be uttered with such relief, for the book is full of
schoolboy and adolescent variants of love, sexual and asexual,
that reveal Green as the prey of a full range of emotions, from
disgust to amusement to fascination to obsession to torment and
beyond. 'Pack My Bag' explores every inch of the road from love
as loneliness to love as fellowship, but only achieves, or appears
to achieve, the latter in the last words of all.

There are of course lighter touches also, the embarrassed headmaster dealing with the facts of life with a brutishness that leaves
his hearers 'thunderstruck',(27) and Green's embarrassment at
being seen naked by his mother's maid. But regret is the dominant
feeling, mixed with a pained astonishment at the naivety of childhood, as in the story of his Dutch cousin:

She had no English and burst into giggles and I giggled too.
As one sees it now she meant me to kiss her which I never
did and of course this kiss which was not exchanged has
lasted on where others given or received would have escaped
the memory. Indeed it has grown, for better or for worse
this incident now at this moment looms quite large and that I
believe because of its impact; one was new then.(28)

Green only fills in the psychological background to this incident
later. But when he does so, it is devastating:

One sister who was often down to see her brother was fond,
or so it was said, of kissing. When I saw her after I had
heard this, I thought she was a prostitute, it seemed so
horrible that she could like it. Some time later when I learned
they wore nothing under their evening dresses I almost
fainted.(29)

Not surprisingly, Green's accounts of schoolboy voyeurism are
themselves not free of a certain voyeuristic relish, as though the
damage and distortion of his cloistered upbringing have not yet
been left behind:

It was their skin got me which I had never touched except
on hands and which I thought to be softer than I afterwards
found....I watched as does a cat which has not yet caught

a mouse sitting over an old hole expecting at every
minute...(30)

Symptomatic of his problems is the fact that the only contact he
can have at this stage is collision:

I came blind round a corner slap into the arms of a girl....
After apologising I went away dazed for this then was what
it must be like, this softness like a tight bolster and over
her chest some sort of shirt covered with starched frills
which had pricked my chin. I told no one, and come to that
have never told anyone before.(31)

When later Green imposes his frustrated will on a girl in a trivial
matter by snatching a spade from her and accidentally cutting her
leg to the bone, we are not altogether surprised to find him
treating the event more in suicidal than homicidal terms, less as
an act of revenge than of symbolic castration: 'It seemed to me
more a final act as though I had been cut off for ever.'(32) The
element of unconquered voyeurism remains on into his young manhood: when he goes to see Mary Pickford at the cinema, he
assuages his guilty desire for her by indulging his taste for
'those heads more intent on each other's breath as in the oldest
gesture they inclined one to the other against the lighted screen.'
(33) Green is matchless at describing the fascination mingled with
desolation that is part and parcel of the voyeur's plight.

The mature Green suffers, like the child, from a horror of the
body which derives from being required to bathe naked with
others at school: 'that shrink from mass nudity I still have, that
shock, that feeling this is wrong which in my case is the strong-
est of all instinctive feelings.'(34) If he is delighted by a glimpse
of girls bathing naked in a river, he is painfully vulnerable to
the girls returning his glance. His absurd withdrawal into himself
on the occasion of first travelling alone with a young female in a
train compartment is especially poignant, but perhaps even more
telling is his account, obviously intended as a reverse image, of
how he chased after a complete stranger and had to apologize
abjectly when she seemed to be on the point of confronting him
with his crime. Green cannot face confrontation: it leaves him no
hole to bolt into. Much better to read books and have vicarious
experiences or, better still, write them oneself and reduce still
further the likelihood of females causing one heartache. All Green's
difficulties with the fair sex are encapsulated in a brilliant and
complex description of one of the girls he met when he was beginning to become a writer:

The dark one had vast dark eyes with a kind of way she used
to look at you as though you were standing blinded in the sun
while she had caught you trying to look in where she was in
that echoing shade, as though she had all that glare which
was about you inside her and knew it well, inviting you even
to match yours with her, mocking you for standing out while
absolutely refusing to let you come inside.(35)

This is obviously a case of the voyeur trapped and outfaced by a
superior being, daring him to some sexual conquest and yet

invested with a curious radiance, almost like a goddess. Its
potency is such that we feel no strain in Green's mimetic adoption
of a 'stunned' prose in which so many unpunctuated words jostle
uncomfortably against one another, although it is a 'tour de force'
almost unmatched in Green's other writings. Green is telling us
something about literature here as well as something about life,
for he has by now added the career of literature to his repertoire
of reasons for not approaching women, and the glazed surface of
the prose is a recognition of, and a dramatization of, this fact.

After this it is almost predictable that Green's 'first complete
exchange of views'(36) with a woman should be with a Parisian
'cocotte' for it is only with those who do not represent a threat to
his expectations that Green can express himself confidently. A
familiar literary configuration is here made once again real in a
heartrendingly acute psychological analysis that is quite without
any cognizance, on Green's part, that the things he has told us
elsewhere lead up to this and help to account for it. At the same
time the ironic underpinning that makes all Green's descriptions
of Hunt Balls and Oxford colleges seem faintly ridiculous is begun
here; the 'cocotte' is a liberator in this regard as well. From here
on Green allows the subject of womankind to be decently laid to
rest and begins to stress the male-dominated world of drinking
clubs and common-rooms. The last third of 'Pack My Bag' is a
much less intense affair altogether; the dominant theme has become the abstract one of whether or not change is to be feared or
welcomed, and no longer the painfully specific one of sexual
struggle.

One of the most interesting aspects of Green's treatment of
sexual issues, and one of the most telling illustrations of his
'gathering web of insinuations' technique, is a passage that uses
the image of the contest between the huntsman and the fox. This
is more than just an unspoken gloss on the young Green's frenetic pursuit of the frightened girl; it helps to explain why he is
writing at all:

We who must die soon, or so it seems to me, should chase
our memories back, standing, when they are found, enough
apart not to be too near what they once meant. Like the
huntsman, on a hill and when he blows his horn, like him
some way from us...our memories when they are written
should like the huntsman tell that the chase is on, like the
sirens that it will soon be too late and in the way that both
these are at a distance they should be muted so that they
shall not break upon a reader's communion with his own but
only remind him by the sound so faint of ours.(37)

Of course this is much more than a mere rationale for writing 'Pack
My Bag'; it is an admission of the need to write and a recognition
that writing is, like hunting, a public and collective activity.
Green makes clear at the end of the section that begins with this
hunting image that not only art but also life must be conceived as
a hunt of sorts:

Later, when the accident I have described [in which he cuts

the leg of a girl to the bone] disrupted me, I felt, and it
is hard to explain, as though the feelings I ought to have
had were hunting me.(38)

It gradually dawns upon us that this is exactly what the death-
orientated images have been doing also, and it is clear that the
book has reached a resolution point in which 'the gathering web
of insinuations' can be forgotten about for a while. The more conventional aspects of self-portraiture - the high jinks of university
life, the formation of a personality that will enable one to survive
the world - take over, and 'Pack My Bag' is never quite so good
again, not even in the carefully cadenced phrase that concludes
the book and brings him the love he has been longing for. But
Green's management of this climax is masterly:

I was as much alone as any hunted fox. Only as my feelings
turned and doubled in their tracks to the loud blast of news
each cable brought [from his parents in Mexico], as conscience the huntsman cast my feelings forward and then back
until the fox I was was caught, bowled over at last into general surrender, there was something desperate in the noise,
the howling at my heels. At this distance the noise of the
pack is stilled, their music as it is called comes from over the
hill, the huntsman, now an older man, blows his horn gently,
and the note, now so distant it is no longer than a breath to
bring forgotten embers to a glow, is shame remembered, a
run across familiar country.(39)

This is in some ways a gruesome image, but not a gratuitous one;
Green knows how grotesque the hunt can be. He has been the fox,
although he is now the huntsman. There are compensations,
clearly, in growing older, even if the recollection of the past leads
finally to the recognition of how little one has changed. The last
part of the book takes up this question of change and changeless-
ness as if Green is intent upon spinning another web of insinuations, but it never crystallizes again in quite such a compelling
way. There is nothing complacent about Green's writing here: the
resolution is adroit and to some extent stage-managed, but no
more lacking in tension than the rest of the paragraph. Huntsman
and fox, free man and prisoner, individual and society remain
locked in combat; the glow, and the shame, are part and parcel of
a continuing process.

Green's 'self-portrait' is, like all the great self-portraits, more
than simply a portrait of the self. It is nothing like as impersonal
as it pretends to be, and there are moments when its candour is
surprisingly naked and unprotected. It is not, to use Green's own
words,(40) a book to be read aloud (though only that way, perhaps, could one prove to someone else what seductive rhythms it
has) and it is not 'quick as poetry', being sometimes turbid and
muddy and slack. But it has the great virtue of leaving its readers
free to make up a portrait for themselves, by - as Green claims
prose should do - appealing slowly to feelings unexpressed, and if
it will never quite draw tears out of the stony, that will be because

they have stopped reading long ago. Green the real man remains,
despite his articulacy and his openness, a stranger; the intimacy
that we have with him is an entirely selective one, in which he
decides how much to reveal and how much to conceal. But the
gathering web of insinuations does make 'Pack My Bag' a work of
art, not a mainstream classic, certainly, but without question
something to be rescued from a backwater. And like any true
work of art it goes, in Green's phrase, 'further than names however shared can ever go.' We would do well to remember this, in
view of the way Green's adoption of a low-key pseudonym seems
to have conspired to keep him, until very recently, out of the
spotlight he so plainly deserves.

B ADRIAN STOKES: 'INSIDE OUT'

At a time when the writings of Adrian Stokes are eliciting an unprecedented interest among commentators,(41) there are any
number of good reasons for reassessing his outstanding contribution to the genre of autobiography. But the specific reason for
my studying it within the context, but outside the text, of the
main body of this book is to demonstrate that the manner in
which Stokes came to terms with this intractable genre has both
an intrinsic and extrinsic interest - intrinsic in the sense that his
autobiographical writing contains (as Richard Wollheim has said)
'representations, unexcelled in our literature, of the artist and
the aesthete in the making',(42) extrinsic in so far as the imaginative strategies that Stokes employs are part of a pervasive tendency in the literature of self-scrutiny in this century. Like the
other works I consider here, 'Inside Out' is not so much an autobiography as an attempt to get beyond the facts of an individual
life and to state what Stokes calls, in the preface to the book,
'the themes of human nature'.(43) Although it gives no sense of
the richness of Stokes's scrutiny of the experiences that have
conditioned his personality, his subtitle for the book - 'An Essay
in the Psychology and Aesthetic Appeal of Space' - is an eloquent
reminder that 'Inside Out' is not to be construed as a kind of
memoir, but rather as an analysis of 'the deeper sources of human
action'. In Stokes's own words: 'This is not a book about childhood, except for a little of my own. The working out as the title
suggests, a certain relation to the external world, provides the
subject.'(44) As we shall see, Stokes's complex treatment of this
subject has the effect of turning our expectations of what autobiography should be 'inside out' and thereby reminding us - like
the writers I have already considered - that we have to do here
with a special kind of imaginative literature.
    Stokes began the composition of 'Inside Out' in August 1943 at
a time when his mind was, even more profoundly than usual, 'busy
with the correlation of its patterns'.(45) As someone who had for
several years been undergoing psychoanalysis with Melanie Klein,
(46) Stokes naturally turned to his memories of childhood as the

most promising material for an enterprise of this kind, partly in
an attempt at self-analysis and partly in a disinterested spirit of
laying bare 'the single experience that typifies'. The peculiar
structure of 'Inside Out', in which self-portraiture is finally subsumed in an extended meditation on Cézanne, reflects Stoke's
need to subject the relationship between 'self' and 'unself' to the
kind of scrutiny which would make sense of both his own life and
the lives of others, and which would explain how the volatile
inner world can be tempered by the curative properties of objectification. The interest of 'Inside Out', even for a reader who
knows nothing of psychoanalysis, resides in Stokes's purposeful
but never purely rational (47) 'elaboration of the mental life'. A
purely rational presentation of this material, assuming this were
possible, would be of very limited value and of dubious authenticity. An account that possessed the irrationality of a dream
would simply throw the onus of interpretation upon a professional
analyst. 'A man', Stokes wrote in his notebook, 'is the sum of all
meanings he has experienced. But it is very rare that he speaks
and feels in complete equilibrium....' 'Inside Out' is an attempt
to conjure at least partial equilibrium from the 'subtle structures
of correlation and distortion'(48) that were characteristic, for
Stokes, of any mental act.

Stokes begins his book with a childhood memory that retains a
childlike quality, even in the face of an adult gloss:

Going down the hill one morning towards Lancaster Gate, my
eldest brother remarked on an orange cloud in a dark sky:
a thundercloud, he said. And sure enough, that afternoon
there was a thunderstorm. At nearby Stanhope Gate, an old
woman sold coloured balloons. It was as if the lot had burst.
I think I remember well this small event since it symbolizes
an exceptional happening. For once the glowering suspense,
the feeling of things hardly redeemed, was contradicted by
a menace that came to violent fruition. The thing was done and
finished with: the storm happened and past, and the small
orange cloud had shown it was to happen. None of the other
omens I can remember was either read or fulfilled as was this.
The year would be 1908 or so, when I was six.(49)

Stokes's opening paragraph sets not only the tone of what will
follow but also the terms in which the subsequent narrative must
be viewed. The experience is at once an exception and a promise
of other privileged moments; and equal weight is placed upon violence and fruition or, in parallel terms, menace and redemption.
The young Stokes's inability to read his predicament - which becomes the subject of the whole Hyde Park section of the book - is
tempered by his proximity to an authority figure who possesses
mundane - but to his younger brother, magical - powers of prophecy. The adult Stokes's fascination with the explosive properties
of colour (50) is prefigured in a metaphorical transfer that reminds
the reader that the world of childhood will have to be left behind.
(51) The tension between the child's understanding of the event
and the adult's sophisticated gloss on it acts as a signal that in the

subsequent narrative there will be as much unconscious distortion
(or conscious disguise) as there will be disclosure.

Stokes proceeds to articulate the less exceptional events of
childhood which, for complex reasons, offered menace without
fruition. The dominant motif of the second paragraph is the railings within and around the Park. These railings are seen in terms
of privation (they keep out the tramps) and prohibition (they in-
hibit the couples who are looking for a place for love-making).
The small boy is overwhelmed by a feeling of massive impoverishment and desolation in the face of a world in which there seems to
be no love. Though Stokes does not tell us this, it is clear that
he is projecting, in a manner that can only harm his subsequent
development, his own feelings onto the things outside himself.
Since it gradually becomes obvious that the Park is a kind of
mother-figure it is quite permissible to see these feelings as a
function of a deep-seated Oedipus complex, with the boy both
prohibited from satisfying one type of love for his mother and
deprived of her maternal affection. (Stokes's actual mother is
completely absent from his account of his childhood.) As Stokes
modulates (52) from the iron railings to the iron seats on which
the destitute sit - against which there is a similar prohibition -
his account takes on a more positive character as he entertains
'the possibility of constant acts of restitution'.(53) (This is a
perfect illustration of the syndrome postulated by Melanie Klein,
who is nowhere mentioned in 'Inside Out', but whose theories
clarify almost every puzzling detail of the book.) The child's
initial act of restitution is seen as a kind of game, a game which,
at this point of development, and under these traumatic conditions,
must certainly be lost.(54) The child's desire to 'keep the underneath alive and thus cause the animation of the whole' is com-
promised by the fact that he does not know the real underneath
(the repressed Oedipus complex) and also by 'the clanking of the
lethal cylinders' of the machine-house that operates the Park's
fountains. The boy sees this as an 'entirely mechanical restitution'
although he is attracted by the 'eager pumping pulse' of the
sprays of water. But he associates the water also with the suicides
in the Serpentine and admits that his 'predominant impression of
the Park as a whole' is encapsulated in 'a police description of a
dead body'. Stokes's description of the fountains leaves no room
for doubt that we are being confronted here by a correlative of
the Oedipus complex, the fascination with (and yet fear of) the
sexual organ of the father that, in conferring life, commits its
offspring to ultimate death. Indeed Stokes subsequently speaks,
in connection with the whistles blown by the park-keepers, of 'a
cold, punishing little organ that it was a positive duty to handle,'
(55) as a way of dramatizing the child's subservience to authority,
and reluctance to admit that the organ could be an instrument of
pleasure. (Later, in one of his most subtle correlations, Stokes
shows how a barrel-organ can provide not only pleasure, but an
integrating principle.)

Stokes has said nothing as yet of his 'seven years' analysis'.(56)

But in order that the reader should not lose himself among the
child's distortions, he admits quite openly that his feelings are
projections of fantasy. After recounting the way in which he fell
among and could not escape from the 'parkees' or tramps, the
adult voice provides an important corrective view: 'I have little
doubt that no such actual thing happened. Probably the context
existed....'(57) These more rational adult comments are sprinkled
throughout Stokes's narrative, but not in any spirit of supporting
the adult's as against the infant's view of the world. The comments of the adult Stokes are indicative that, even in maturity,
there is a residue of trauma and neurosis, and that the child is
father of the man in a manner that is in some respects irremediable. But it is at the same time clear that the battle that is going
on in the mind of the child (58) must in some way be resolved,
and Stokes turns his attention to the child's attempts to bring
this about.

The architecture in the Park only exacerbates the child's mor-
bidity, and the imagery that Stokes uses to describe it consolidates the images of excretion that Stokes has already set in train
in his description of the fountains: 'The tall, disproportionate
alcove, shallow, high and cold, with toddlers squirming on a low
brown seat, was, and is today (though it be attributed to Wren)
an image to me of blindness.'(59) The child seeks relief from this
'ethical ugliness' in 'forms of life', the natural life of the Park.
But in the case of dogs let off the lead, 'their curiosity about
each other appeared particularly morbid' and an old man feeding
sparrows seems only to be expressing 'his own accumulated
evasions'.(60) Only the cries of the 'disconsolate' peacocks and
the sudden violence of the swans seem to offer an escape from the
restrictions of the Park. But in psychoanalytical terms they are
at odds with one another, for although the yelling of the sexually
explicit peacocks (61) 'dislodged for a time an imputed curriculum',
the violence of the swans is predicated on the protection of the
family unit. Stokes's description of a swan, 'in minatory Edwardian stateliness', sitting on a nest beside a 'dangerous overflow'
acts as an index of not only his own repression, but also of the
repression of an age, a theme later dramatized in his account of
the funeral of Edward VII and the coronation of George V. In describing the low white bridge that divided the Serpentine from the
water beyond it, Stokes contrives to correlate his own castration
complex, his own (and the reader's) desire to 'penetrate the mystery', the controlling power of the crown and the even more
decisive power of the Unconscious to disgorge its contents. This
is one of Stokes's more dazzling sleights-of-hand, rounded off by
an open declaration that the traumas of childhood survive into
adult life:

> This white stone bridge had a certain grace: the exceed-
> ingly low arches, however, were associated in my mind
> with a challenge to any inquisitive head whether of water-
> fowl or man, who tried to share the fate, whatever it might
> be, of the water beyond the Serpentine.

On the further side of the white bridge there was a sharp
declivity and a high though meagre waterfall. I don't think I
connected this water with a flow from the Serpentine. Later,
I was to hear that most of the Serpentine water passed under-
ground and came up in the park of Buckingham Palace. I was
to be told that the Serpentine could be drained, that everything flung into it could be brought to light. All the miseries
of the torn, attacked and divided mother without me and
within, she who was the Park and all that happened there, to
be known, controlled and restored? No wonder that in many
later writings I have sought for the clean sweep. I have had
an absurd faith in the efficacy of generalization and, at times,
a neurotic subservience to the behests of an apparent logic.
(62) By this would-be control I have been subservient to the
same relentless animus that informed, to my mind, the face of
the Park.(63)

The compensatory fantasies of the child continue. But the atmosphere is slightly less oppressive after this outburst. The narrative
moves beyond Hyde Park proper and into Kensington Gardens, and
the imagination begins to operate in a more positive way, with increased detachment, and yet with a desire to make the world
habitable again:

In the course of time I grew very curious concerning...a well-
sized house in the middle of Kensington Gardens. I had never
seen anyone go in or come out....Later I used to imagine myself inhabiting the house (64) in the middle of Kensington
Gardens; walking in the Park in the early morning, watching
the dawn and later seeing the lines of trees, an unspoilt natural panorama; living in the country in the middle of London.
From adolescence onwards I did what I could with my imagination to restore the Park. Standing at the Round Pond, I
looked across the Long Water and conjured up the vista of an
eighteenth-century park, a royal park having no essential
connection with the lives of children.(65)

This increase in detachment allows the maternal and paternal em-
blems (66) to disappear from the narrative, if only momentarily.
Stokes now pictures himself in the context of other children,
having picnics on the grass, and although London still seems like
a malevolent force, its ceaseless traffic begins to symbolize the
possibility of a more profitable commerce between the inner and
the outer world:

This circular flow of traffic served as a kind of watchful coast-
ing on the fringes of consciousness: at times, also, as vehicles
which carried correspondence to the deeper depths of the mind,
bringing thence the matter for new affinities....There is
pleasure, there is life, when movement, particularly even movement in space, when the outward world at large, takes for
us the form of the jagged shifting promontories of the mind.
It is notable, however, that the first glimpse of the sea, that
closer parallel to the tossing mind, has a meaning of limitless
release, and words wrested from a life at sea (67) ring true of
the mind.(68)

Stokes prefigures here, and again a few paragraphs later, the abiding satisfaction to be derived from a relationship with the 'outward world at large'. But London and Hyde Park and Edwardian England cannot provide that satisfaction. The statuary of Hyde Park does not even offer the consolations of a vibrant contemporary culture:

I had high hopes of the Watts [equestrian statue] because it was new; I remember it veiled and then unveiled. Such figures were to me stern yet impotent; figures of a father, then, who both attacked and had been attacked. These statues attempted to affront the shy yet they were recipients of fog, of bird droppings and of soot: they seemed unconnected with light.(69)

In reaction against the malaise of the contemporary environment, the boy continues to seek solace in projections onto the landscape that is available to him. He even constructs a Paradise of sorts on the west side of Kensington Gardens, which by virtue of the 'magic' that he invests in it seems to offer him a freedom from limits and limitations: 'I thought of this piece of ground as outside the Park, yet at the same time, inside it, like a historical association pursued into the present.'(70) This is an important prefiguration of the effect that the Mediterranean will have on Stokes, but nothing more than that. Stokes immediately widens his perspective to show that the associations of history are merely a placebo, without really curative properties: 'I was later to take great comfort in history, as if the things of the Park, as if all that was carried inside my mind, could be pinned down, arranged, comprehended.'(71) There is even an implicit suggestion, conveyed by the juxtaposition of this quietly bitter remark with the section that follows it, that it would be better if history were brought to a halt by a massive and cataclysmic explosion by the Magazine at the end of the Serpentine bridge, at the very heart of 'the Edwardian centre of Empire.'(72)

Despite this, the soldiers who patrol the Magazine retain a special fascination for the child. The sentry, like the boy, is 'controlling the explosive powers within by his drilled movements' and the boy, by projecting his more positive fantasies with the fanaticism that has already marked his negative ones, is no nearer to establishing a modus vivendi that will bring the inner and outer worlds into a less frictional opposition: 'the very encouragement by the onlooker of pastoral things', Stokes writes, 'denied them a reality that was supreme.' The quest for a supreme reality now takes on a religious colouring, with the boy placed in the more or less pastoral care of a sequence of governesses. But the governesses, and one governess in particular, prove to be only another version of the repressive forces that have previously been imaged in terms of park-keepers and sentries:

Miss Harley used to sing me hymns. She was for me the Salvation Army of morbid streets and morbid walks. Even the Park sheep looked wicked and guilty, particularly the sheep, poor, smelly and sniffing. There was, I think, no talk of Christ.

The only salvation that this army can offer is the inevitability of
death:
>'Time like an ever-rolling stream, bears all her sons away.'
>We used to sing that hymn, the thin sounds torn by the wind.
>I had never seen a rolling stream. I thought of it as the low
>thunder of the London traffic. And Time was the gloomy sky
>over the Park, which, by turning into night, bore away the
>soiled fretfulness of all happenings there each day.

The gap between this blind and fatalistic philosophy and the 'all-
seing eye' of the boy's simple theism is of the kind that no amount
of imaginative energy could hope to bridge. And the memory of
the way the monumental masonry of the Park became for him a
monstrous parody of a life-giving source moves the adult Stokes
to a childlike outburst at the way his environment failed to nour-
ish him:
>Between Marble Arch and Albion Gate there is a kind of
>Gothic steeple whose function is to provide several vents of
>drinking water. To this globuled monstrosity in particular
>I attributed a horrible masochism....Here stood no source,
>no spring....It is horrible that a flow of water, thin though
>the trickle, should come to represent a blindness.(73)

In accordance with the pattern of flow and recoil that makes this
section of 'Inside Out' so compelling and yet so complex, Stokes
completes his account of the Hyde Park experience with the 'rare
moments when the purlieus known to me had stature.'(74) These
'moments of pageantry' are moments of vision within the prevail-
ing blindness and are intrinsically colourful:
>What stays in mind were the long thin festive poles swathed
>in scarlet cloth, tipped with golden spear-heads, that lined
>both sides of Bayswater Road. Even railings were tipped
>with gilt. It was not the gaudiness so much as the picking
>out of features, the slight rearrangement of the London for-
>getfulness, which gave the street a life to me. I saw, as it
>were, for the first time that Bayswater Road was a thorough-
>fare: some kind of plan appeared.

Stokes associates this partial liberation from trauma with a foreign
governess with whom he would watch the ceremonies associated
with the end of the Edwardian empire and the beginning of a new
dynasty. But the governess, in becoming an almost erotic object
for the boy, reactivates the boy's dormant Oedipus complex:
>She brought a homesick warmth. But the Park held sway, and
>when we ate a raspberry cream-filled chocolate bar which I
>had been forbidden, sitting in the Park on one of the for-
>bidden seats, my pleasure was not exactly sweet. I remember
>particularly some bedroom slippers on which had been spilt
>an extremely sticky spread which I liked, called Frame food
>jelly. This sweetness in the wrong place was agonizing. I
>used to wear those slippers because the nursery stood over
>my parents' bedroom and my father, at that time, lay fighting
>for his life...

Although the King dies, the boy's father survives, and his sur-

vival arrests the boy's own morbid drifting. Once again Stokes's
narrative can be seen as an almost perfect illustration of the
struggle between the life and death instincts that first Freud,
and then Melanie Klein, had been concerned to identify as central
to the treatment of neurotic trauma. The Hyde Park section of
'Inside Out' ends with a memory of the 'dirty, echoing tunnel'
that the boy had to walk through on his way home from the Park,
an 'obscene' and hellish hole that is suddenly revealed as 'the
home of the animus that tore the body of the Park to shreds.'(75)
But previous to this final reminder of the need to conquer the
Oedipus complex, the boy is granted a fantastic experience that
gives him the strength to stand on his own and the promise of a
more satisfying relationship with the outside world. In a passage
of great colour and drama, Stokes shifts, as he has done at less
crucial moments previously, from the past to the present tense:

I have a pictorial, almost a Renoir-like image (76) - the only
one - of those times, based, I have little doubt, on much
later experience. For it is night, a dark, still night with rain
in the air. The speakers at Marble Arch are lit with their
torches; the outer fringe of whispering couples are lit by the
lamps. Where it is dense the crowd is dark. Hats are in sil-
houette, so too the railings behind the speakers. Beyond,
unwhispering grass is black except where a beam of light
turns an outer fringe to emerald, the tired-smelling grass
that otherwise would have been long obscured.

A soldier in a red tunic detaches himself from the crowd,
takes the path across the Park, probably making for the
Knightsbridge barracks. I watch him going between the far-
flung lamps, making for the centre of the Park and, so it
seems, for the centre of the night, since the Park symbolizes
all. I watch him go, getting less scarlet. Steadied by the
lamps, my thoughts follow him into an immense space: for he
has reached the open space where the enfolding pulse of the
traffic is best felt. The lights, both near and distant, stare:
an iron urge is to be attributed both to the soldier and to the
preacher. Once and for all, I now put up the railings inside
myself. I have an inspired feeling of Destiny, of Duty. I will
follow out the most exacting inner imperative. With consistent
dutiful fire I will equal the coldness and steadiness of the
lamps: with a certain inner talisman I shall part the murmur-
ing London sea: I shall prolong a selfless path with such
resolution that the astonishing hideous pile of the Hyde Park
Hotel, so often figuring on the limits of vision, shall fall
defeated below man's horizon....(77)

This extraordinary passage, replete with analogues of the crossing of the Red Sea and the collapse of the Tower of Babel,
dramatizes the most crucial of the 'introjective' fantasies that the
child has to undergo in order to balance the preponderance of
'projective' ones that have thus far distorted his sense of things.
But it requires completion; the optimum objective environment
must still be sought. As the rest of the first part of 'Inside Out'

demonstrates, the Mediterranean, and specifically Italy, provides the necessary complement. The boy disappears into the Hyde Park tunnel and is reborn as he emerges from the Mont Cenis railway tunnel into the Italian sunshine. A great weight is lifted, for both Stokes and the reader, as a more expansive and translucent prose takes over from the contorted and somehow rootless tensions of the Hyde Park section. And the very first paragraph of this discursive prose is devoted to a summary of what the rest of 'Inside Out' will be concerned with:

Each man invents a myriad states to counter his inferno.... But a truly exacting person, anxious to discover a reparation of even the smallest detail, is likely to construct a state parallel to that by which inferno is summed. And indeed, it is the initial imputation, in such a strong degree, of emotional states to the external world, inferno or paradiso or both at once, that characterizes the person who will primarily be an artist, even when childhood is passed. In this, however, I do not think he is peculiar, but only extreme and exacting in the use of a compulsion commensurate with his anxiety.(78)

This section of 'Inside Out' is essentially a bridge-passage, in which the experience of Italy is suddenly 'revealed' to have been a hidden potential in the English experience. The learning of Latin grammar during 'the years of Mathilde' and the creative power of a London barrel-organ are brought out, as in an analysis, as the latent positives in what had seemed an irremediable neurosis. The homeless struggle against inner and outer cruelties is superseded by a crystalline clarity and benevolence:

Of the table, for the table, by the table, each expressed by one simple word. The genitive case was the possessiveness of a simple love.

It is a scrubbed, sturdy, deal kitchen table, very bright: the fact that it is solid, that it stands on the floor, is beautiful....With one word I possessed in embryo the Virgilian scene; a robust and gracious mother earth.

The organized focus of the Latin language is supported by the equally homely barrel-organ:

I found in sound a most effective qualification of the visual world. A street became *informed* for me by the sounds of a barrel-organ. Everything had a new angle of light upon it, a new arrangement with a centre pulsating like a heart. Thus the street was not only organized; it became an organism, it came alive.(79)

These English experiences modulate into analogous but distinctively Italian ones in obedience to the principle of 'identity in difference' that Stokes had been attracted by in the philosophy of F. H. Bradley.(80) But sound is only a qualifier for Stokes, it does not possess the substantive qualities of mensa (the table) and the world perceived by the eyes. Stokes even goes so far as to illustrate how sound alone returns the psyche to the vicious circle of provocation and projection that has been the hallmark of the Hyde Park experience. It is the table that is the true prolepsis of the earthly Paradise that Italy represents:

I had half forgotten about my table for more than ten years.
At once I saw it everywhere, on either side of the train,
purple earth, terraces of vine and olive, bright rectangular
houses free of atmosphere, of the passage of time, of imped-
iment....The hills belonged to man in this his moment. The
two thousand years of Virgilian past that carved and habit-
uated the hill-sides, did not oppress: they were gathered
into the present aspect...time was here laid out as ever-
present space.(81)

Throughout Stokes's description of his journey towards Rapallo,
we find motifs that are echoes, conscious or unconscious, of the
Hyde Park experience. But they are the obverse of the coin: the
day gives way to night without misgiving, the emphasis is all on
seeing and being seen instead of blindness: 'The inhabitants had
no need of blinds: since no dominant misery and no surfeit of unexpressed emotion lurked inside them, there was nothing beyond
the houses to be shut out.'(82) Within the world of suspended
juxtapositions is a world of reciprocations and commonweal:

I had the new sensation that the air was touching things;
that the space between things touched them, belonged in
common; that space itself was utterly revealed. There was
a neatness in the light. Nothing hid or was hidden....Here
was an open and naked world...I had, in fact, incorporated
this objective-seeming world and proved myself constructed
by the general refulgence.(83)

Stokes acknowledges here that the world he is describing is as
much a construction of the mind as the Hyde Park he is so pleased
to be rid of. But the lines of force are utterly reversed: instead
of spiralling endlessly inward by false projections outward, the
inner and outer worlds relate symbiotically, in a creative dynamism:

I have here the means of action, a demonstration, not of the
purpose of life but of the power of life to be manifest; not of
one thing but of the calm relationship of many things, concrete things, each bound to each by an outwardness that
allows no afterthought to the spectator: an outward showing
goes within him. An answering life wells to the surface and
he feels - hence the great beauty of the Mediterranean landscape - that the process of man's existence is outward, giving
shape, precise contour to the few things that lie deepest;
whatever the distortion they mutually endow, making the
expenditure in terms of a surface we call expression, be it in
action, art or thought.(84)

Stokes does not deny the element of distortion; indeed he stresses
it. But it is clear that a kind of marriage has been effected between the 'genius loci' and the genius of the person concerned.(85)
It is the exactness of the 'concatenation' that Stokes is struck by,
and it entails the disappearance of the merely personal.

The remainder of 'Inside Out' is concerned with 'matters less
immediate...but often more profound than are revealed by reminiscences' or, as Stokes later describes it, 'a generalized confron-

tation, however personal the reference'.(86) Other than the opening paragraphs of part two (which merge Stokes's train journeys (87) to preparatory school and public school), the remainder of 'Inside Out' is essentially 'an abstract setting of the mind over against the visual world',(88) first (in what remains of part one) by means of a vigorous defence of psychoanalysis, second (in part two), through a reassessment of the life and work of Cézanne. This is a necessary consequence of the 'working out' of which the preface has spoken, and not the result of an atrophy of the autobiographical impulse. The 'generalized confrontation' is, in any case, a profoundly personal one; few writers have excelled Stokes in the ability to make discursive writing as intimate as autobiography.

The composition of 'Smooth and Rough' in 1948-9(89) indicates indeed that the impulse to confront the configurations of his life was an almost permanent preoccupation with him, as his commitment to psychoanalysis made almost inevitable. 'Smooth and Rough' follows on from 'Inside Out' only in the sense that the period described is later than the childhood and adolescence of the earlier book; formally, it is quite distinct from and quite as idiosyncratic as its predecessor. In part two of 'Smooth and Rough', for example, rather than (as in 'Inside Out') secreting his own beliefs behind the narrative of someone else's life, Stokes stands outside himself and plays the role of hypothetical commentator.(90) But this second book ends, like the first, with a long, discursive section. There are moments of great beauty in 'Smooth and Rough', and it is a more equable book as a whole, smooth, in fact, rather than rough. But this is because it is not composed, like that part of 'Inside Out' that I have attempted to present a simulacrum of here in accordance with the principle of an 'ever increasing complication in correspondence'.(91)

NOTES

Introduction

1   Herbert Read, introduction to Paul Nash, 'Outline: an Autobiography and Other Writings', Faber & Faber, London, 1949, p. 14.

2   See, for example, Mutlu Konuk Blasing, 'The Art of Life', University of Texas Press, 1977, p. xiii: 'autobiographical literature has the status of a metaliterature'; Louis Renza, The Veto of the Imagination: a Theory of Autobiography, 'New Literary History', vol. 9, no. 1, Autumn 1977, p. 1: 'Perhaps more than any other literary concept, autobiography traps us into circular explanations of its being.'

3   As long ago as 1964, Robert F. Sayre wrote: 'our distinctions between... [autobiography] and the novel...strike me as shamefully unanalyzed' (The Examined Self: Benjamin Franklin, Henry Adams, Henry James', Princeton University Press, 1964, p. ix). Cf. Philippe Lejeune, Autobiography in the Third Person, 'New Literary History', vol. 9, no. 1, Autumn 1977, p. 47.

4   Roy Pascal, 'Design and Truth in Autobiography', Routledge & Kegan Paul, London, 1959.

5   See, e.g., the criticisms of Stephen Shapiro, The Dark Continent of Literature: Autobiography, 'Comparative Literature Studies', vol. 5, 1968, p. 426. Cf. the introduction to Philippe Lejeune's 'Le Pacte Autobiographique', Seuil, Paris, 1975

6   Jean Starobinski, The Style of Autobiography, in 'Literary Style: a Symposium', ed. Seymour Chatman, Oxford University Press, London, 1971, pp. 285-96.

7   These are the titles of works by, respectively, John Morris (New York, 1966), James Olney (Princeton University Press, 1972), Mutlu Konuk Blasing, op. cit. Roger J. Porter and H. R. Wulf (Knopf, New York, 1973) and Elisabeth Bruss (Johns Hopkins University Press, Baltimore, 1976).

8   'New Literary History', vol. 9, no. 1, Autumn 1977; 'Genre', vol. 6, nos. 1 and 2, March and June 1973; 'Modern Language Notes', vol. 93, no. 4, May 1978.

9   Cf. David Gervais, Leonard Woolf's Autobiography, 'Cambridge Quarterly', vol. 7, no. 1, Spring/Summer 1970, p. 82: 'It is, in England at least, a branch of literature which is not often closely thought about. An exasperating symptom of this is that every time an important autobiography appears, somebody is ready to tell us that it equals Rousseau's.'

10 'Manhood', trans. Richard Howard, Jonathan Cape, London 1968, p. 15.

11 Ibid., p. 19.

12 Henry James, 'Autobiography', W. H. Allen, London, 1956, p. 65.

13 'Henry Adams and his Friends', ed. Harold Dean Cater, Houghton Mifflin, Boston, 1947, p. 614; 'Letters of Mrs. Henry Adams', ed. Ward Thoron, Little Brown, Boston, 1936, pp. 458-9.

14 'Letters of Henry Adams, 1892-1918', ed. W. C. Ford, Houghton Mifflin, Boston, 1938, vol. 2, p. 476.

15 See my Aspects of Kafka, 'Poetry Nation Review', no. 10, 1979.

16 Richard Wollheim, introduction to 'The Image in Form: Selected Writings of Adrian Stokes', Penguin, Harmondsworth, 1972, pp. 27-8.

17 Paul Nash, 'Outline', op. cit., p. 18.

18 See Anthony Stephens, 'Rilkes Malte Laurids Brigge: Strukturanalyse des Erzählerischen Bewusststeins', Verlag Herbert Lang et Cie., Bern, 1974.

19 The decapitation motif of 'L'Age d'Homme' is found again in 'Speak, Memory': the quotation from the Marguerite section of part one of Goethe's

'Faust' in 'L'Age d'homme' is found again in 'The Education of Henry
Adams', and so on.
20 Blasing, 'The Art of Life', op. cit., p. xxviii.

Chapter 1 Henry Adams: 'The Education of Henry Adams'
1 'Letters of Henry Adams, 1892-1918', ed. W. C. Ford, Houghton Mifflin,
   Boston, 1938, p. 414; hereafter Ford II. Cf. a letter of 1915 to William
   Roscoe Thayer: 'I felt a little as though you had written a life of me as
   well as Hay' (Ford II, p. 633; cf. p. 632).
2 'Letters of Henry Adams, 1858-1891', ed. W.C. Ford, Houghton Mifflin,
   Boston, 1930, p. 347; hereafter Ford I.
3 'Henry Adams and His Friends', ed. Harold Dean Cater, Houghton Mifflin,
   Boston, 1947, p. 592; hereafter Cater.
4 Ford II, p. 416, cf. Cater, pp. 486-8.
5 Ibid., pp. 412, 416. Cf. ibid., pp. 271, 526 and Cater, pp. 592, 649.
6 Ibid., p. 473.
7 See Earl N. Harbert, 'The Force So Much Nearer Home', New York University Press, 1967, *passim* for extended analysis of this subject.
8 Ford I, pp. 156-7. Cf. Adams's later 'editing' of Queen Marau of Tahiti's
   memoirs.
9 Ford II, pp. 70-1.
10 Ford I, p. 344.
11 Cater, p. 580.
12 Ford II, p. 495. When James did indeed 'take his own life', but in a very
    different way, Adams had reservations about the outcome. See Ford II,
    p. 622 and Percy Lubbock (ed.), 'The Letters of Henry James', Macmillan,
    London, 1920, vol. II, p. 373 for James's riposte.
13 Thomas Cooley calls the 'Education' 'the most egocentric of books'
    ('Educated Lives: the Rise of Modern Autobiography in America', Ohio
    State University Press, 1976, p. 45).
14 Ford I, p. 51.
15 Ibid., p. 261.
16 Ibid., p. 261.
17 Ibid., p. 318.
18 Ibid., p. 262.
19 Ibid., p. 132.
20 Ibid., p. 269.
21 Ibid., p. 352.
22 Cater, p. 547.
23 Ford I, p. 313.
24 Ernest Samuels, 'Henry Adams: the Major Phase', Harvard University
    Press, 1964, p. 329.
25 Ford I, p. 322.
26 Ibid., p. 337.
27 Cater, p. 137.
28 Ford I, p. 377. Cf. Ford I, p. 468, where Adams compares his nine-volume
    'History' unfavourably with 'Esther'.
29 Ibid., p. 343.
30 Cater, p. 262.
31 Ibid., p. 37.
32 Ford II, p. 495.
33 Ford I, p. 341.
34 Ibid., p. 401.
35 Ibid., p. 333.
36 'I believe silence to be now the only sensible form of expression' (Ford II,
    p. 70; cf. ibid., pp. 122, 552, 642, Cater, pp. 114 etc.)
37 Cater, p. 243.
38 Ibid., p. 237.
39 Ford II, pp. 559-60.
40 Ibid., p. 567.
41 Ibid., p. 565.

42 Cater, p. 614.
43 Ford II, p. 490. This letter is eloquent proof of Adams's inability in, or lack of interest in distinguishing between different types of literature. The 'ten years' here is doubtless an exaggeration. On the 'Education' as a romance, see another letter of the same year: 'the path is sugar-coated in order to induce anyone to follow it. The nearer we can come to romance the more chance that somebody will read – and understand' (Cater, p. 622).
44 Cater, p. 614.
45 Ibid., p. 644.
46 Ibid., pp. 645–6.
47 Ford II, p. 490.
48 'I have written you before...that I aspire to be bound up with St. Augustine. Or rather, I would have aspired to it, if it were artistically possible to build another fourth-century church. It cannot be. The *Leit motif* is flat. One can get one's artistic effects only by flattening everything to a level' (ibid., p. 525).
49 Ibid., p. 490.
50 Cater, p. 622.
51 Ford II, p. 485. See also the letters to William James of 9 December 1907 (Ford II, p. 485) and 17 February 1908 (ibid., p. 490). In a letter of 6 May 1908 to Henry James Adams stressed both the historical and the literary elements (ibid., p. 495).
52 Ibid., p. 472.
53 Cater, p. 610.
54 Ibid., p. 472.
55 Ibid., p. 614. In the same letter Adams restates his claim that the 'Education' (and indeed the 'Mont Saint-Michel and Chartres' volume) had 'not been done in order to teach others, but to educate myself in the possibilities of literary form' (ibid., p. 614; cf. p. 610).
56 Ibid., p. 619.
57 Ibid., p. 559.
58 'Letters of Mrs. Henry Adams', ed. Ward Thoron, Little Brown, Boston, 1936, pp. 458–9.
59 Ford II, p. 495.
60 Melvin Lyon, 'Symbol and Idea in Henry Adams', University of Nebraska Press, Lincoln, 1970, pp. 285–6.
61 Vern Wagner, 'The Suspension of Henry Adams: a Study of Manner and Matter', Wayne State University Press, 1969.
62 Cater, p. 732.
63 Wagner, op. cit., p. 86.
64 'The Education of Henry Adams', ed. Ernest Samuels, Houghton Mifflin, Boston, 1974, p. xxx; hereafter 'Education'.
65 In each paragraph almost; see Wagner, op. cit., p. 100.
66 Adams repeatedly calls this point the 'term' in order that its educational connotations should not be forgotten (see Lyon, op. cit., p. 292).
67 'Education', pp. 53, 69.
68 Ibid., pp. 97, 127.
69 Adams saw himself as a 'professional wanderer' (Ford II, p. 36) and told John Hay in a letter of 1891: 'the true wanderer cannot stop' (Cater, p. 234).
70 'Education', p. 500. This is a variant on Wordsworth's 'child is father of the man' idea. Adams discovered Wordsworth late (see Samuels, op. cit., p. 262) but made amends in the 'Education', and also in 'Mont Saint-Michel and Chartres', in which, at the beginning of chapter one and at the beginning of chapter six, he alludes to the 'Immortality Ode'.
71 Ibid., p. 209.
72 Ibid., p. 289.
73 Ibid., p. 413.
74 Ibid., pp. 413–14.
75 Henry James, preface to 'Roderick Hudson' (New York edition), p. x.
76 'Education', p. 91.

77 Ibid., pp. 94-5.
78 Ibid., p. 20.
79 Ibid., p. 95.
80 T. S. Eliot, A Sceptical Patrician, 'The Athenaeum', no. 4647, 23 May 1919, p. 362.
81 'Education', pp. 4-5.
82 Ibid., p. 4.
83 Ibid., p. 329.

Chapter 2 Henry James: 'A Small Boy and Others'
1 F. O. Matthiessen, 'Henry James: the Major Phase', Oxford University Press, London, 1946.
2 'Letters of Henry James', ed. Percy Lubbock, Macmillan, London, 1920, vol. 2, p. 373.
3 Ibid., p. 508.
4 Most accessible in 'Parodies', ed. D. Macdonald, Faber & Faber, London, 1961.
5 Most recent criticism has attempted to disprove the contention that James was only an 'old Pretender' in his later work.
6 Henry James, 'Selected Letters', ed. Leon Edel, Rupert Hart Davis, London, 1956, p. 234.
7 See, e.g., Seymour Chatman, 'The Later Style of Henry James', Blackwell, Oxford, 1972.
8 Henry James, 'Autobiography' ('A Small Boy and Others', 'Notes of a Son and Brother', and 'The Middle Years'), ed. F. W. Dupee, W. H. Allen, London, 1956, p. 65. All further references are to this one-volume edition.
9 Ibid., p. 105.
10 Ibid., p. 105.
11 Ibid., p. 4.
12 Ibid., p. 65.
13 Ibid., p. 105.
14 Ibid., p. 105. Cf. the discussion in 'William Wetmore Story and his Friends', (1903; reprinted Thames & Hudson, London, 1957; hereafter 'Story'), where James concludes that there can be no line of division between the absorption and effusion (vol. 1, p. 347).
15 Ibid., p. 105. Cf. the preface to 'The Awkward Age' (New York edition, p. xi) and the preface to 'What Maisie Knew' (New York edition, p. xi).
16 'Autobiography', p. 105.
17 Ibid., p. 104. Cf. ibid., p. 26: 'mere mite of observation'.
18 Except in so far as James believes he is 'seeing the whole...in each enacted and recovered moment' (ibid., p. 4).
19 Ibid., p. 65.
20 Ibid., p. 105.
21 James's prime difficulty was that 'aspects began to multiply and images to swarm' (ibid., p. 3). Cf. ibid., pp. 436, 449, 551, 554, 563, 564 etc. At the beginning of 'The American Scene' (1907; reprinted Indiana University Press, 1969), a book in which he repeatedly describes himself as a 'restless analyst' (e.g. pp. 11, 29, 33, 43, 47, 164), James admits that treating his material properly is 'going to be a matter of prodigious difficulty and selection' (p. 3) and throughout the book he reverts to the way in which vivid images tend to multiply and intensify (e.g. pp. 50, 108, 122, 143, 422). Cf. the 'complications' of 'The Awkward Age' (op. cit., p. viii) and the 'multiplications' of the story The Point of View (vol. 19 of the New York edition, p. xxiii). The other major obstacle to completing the task satisfactorily was, in James's view, the questions that could not be answered; see, for example, the prefaces to vol. 19 (p. x) and vol. 22 (pp. xxv and xxx) of the New York edition, and 'Story', vol. 1, p. 312.
22 'Autobiography', p. 65.
23 Cf. ibid., pp. 28, 32, 54, 79, 155, 171, 263, 434; 'The American Scene', op. cit., pp. 68, 99, 220, 244, 378; and 'Story', vol. 1, pp. 16, 75-6, 109-10, 144, 219. The preface to vol. 22 of the New York edition is James's

most extended discussion of why the ghost-story was his favourite kind of fairy-tale (see especially p. xix).

24 'Autobiography', p. 65.
25 Cf. ibid., p. 80: 'I am, strictly speaking, at this point, on a visit to Albert'.
26 For other instances of James's 'organicism', see ibid., pp. 236, 567; also the preface to 'The Awkward Age', which speaks of a 'principle of growth' (op. cit., p. v) and the preface to 'What Maisie Knew' (op. cit., p. v).
27 'Autobiography', p. 65. The image of 'swarming' is habitual in late James; see, for one example among many, ibid., p. 554.
28 Ibid., p. 65.
29 Ibid., p. 65.
30 Ibid., p. 198. James was obviously aware of Tennyson's poem 'The Palace of Art' and of Dante Gabriel Rossetti's sonnet-sequence 'The House of Life'.
31 Cf. James's remarks on 'fusions', ibid., pp. 477, 494; and the preface to vol. 18 of the New York edition: 'everything I "find", as I look back, lives for me again in the light of *all* the parts...of my intelligence....The musing artist's imagination...makes the whole occasion...comprehensively and richly *one.*'
32 'Autobiography', p. 38. The image is habitual in James's later works; see for one example among many, the preface to vol. 18 of the New York edition, p. v.
33 'Autobiography', p. 4.
34 Ibid., p. 54.
35 See, for an assessment of it, Elizabeth Stevenson, 'The Crooked Corridor: a Study of Henry James', Macmillan, New York, 1961, pp. 160ff.; Thomas Cooley, 'Educated Lives: the Rise of Modern Autobiography in America', Ohio State University Press, pp. 112-13; Leon Edel, 'Henry James: The Master 1901-16', Rupert Hart-Davis, London, 1972, pp. 459, 478.
36 'Autobiography', p. 195.
37 Ibid., p. 161.
38 Ibid., p. 161. The whole subject of James's opposition of 'Europe', as he persistently marked it off, and America is, of course, much more complex than this. Cf. ibid., pp. 23, 42, 43, 219, 230. The specific role of Italy has been discussed by Carl Maves in 'Sensuous Pessimism' (Stanford University Press, 1969), and the travel books - 'English Hours', 'Italian Hours', and 'A Little Tour in France' - are full of vivid responses to each country, as is the collection of early journalism, 'Parisian Sketches'. See also the preface to 'The Awkward Age' (op. cit., pp. xi-xii), the preface to 'What Maisie Knew' (op. cit., pp. xix-xx), the preface to vol. 19 of the New York edition, pp. v et seq., xv-xvi, and the preface to vol. 18 of the New York edition, pp. xiii, xvi. Cf. also 'Story', vol. 1, pp. 4, 187, 295-6, 333, and 'The American Scene', op. cit., pp. 312, 321, 365ff., 399, 406ff.
39 'Autobiography', p. 196.
40 Ibid.
41 Cf. James's sensitivity to the country as a natural place for the common people in 'The American Scene', op. cit., p. 178.
42 'Autobiography', p. 196.
43 Ibid., p. 195.
44 Ibid., p. 196.
45 Ibid.
46 Ibid.
47 Ibid., p. 199.
48 Ibid., p. 196.
49 Ibid., p. 197; James's italics.
50 Ibid., p. 196. The imagery of doors is very common in late James, often (as in 'Story', vol. 1, p. 336) in the context of multiplying impressions.
51 'Autobiography', p. 224.
52 Ibid., p. 197.
53 Ibid.

54 Cf. James's preface to 'What Maisie Knew' on the 'great gaps and voids' of 'the infant mind' (op. cit., p. x), and 'The American Scene', op. cit., p. 171, on 'the incoherence and volatility of childhood'.
55 'Autobiography', p. 194.
56 Ibid., pp. 195-6.
57 Ibid., p. 103.
58 Ibid., pp. 207, 212, 225.
59 Ibid., pp. 10,42,50, 59, 68, 160. Cf. 'Story', vol. 1, p. 95.
60 'Autobiography', p. 52.
61 Ibid., p. 38. Cf. ibid., p. 294: 'the dawning perception that the arts were after all essentially one.'
62 Ibid., p. 117. This is only one of many references to Dickens; see Dupee's index to this end.
63 Ibid., p. 175.
64 Ibid., p. 118.
65 Ibid., pp. 147-8.
66 Ibid., pp. 20, 29, 89, 119.
67 Ibid., p. 33.
68 Ibid., p. 5..
69 Ibid., p. 48. The imagery of 'filling in' and 'thickening' is very common in late James; see, for example, 'Story', vol. 1, pp. 219, 273.
70 'Autobiography', p. 92.
71 Ibid., p. 107. Cf. ibid., p. 434, the 'little constituted dramas' that make up the 'scenic law' as described in the preface to 'What Maisie Knew' (op. cit., pp. xxiv-xxv) and the 'peopled scene' of 'Story', vol. 1, p. 96.
72 'Autobiography', p. 73.
73 Ibid., p. 57.
74 Ibid., p. 149.
75 Ibid., p. 161.
76 Ibid., p. 32.
77 Ibid., p. 131.
78 Ibid., pp. 158, 159, 164.
79 Ibid., p. 156.
80 Ibid., p. 214.
81 Sayre, op. cit., p. 149.
82 For the differences between them, see Robert F. Sayre, 'The Examined Self: Benjamin Franklin, Henry Adams, Henry James' (Princeton University Press, 1964), pp. ix, 61, 83, 95, 140, 194, 203ff.
83 'Autobiography', p. 13.
84 Ibid., pp. 77ff.
85 Ibid., p. 235.
86 Ibid., p. 126.
87 Ibid., p. 99.
88 Ibid., pp. 23, 26.
89 Cf. 'The American Scene', op. cit., pp. 452ff. See 'Story', vol. 1, p. 199 and 'Autobiography', pp. 13, 78, 125, 235 for a selection of 'types' and 'cases'.
90 Ibid., p. 104. Cf. 'The American Scene', op. cit., p. 8 and the preface to vol. 18 of the New York edition, p. xxi.
91 'Autobiography', p. 158.
92 Ibid., p. 135. Cf. the 'ancient order' of ibid., p. 569 and the 'old order' of ibid., p. 597, 'Story', vol. 2, p. 209 and the preface to vol. 18 of the New York edition, p. xv.
93 'Autobiography', p. 81.
94 Cf. the 'long nostalgia' of a maternal aunt (ibid., p. 49), 'Story', vol. 1, pp. 111-12, 248, and the 'nostalgic poison' of the preface to vol. 18 of the New York edition (p. xxi).
95 Ibid., p. 112. Cf. the preface to 'The Awkward Age' (op. cit., p. ix) and the preface to vol. 18 of the New York edition, pp. viii-ix.
96 'Autobiography', pp. 16-17.
97 Ibid., p. 137. Cf. the 'rage for connections' of ibid., p. 578, and the

concern for 'the mutual relation of parts' in 'Story', vol. 1, p. 341.
98 Cf. Sayre, op. cit., p. 152, for discussion of this aspect.
99 'Autobiography', p. 128.
100 Ibid., p. 129.
101 Ibid., p. 231.
102 Ibid., p. 8.
103 Ibid., p. 134.
104 Ibid., p. 71.
105 Ibid.
106 Ibid., p. 230. Cf. the 'fine old native basis' of the preface to vol. 18 of the New York edition, p. ix.
107 'Autobiography', p. 40.
108 Ibid., p. 114.
109 Ibid., pp. 68, 198.
110 Ibid., p. 198.
111 R. W. Stallman, 'The Houses that James Built and Other Essays', Michigan State University Press, 1961.
112 The title of a story in vol. 21 of the New York edition.
113 'Autobiography', p. 57.
114 Ibid., p. 3.
115 Preface to 'Roderick Hudson' (New York edition, p. x).
116 'Autobiography', p. 4.
117 'Letters of Henry James', op. cit., vol. 1, p. xiii.
118 Ibid., vol. 2, pp. 214-15.

Chapter 3 W. B. Yeats: 'Reveries Over Childhood and Youth'
1 Joseph Ronsley, 'Yeats's "Autobiography": Life as Symbolic Pattern', Harvard University Press, 1966.
2 Peter Ure, 'Yeats and Anglo-Irish Literature', ed. C. J. Rawson, Liverpool University Press, 1974, p. 48.
3 L. A. G. Strong in a review of 'Autobiographies', 'London Magazine', vol. 2, no. 6, 1955, p. 84.
4 Ian Fletcher, in Rhythm and Pattern in 'Autobiographies' (in 'An Honoured Guest: New Essays on W. B. Yeats', ed. D. Donoghue and J. R. Mulryne, Edward Arnold, London, 1965, pp. 165-90), suggests that 'The Trembling of the Veil' is the most satisfying.
5 'Autobiographies', Macmillan, London, 1955, p. 3; all subsequent references are to this edition of 'Reveries'.
6 The watercolour is referred to in section X of the text and was published in the editions of 1915 (Cuala Press), 1916 (Macmillan) and 1926.
7 Rousseau, 'Reveries of a Solitary', trans. John Gould Fletcher, Routledge & Kegan Paul, London, 1927, p. 31.
8 The analogy is only an analogy. Yeats may have read Joyce's 'Portrait of the Artist as a Young Man' as serialized in the 'Egoist'; at the time he was living with Pound, who had arranged for its publication. But the idea of an autobiography had been in Yeats's mind at least since 1908, as his letters show, and the term 'epiphany' is, in any case, confined to Joyce's first version, 'Stephen Hero', which Yeats could not have read. Cf. however David G. Wright, The Elusive Self: Yeats's Autobiographical Prose, 'Canadian Journal of Irish Studies', vol. 4, no. 2, December 1978, pp. 42-3.
9 Wolf Künne, in his 'Konzeption und Stil von Yeats' "Autobiographies" ' (Bouvier Verlag, Bonn, 1972. pp. 198-201; hereafter Künne), finds no less than seven different meanings of the word 'dream' in Yeats's oeuvre.
10 'Autobiographies', p. 2. The eight volumes of Yeats's 'Collected Works' published in 1908 would have facilitated this.
11 'Autobiographies', p. 3.
12 Cf. ibid., p. 172.
13 Cf. Louis Renza's interesting discussion of the 'absent' reader who is 'autobiography's version of a Muse' and who nevertheless 'aggravate[s] the project's realization' (The Veto of the Imagination; a Theory of Autobiography, 'New Literary History', vol. 9, no. 1, Autumn 1977, pp. 20, 21).

14 Compare the sudden shifts in syntax, sometimes extremely awkward, in Yeats's poetry. Künne and Marjorie Perloff ('The Tradition of Myself': the Autobiographical Mode of Yeats, in the special Yeats number of the 'Journal of Modern Literature', vol. 4, February 1975, pp. 529-73) both write well on this aspect.

15 It is important to notice that Yeats leaves this suggestion entirely neutral: to be upset about it would imply Romantic 'Schadenfreude'; to be glad about it would imply that interactions between the real world and the spirit world are to be avoided, whereas the rest of 'Reveries' proves the opposite to be the case.

16 Künne, p. 93, notes the return in the last three sections, of stylistic features associated with the opening of 'Reveries'.

17 The title of a section of 'The Celtic Twilight' (1893) collected in 'Mythologies', (Macmillan, London, 1959). Daniel Harris writes: 'A deep uncertainty hovers over the final section...Yeats had somehow reached a point of transition with no Miltonic "place of rest" [the allusion is to section XXXI, where Milton is quoted] in sight' ('Yeats: Coole Park and Ballylee', Johns Hopkins, Baltimore, 1974, p. 89; hereafter Harris); Mary Flannery refers to the 'strangely uncertain note' of the conclusion, but would have us believe that 'by 1912...Yeats had integrated his thought, his magic and his poetics' ('Yeats and Magic; The Earlier Works', Colin Smythe, Gerrards Cross, 1977, p. 139). The first part of 'Per Amica Silentia Lunae', dated February 1917, tends to disprove Flannery's contention; Harris refers to 'Per Amica' as part of the evidence for his contention, but without specifying which section is relevant.

18 Cf. Fletcher, op. cit., and 'The Letters of W. B. Yeats', ed. Allan Wade, Rupert Hart-Davis, London, 1954, p. 607: 'The element of pattern in every art, is, I think, the part that is not imitative, for in the last analysis there will always be somewhere an intensity of pattern that we have not seen with our eyes.' The whole of Yeats's system in 'A Vision' revolves around ideas of rhythm and pattern, which are associated with 'vision' at the end of 'Anima Hominis' in 'Per Amica'. 'Dream' and 'vision' are placed in opposition in 'Mythologies', p. 277.

19 'Autobiographies', pp. 40, 42.

20 Stephen Shapiro, The Dark Continent of Literature, 'Comparative Literature Studies', vol. 5, 1968, p. 436.

21 'Mythologies', p. 277.

22 Ibid., p. 347. The 'nunc stans' and 'tota simul' of Boethius, resuscitated by Schopenhauer in 'The World as Will and Idea', are analogous. In the essay on Swedenborg which dates from 1914 and which Harris relates to 'Reveries' (p. 89), Yeats quotes the idea as Villiers de l'Isle Adam's, borrowed from Aquinas ('Explorations', Macmillan, London, 1962, p. 37).

23 Cf. the discussions of chronology in autobiography in J. Sturrock (The New Autobiography, 'New Literary History', vol. 9, no. 1, pp. 55, 56); R. M. Dunn ('Les Mémoires d'outre-tombe': Chateaubriand's alter ego 'Genre', vol. 6, no. 2, June 1973, p. 180); M. K. Blasing ('The Art of Life', University of Texas Press, 1977, p. xxvi).

24 Cf. Peter Ure's account of the play 'Purgatory' in 'Yeats the Playwright', Routledge & Kegan Paul, London, 1963, pp. 103-113.

25 Harris, p. 90.

26 'Autobiographies', pp. 40, 42.

27 Cf. Julien Green's opening to 'To Leave Before Dawn', trans. Anne Green, Peter Owen, London, 1969, p. 13.

28 Harris, p. 88. Harris finds this opening 'embarrassed'; it seems to me better described as 'ingenuous'. Curtis Bradford has pointed out that Yeats 'did not make changes in order to spare himself' ('Yeats at Work', Southern Illinois University Press, 1965, p. 348) which suggests he was not easily embarrassed. But perhaps Harris means that Yeats is embarrassed about something else, as Brenda Webster (in 'Yeats: a Psychoanalytic Study', Macmillan, London, 1974, passim) suggests.

29 Künne, p. 83, also discusses how important certain places are.

30   'Autobiographies', pp. 6, 103-5.
31   Ibid., p. 5.
32   For an excellent breakdown of the first ten sentences of 'Reveries', see
     Künne, p. 83, who points out that space is much clearer than time at the
     beginning and that figures only gradually come into focus and are named.
     Künne stresses the way Yeats tries, in 'Reveries', to achieve a childlike
     way of seeing (p. 69), analyses the polysyndeton that helps him to do
     this (pp. 89ff.), and concludes that Yeats 'has, as it were, naivetized the
     text' (p. 102). Ronsley compares the beginning to Genesis and calls it
     Edenic (p. 34); but Künne (p. 192, note 6) rightly objects that there is
     nothing Paradisial about Yeats's childhood. Much the most imaginative and
     profitable interpretation of the opening of 'Reveries' is Shirley Neuman's
     in her 'Some One Myth: Yeats's Autobiographical Prose' (The Dolmen Press,
     Dublin, 1981). She refers to the Sturge Moore cover design for the 1916
     Macmillan edition (which, like the Jack Yeats watercolour, has unfortunately
     not been retained in modern editions):
> That design, a 'stylistic arrangement' of rectangles and arcs, is
> vertically symmetrical around an abstractly rendered tower....At the
> top of the tower, a recumbent baby clutches the forefinger of the
> divine hand descending through the circles of heaven. At its foot, a
> young man descends the tower stairs through a door he holds half
> open...The journey down the tower stairs, from earliest childhood to
> youth; the moment of Creation ends with the young man's stepping
> into the world delineated in 'Four Years' [the first section of 'The
> Trembling of the Veil']. The waves surrounding the tower's base
> present visually the metaphor of the time of 'Reveries' as a period of
> gestation for they recall both Porphyry's 'waters of generation' and
> the Judaeo-Christian creation myth. In the Philosophus 4=7 ritual of
> The Order of the Golden Dawn, the Hierophant invokes Genesis....
> By introducing himself both visually and verbally by allusion to the
> Creation, Yeats directs us as to the manner in which he wishes his
> autobiography to be read: he signals that his design is to be mytho-
> poeic rather than mimetic....

     Professor Neuman's approach, not only to 'Reveries' but to 'Autobiographies'
     as a whole, is of exceptional interest, and I am very grateful to her for
     giving me permission to make these quotations here.
33   'Autobiographies', p. 14.
34   Ibid., p. 15.
35   Harris, p. 87.
36   'Autobiographies', p. 60.
37   Ibid., pp. 8-9.
38   Ibid. pp. 12-13, 16. It is noticeable that in section XIV Yeats describes
     how he identified with the protagonist of Shelley's 'Alastor' who is also a
     boat-traveller (ibid., p. 64).
39   Ibid., p. 18.
40   Ibid., p. 63.
41   Ibid., pp. 71ff.
42   Ibid., p. 78.
43   Ibid., p. 49.
44   Cf. John Unterecker, 'A Reader's Guide to Yeats', Thames & Hudson,
     London, 1959, p. 39. Yeats began the book in London but finished it at
     Coole Park.
45   'Letters', p. 589.
46   Künne stresses that Yeats's father is introduced late in 'Reveries' (p. 57).
47   'Autobiographies', p. 31.
48   Ibid., p. 34.
49   Ibid., p. 62.
50   Webster, p. 128, relates this 'cracked wall' to the 'gap in the wall' in the
     late play 'Purgatory'.
51   'Autobiographies', p. 5.
52   Ibid., p. 33.

53 Ibid., p. 106.
54 Künne, p. 139, points out that references to theatre become more numer-
    ous as the world becomes clearer to the young Yeats, and even more
    numerous beyond 'Reveries', most obviously of course in 'Dramatis
    Personae'.
55 'Autobiographies', p. 5.
56 Ibid., pp. 90, 102.
57 Ibid., pp. 8, 9.
58 Ibid. pp. 93, 94. For a quite different reading of Yeats's struggle for
    self-possession see Daniel O'Hara, The Irony of Tradition and W.B.
    Yeats's 'Autobiographies': an Essay in Dialectical Hermeneutics, 'Boundary', vol.
    5, no. 3, Spring 1977, pp. 679–709.
59 Ibid., p. 13.
60 Ibid., pp. 40, 41.
61 Ibid., pp. 58ff.
62 Ibid.. p. 89.
63 This was one of the sections revised between the private press edition
    brought out by the Cuala Press and the Macmillan trade edition. See Curtis
    Bradford, 'Yeats at Work', pp. 346ff.
64 Ibid., p. 22.
65 Künne, p. 215, points out that the description of O'Leary leads on to the
    all-important question of a National Literature.
66 'Autobiographies', p. 14.
67 Ibid., p. 95.
68 Ibid., p. 96.
69 Ibid.
70 Ibid., p. 99.
71 Ibid., p. 27.
72 L. A. G. Strong says: 'It is surprising how often the word "violent" occurs
    in "Reveries Over Childhood and Youth" and how many references there are
    to violent action' (op. cit., p. 85).
73 Letter of 29 December 1914 quoted by Joseph Hone in 'W. B. Yeats: 1865 –
    1939', Macmillan, London, 1962, p. 288.
74 Cf. Künne, p. 53, who reads the section differently as Yeats's drama-
    tization of the entrance into the adult world.
75 'Autobiographies', p. 27.
76 On Pollexfen see William Murphy's article in the 'Irish University Review',
    vol. 1, Autumn 1970. Yeats clearly fears madness and being accounted mad,
    which helps to explain why he cut section VII.
77 'Autobiographies', p. 10.
78 Ibid., p. 12.
79 Ibid., p. 67.
80 Ibid., p. 72.
81 Ibid., p. 55.
82 Ibid., p. 18.
83 For the association of Juno Regina with peacocks, see the 'Larousse
    Dictionary of Mythology'.
84 'Autobiographies', p. 83.
85 See 'Mythologies', pp. 64, 98, 116 and indeed passim for the close contact
    between life and death in Yeats's Sligo world.
86 'Autobiographies', p. 106.
87 Cf. Künne, p. 192, who points out that Yeats leaves out all the events
    later dealt with in 'Four Years' (in 'The Trembling of the Veil') in order
    to end thus.
88 'Autobiographies', p. 106.
89 Harris seems to me to misread the end of 'Reveries'; it does not, I think,
    end with 'symbolic events which displace what Yeats might have written of
    himself' (p. 88). It is both personal and symbolic at once. Compare also
    Hazard Adams's reading of the last section in 'An Honoured Guest', op.
    cit., p. 169.
90 'Autobiographies', pp. 26, 27.

91   Cf. 'Memoirs', ed. D. Donoghue, Macmillan, London, 1972, pp. 71–2,
     where Yeats is much less guarded.
92   'Autobiographies', pp. 26, 27.
93   Yeats describes himself thus in the last stanza of the poem 'Coole Park and
     Ballylee, 1931,' but there is a phrase in section VIII of 'Reveries' which
     prefigures it – 'the romantic movement drawing to its latest phase' ('Auto-
     biographies', p. 46).
94   Ibid., p. 42.
95   Ibid., p. 62.
96   The word surfaces later, as an adverb, in poems like 'Are you content?'
97   It is surprising that Brenda Webster ('Yeats: a Psychoanalytic Study', op.
     cit.) does not refer to this, since it has obvious possibilities if one is con-
     vinced by her 'primal scene' speculations.
98   Yeats discusses cave imagery in Shelley in the essay The Philosophy of
     Shelley's poetry ('Essays and Introductions', Macmillan, London, 1961,
     pp. 65–95) and describes another favourite cave in Drumcliff and Rosses,
     'Mythologies', pp. 88ff.
99   Cf. The end of section II for another reference to eggs, this time in con-
     nection with a love letter ('Autobiographies', p. 17).
100 Ibid., p. 63.
101 Ibid., p. 26.
102 Yeats's discomfiture was obviously sufficient to make him cut the original
     text of section XIV, the beginning of which was once (as Curtis Bradford
     has shown, 'Yeats at Work', op. cit., p. 346) much closer to the account
     in 'Memoirs'.
103 'Autobiographies', p. 87.
104 Ibid., p. 72.
105 Ibid., pp. 71, 69.
106 This play occupied, not to say obsessed, Yeats from 1907 to 1919.
107 'Autobiographies', p. 75.
108 Künne, p. 83, notes the many combinations of 'some–in 'Reveries'.
109 'Autobiographies', p. 76.
110 The woman is not, as might be expected, Maud Gonne, although she is
     obviously useful as a surrogate figure for Maud. As Brenda Webster has
     shown (op. cit., p. 11), she is actually Laura Armstrong, with whom
     Yeats fell in love in 1884.
111 'Autobiographies', p. 40.
112 Yeats has, like his uncle George Pollexfen, 'a mind full of pictures'
     ('Autobiographies', p. 69), partly no doubt because his father was a
     painter. Section VII of 'Reveries' consists of 'two pictures' (it was origin-
     ally, as Curtis Bradford ('Yeats at Work', op. cit.) has shown, three
     pictures) and section III is mainly 'miniatures' (Autobiographies', p.23).
113 'Autobiographies', p. 106.
114 Künne, p. 191.
115 'Letters', p. 922; 'Mythologies', p. 269.
116 'Mythologies', p. 267.
117 Recent Yeats criticism, notably the books written or edited by George
     Mills Harper, have done much to rehabilitate Yeats's interest in magic. Cf.
     also J. L. Allen's confrontation of Ellmann's divergent positions in 'The
     Man and the Masks' and 'The Identity of Yeats' in an article in the special
     Yeats number of the 'Journal of Modern Literature', vol. 4, February
     1975.
118 Yeats's poem 'The Balloon of the Mind' is presumed to be contemporaneous
     with 'Reveries' by A. Norman Jeffares in his 'Commentary' (Macmillan,
     London, 1970) on the 'Collected Poems'.

Chapter 4 Boris Pasternak: 'Safe Conduct'
 1   Nine Letters of Pasternak, 'Harvard Library Bulletin', vol. 15, no. 4,
     October 1967, p. 322.
 2   Pasternak's second (1959) attempt at a narrative of his life is titled 'Avto-
     biografecheskii ocherk'.

3 In his famous 'marginal notes' of 1935, to which all subsequent commentaries have been little more than marginal notes indeed. Translated and
   included in 'Pasternak: Modern Judgements', eds. Donald Davie and
   Angela Livingstone (Macmillan, London, 1969).
4 The subtitle of 'Zhivago' alludes to the subtitle of Pushkin's 'Eugene
   Onegin'; Pasternak called 'Spektorsky' 'my novel in verse' ('The Last
   Summer', trans. George Reavey, Penguin, Harmondsworth, 1960, p. 19).
   Cf. Some Statements, trans. Angela Livingstone in 'Modern Russian Poets
   on Poetry', Ardis, Ann Arbor, 1976, p. 84.
5 'An Essay in Autobiography', trans. Manya Harari, Collins, London, 1959,
   pp. 110-111.
6 Moreau ('Books Abroad', vol. 44, no. 2, Spring 1970, pp. 239-40) points
   out that in a letter to a French friend written shortly before his death,
   Pasternak said that all his life he had had the feeling of unintentionally
   copying Rilke: cf. the letter to Renate Schweizer of 1958 quoted by Olga
   Ivinskaya, ('A Captive of Time: My Years with Pasternak', trans. Max
   Hayward, Fontana, London, 1979; hereafter Ivinskaya) (p. 238).
7 This passage is unaccountably omitted from one of the three English trans-
   lations, that of Alec Brown (Elek Books, London, 1959). All my quotations
   are from the Beatrice Scott translation in 'Prose and Poems' (Benn, London,
   1959; hereafter 'Safe Conduct') which, despite being out of print, may be
   marginally more accessible than the excellent Angela Livingstone translation in the 'Collected Prose' (Praeger, New York, 1977) ed. and intro.
   by Christopher Barnes.
8 'Safe Conduct', p. 24.
9 Ibid.
10 One irony that might be lost on an English reader is that Okhranka was
   the name of the secret police in Tsarist Russia.
11 The Russian title 'Sestra Moya - zhizn' resists accurate translation into
   English. The English reader has to think of the title as meaning 'My Sister
   Is Life', 'My Sister, Life', 'Life, My Sister' and so on. Cf. my later discussion of section fifteen of part three (p. 56).
12 Cf. the essay The New Georgian Poetry ('Letters to Georgian Friends',
   Penguin, Harmondsworth, p. 16) and a letter of 1957 to Chikhovani (ibid.,
   p. 159). Compare the correspondence with Kaverin to which Olga Hughes
   refers ('The Poetic World of Boris Pasternak', Princeton University Press,
   1974, p. 59) in which Pasternak insists on the interrelation of poetry and
   everyday prose, and 'The Last Summer', p. 75: 'the intercourse of
   ecstasy with the everyday'. Cf. also the letter to E. D. Romanova of 23
   December 1959 quoted by Ivinskaya, p. 201, and the speech of 1934 (ibid.
   p. 200).
13 A. Gladkov, 'Meetings with Pasternak', Collins & Harvill, London, 1978,
   p. 57. Dated by Gladkov Christmas Day 1941.
14 'Safe Conduct', p. 24. Krystyna Pomorska (in 'Themes and Variations in
   Pasternak's Poetics', Peter de Ridder Press, Lisse, 1975) glosses this
   excellently: 'The hero tends to identify with each person he meets...[but]
   what was supposed to be the element of similarity...remains only as his
   metonymy. In this sense he leaves his own biography under the names of
   others' (p. 71).
15 Cf. Hughes, p. 41 on Pasternak's 'subjectivity'.
16 See, for an excellent account of this, the 1927 article by A. Lezhnev, The
   Poetry of Boris Pasternak, in 'Pasternak: Modern Judgements', op. cit.,
   pp. 99ff.
17 Gladkov, op. cit., p. 63. Dated by Gladkov 24 January 1942.
18 Gladkov, op. cit., p. 59. Dated by Gladkov Christmas Day 1941.
19 See the first paragraph of his second 'autobiographical sketch'. As Victor
   Erlich ('The Double Image', Johns Hopkins Press, Baltimore, 1964, p. 147)
   points out, these rejections should not be taken too literally.
20 Gladkov, op. cit., pp. 134, 133.
21 Gladkov, op. cit., p. 39.
22 In the words of Max Hayward's introduction to Gladkov, op. cit., p. 9.

23 Davie and Livingstone op. cit., p. 95. As with Scriabin, his 'formlessness is more complex than form' ('Safe Conduct', p. 20). But cf. 'Books Abroad', vol. 44, p. 196.
24 Cf. 'Letters to Georgian Friends', op. cit., p. 160, where Pasternak speaks about 'extemporization'.
25 Pasternak's third collection of poems has this title.
26 'Safe Conduct', p. 61. The idea pretty obviously derives from Proust.
27 E.g. 'Safe Conduct', pp. 50, 52.
28 E.g. ibid., p. 62.
29 Ibid., p. 26.
30 Ibid., pp. 62-3.
31 Ibid., p. 62.
32 Ibid., p. 52.
33 'Sochineniya', ed. G. P. Struve and B.A. Klipper, University of Michigan Press, 1961, vol. 2, p. 44. Cf. a letter of 15 November 1935: 'I shun nothing in the whole world more than fanfare, sensationalism, and so-called cheap "celebrity in the press",' quoted by Hughes, op. cit., p. 137, a letter of 22 August 1959 in which he talks of 'the unreal domain of the melodramatic' (Pasternak's English), and 'Writers at Work', (ed. Kay Dick, Penguin, Harmondsworth, 1972) p. 146.
34 'Safe Conduct', p. 13.
35 Ibid., p. 69.
36 Ibid., p. 110.
37 See, for example, the last section of Marina Tsvetaeva's classic essay 'A Downpour of Light', in Davie and Livingstone, op. cit., pp. 56 ff.
38 See Isaiah Berlin's essay in 'Partisan Review', 1950, pp. 748-51, for confirmation of this, and also Tsvetaeva's essay, in Davie and Livingstone, op. cit., p. 58.
39 Krystyna Pomorska ('Themes and Variations', op. cit., p. 71) usefully points out: 'the dynamism of the episodes lies in the fact of their oscillation between the metaphoric and metonymic poles.'
40 Pasternak's last volume of poetry bears the title 'When the Weather Clears' of 'When it Clears Up', depending on the translator.
41 Arguably the best evocation of a railway journey is that undertaken by Zhenia Lyuvers in the first section of the uncompleted 'The Childhood of Lyuvers'. Pasternak's 1943 volume of poetry was titled 'On Early Trains'.
42 'Safe Conduct', p. 86.
43 Ibid., p. 110.
44 As Krysryna Pomorska points out ('Themes and Variations', op. cit., p. 72; her italics): 'Each episode indicates not so much the *continuation* of the poet's life, but his *starting from the very beginning.*'
45 'Safe Conduct', p. 60.
46 One interviewer reports Pasternak as saying that he was 'almost an atheist' ('Encounter', vol. 10, no. 3, March 1958, p. 24), but points out that he had a concept of the divine and that his belief in life had an almost pagan religious quality. Jacqueline de Proyart ('Pasternak', Gallimard, Paris, 1964, p. 41) quotes Pasternak to the effect that 1910-12 was his most intensely Christian period. Pasternak was insistent that 'Doctor Zhivago' 'must not be judged on theological lines. Nothing is further from my understanding of the world.' ('Writers at Work', op. cit., p. 140.)
47 'Second Birth' was the title of the immediately subsequent volume of poems (published 1934).
48 'Safe Conduct', p. 12.
49 Ibid., p. 71.
50 Ibid., p. 73.
51 Ibid., pp. 113-14, 121.
52 Cf. the famous telephone conversation between Pasternak and Stalin regarding the fate of Mandelstam; and cf. 'The Last Summer', p. 23.
53 'Safe Conduct', p. 73.
54 Ibid., p. 73. Pasternak's frenetic activity here, his rushing, is analogous to that which impels him to go to Berlin. But at the very beginning of

part three all Russia is in a hurry (ibid., p. 91) and Mayakovsky's career is a headlong plunge towards disaster. Cf. Vladimir Markov, 'Russian Futurism', Macgibbon & Kee, London, 1969, p. 268: 'Pasternak's soul rushes along the streets and displaces everything.'
55 'Safe Conduct', p. 284.
56 Ibid., p. 41.
57 The comparison is often made; see, for example, Mirsky and Whitfield, 'A History of Russian Literature', Routledge & Kegan Paul, London, 1968, p. 503. Pasternak speaks ('Writers at Work', op. cit., p. 153) of Proust as being close to his own ideas of 1910, Ivinskaya prints (p. 410) a letter of 3 March 1959: 'I didn't like [Proust] very much, you remember. But these final pages ('Time Regained') are infinitely human and brilliant.' Cf. his reaction in the interview in 'Encounter': (vol. 10, no. 3, March 1958, p. 22) 'very beautiful, at times very, very beautiful, but there's something missing in it.'
58 Gladkov, op. cit., p. 60. Dated by Gladkov 31 December 1941.
59 It goes without saying that this could not be further from the tenets of Socialist Realism, and some of the opprobrium heaped on Pasternak in pre-Socialist Realism days obviously stemmed from reaction to opinions like these.
60 I do not intend an allusion to Lermontov here, although Lermontov mattered enough to Pasternak (and later Zhenia Lyuvers) for him to use an epigraph from Lermontov for 'My Sister Life'. See also 'Letters to Georgian Friends', op. cit., p. 123 and Marina Tsvetaeva's discussion in the Davie and Livingstone collection (op. cit.).
61 As Krystyna Pomorska has pointed out, 'Themes and Variations', op. cit., p. 64.
62 Note the metaphor of speed once again.
63 'Safe Conduct' p. 117. If 'this is no metaphor,' then it must (as Jakobson was the first to realize) be metonymy. Pasternak's warning about 'exact resemblance' has not been heeded by those who find only 'coincidences' in 'Zhivago', see above. Cf. Pasternak's anti-Symbolist stress on the 'lack of correspondence' ('Safe Conduct', p. 85). Pasternak did, incidentally, die of a heart attack.
64 'Safe Conduct', p. 26.
65 Ibid., p. 52.
66 Ibid.
67 Ibid. Cf. 'Writers at Work', op. cit., p. 145: 'the old language is transformed from within.'
68 'Safe Conduct', p. 22. The architectural image here recalls Pasternak's description of Scriabin's 'Poème d'extase' as 'a lyrical dwelling not fictitious' ('Safe Conduct', p. 17) and prefigures Pasternak's confrontation with Venice.
69 'Safe Conduct', p. 20.
70 Ibid., p. 40.
71 Max Hayward (Ivinskaya, p. 422) identifies her as Ida Vysotskaya.
72 'Safe Conduct', p. 53.
73 Ibid., p. 58.
74 Ibid., p. 87.
75 Ibid., p. 95.
76 Ibid.
77 Pasternak's way of putting this - 'the *fate* of this material is in [nature's] hands' ('Safe Conduct', p. 51; Pasternak's italics) confirms Lezhnev's shrewd appraisal of the 'materiality' inherent in Pasternak's vision.
78 Ibid., p. 56. Cf. the confidence of the Venetians that 'the future would bear witness to the general participation' ('Safe Conduct', p. 84), which is disappointed. Cf. ibid., p. 49 also. Cf. 'Letters to Georgian Friends', op. cit., p. 163: 'I do not like the past, especially my own. My future is immeasurably larger, I cannot help living by it. I cannot see any point in looking back' and ibid., p. 111 'love of the future is for me as much a constant and intimate thing as love of a woman.' But cf. also Gladkov,

op. cit., p. 60: 'The future is the worst of all abstractions ever.'
79 'Safe Conduct', p. 107.
80 Ibid., p. 126. For a modern reinterpretation of this notion, see John Ash-
    bery's poem 'The Picture of Little J. A. in a Prospect of Flowers' which
    uses this as epigraph and quotes again from 'Safe Conduct' in the body of
    the poem. Ashbery was a friend of Frank O'Hara, who wrote an essay on
    Pasternak.
81 Cf. 'Letters to Georgian Friends', op. cit., p. 130: 'There must be a great
    deal of the feminine, of the passive, in my character'; and ibid., p. 148
    where Pasternak describes himself as 'incorrigibly and inexplicably weak'.
    Serezha in 'The Last Summer', another self-portrait, is described as 'a
    very Christ of passivity' ('The Last Summer', p. 88).
82 Pasternak had a special feeling for childhood, as the marvellous story 'The
    Childhood of Lyuvers' is not alone in showing. Cf. 'Letters to Georgian
    Friends', op. cit;, p. 47: 'I send regrets to the spark of *childishness*
    which runs through...[Leonidze's] manuscripts.' (Pasternak's italics.)
83 'Safe Conduct', p. 123.
84 Ibid., p. 56, cf. ibid., p. 61: 'something which children do not know...
    which I shall call the sense of the *actual*.' (Pasternak's italics.)
85 Ibid., p. 41.
86 Ibid., p. 77.
87 Ibid., p. 60.
88 Cf. 'Letters to Georgian Friends', op. cit., pp. 36, 72.
89 'Safe Conduct', p. 54.
90 Ibid., p. 81.
91 Ibid., p. 88.
92 Ibid., p. 22.
93 The spring is a constant motif in 'Safe Conduct' (see pp. 31, 19, 50), and
    in numerous Pasternak poems.
94 Cf. 'Letters to Georgian Friends', op. cit., p. 122: 'It is, indeed, this
    waiting that is so exciting, like a still unsolved problem or like a flare
    hanging poised in the sky in expectation of the moment of action.' Cf. the
    flare of 'Safe Conduct', p. 95.
95 Ibid., p. 30. Cf. 'the pace of a binding tale' in Pasternak's essay on
    Chopin (English translation in 'Partisan Review', vol. 21, 1964, pp. 405–9).
    The passage quoted is another instance of clear-sightedness, as the first
    sentence quoted obliquely indicates. Marburg's 'fairy-tale' qualities inhibit
    clear-sightedness: 'If the brothers Grimm could come here again, as they
    came a hundred years ago...they would leave here once more as collectors
    of fairy-tales' ('Safe Conduct', p. 45).
96 Ibid., p. 14. It is striking, however, how often Pasternak refers to life as
    a kind of book: see 'Letters to Georgian Friends', op. cit., p. 82 ('I wish
    you a summer like a book'), p. 91 ('[Tabidze's] life...is a poem'); p. 127
    ('a life which, like a book, was full of such quiet, concentrated meaning.')
    Cf. also the reference to 'non-fictional' life on p. 77. Cf. 'Safe Conduct',
    p. 85: 'Once observed, nature opens out in the obedient expanse of a tale.'
97 'Safe Conduct', p. 60.
98 Ibid., p. 19.
99 Ibid., p. 23.
100 Ibid., p. 27.
101 Ibid., pp. 30–1.
102 Ibid., p. 97.
103 Ibid., p. 89.
104 Ibid., p. 41.
105 Cf. the uproar rising 'skywards' (p. 21), the sun rising (p. 25) and the
    stars of p. 64.
106 Ibid., p. 89.
107 Prefigured in ibid., p. 77: 'Khalva and Chaldea, Magi and magnesium,
    India and indigo'; and also on p. 65 (the German pun); p. 52 (the Russian
    verb 'to lie'). Cf. the excursus on the word 'pantaloon' on p. 84.
108 Ibid., p. 108.

109 Ibid., p. 125.
110 Ibid., p. 63.
111 Ibid., p. 26. The imagery of illness is particularly prevalent in part one, where Pasternak's adoration of Scriabin is seen as a fever (p. 11) and where his agitation at the thought of Marburg 'infects' those around him (p. 35). In part two he sees himself as 'a convinced fanatic' (p. 46) full of meaningless ardour (p. 58). Only among the ordinary students at Moscow university is he 'not feverish' and 'at peace' (p.29).
112 Jakobson seems to me to miss this point, although the comparison with Casanova (p. 150) is a very brilliant one.
113 See Pomorska, op. cit. p. 54 and especially Aucoutourier's essay on the short stories in the Davie and Livingstone collection (op. cit.).
114 'Safe Conduct', p. 114.
115 Quoted from The Love Song of J. Alfred Prufrock. Pasternak reminds us of 'how well-trained our facial muscles are' in the context of his visit to Scriabin (p. 19).
116 Pasternak is a remarkably musical writer, however; see 'Safe Conduct', passim: 'The Last Summer', pp. 20, 45; 'Some Statements', p. 84; and 'Writers at Work', p. 138.
117 Cf. 'I was...more posing without a pose than sitting in the compartment' ('Safe Conduct', p. 57) and compare also his admiration for Cohen's 'performance' (p. 48) and his excitement at the 'drama' of the Revolution ('The Last Summer', p. 31).
118 'Safe Conduct', p. 98. Pasternak connects the idea with his notion of the future: 'rapture of the future...realized in the first person, is posing' (p. 98).
119 'Books Abroad', vol. 44, p. 209.
120 Pasternak's own English in a letter to the editor of 'Encounter', vol. 15, no. 8, August 1960, p. 5. Cf. Pasternak's attitude to 'totality' in 'Safe Conduct', p. 100 and 'Writers at Work', p. 144.
121 Pasternak's own description of the book in a letter of 1931, published in the 'Harvard Library Bulletin', vol. 15, no. 4, October 1967, p. 320.

Chapter 5 Michel Leiris: 'L'Age d'homme'
1 Maurice Nadeau, 'Michel Leiris et la Quadrature du circle', Julliard, Paris, 1963, p. 109.
2 From an interview with Raymond Bellour in 'Les Lettres françaises' for 29 September 1966; quoted and translated by Robert Hefner in an article in the special Leiris issue of 'Sub-Stance', nos 11-12, 1975, p. 137.
3 From a 1961 interview with Madeleine Gobeil in 'L'Express' partially translated into English for the special Leiris issue of 'Sub-Stance', p. 51; hereafter Gobeil. I have made some modifications in the translation for the quotations which follow.
4 Gobeil, p. 49.
5 Ibid., p. 52.
6 Ibid., p. 45.
7 Ibid.
8 Ibid., p. 50.
9 Ibid., p. 56.
10 Ibid., p. 44.
11 Ibid., p. 50.
12 Ibid.
13 Ibid.
14 Ibid., p. 44.
15 'Manhood', preceded by The Autobiographer as Torero, trans. Richard Howard, Jonathan Cape, London, 1968, p. 10; hereafter 'Manhood'.
16 Ibid., p. 9.
17 Ibid., pp. 9-10.
18 Ibid., p. 10.
19 Ibid.
20 Ibid., p. 9.

21   Ibid., p. 11.
22   Ibid., p. 12.
23   Ibid., p. 13.
24   Ibid., p. 14.
25   Ibid., pp. 15, 13.
26   Ibid., p. 16.
27   Ibid., pp. 17-18.
28   Ibid., p. 20.
29   Ibid., p. 19.
30   Ibid., p. 20.
31   Ibid., p. 19.
32   Ibid., p. 20.
33   Gobeil, p. 52.
34   Ibid., p. 49.
35   'Manhood', p. 20.
36   Alain-Michel Boyer, 'Michel Leiris', Editions Universitaires, Paris, 1974,
      p. 87; my translations throughout; hereafter Boyer. Philippe Lejeune
      ('Lire Leiris: Autobiographie et langage', Editions Klincksieck, Paris,
      1975, p. 8; hereafter Lejeune) sees it more decisively as 'a kind of swan-
      song to the problems of classical autobiography' (my translations through-
      out).
37   Lejeune, p. 122.
38   'Manhood', p. 185.
39   Ibid., p. 123.
40   Lejeune, p. 44.
41   'Manhood', p. 46.
42   Ibid., p. 187.
43   Ibid., p. 37.
44   Ibid.
45   Boyer describes it thus (pp. 44, 48); Robert Bréchon (' "L'Age d'homme"
      de Michel Leiris', Hachette, Paris, 1973, p. 68; hereafter Bréchon; my
      translations throughout) says 'the chapters are like the articles of a cat-
      alogue or encyclopaedia' but surprisingly does not link this with Leiris's
      fondness for using the 'Nouvelle Larousse Illustré' as a source for epi-
      graphs for the chapters.
46   My italics.
47   'Manhood', p. 143.
48   'Biffures' ('La Règle du jeu', I), Gallimard, Paris, 1948, p. 98.
49   Nadeau, quoted by Bréchon, p. 87.
50   Jeffrey Mehlman, 'A Structural Study of Autobiography', Cornell Univer-
      sity Press, 1974, p. 73; hereafter Mehlman.
51   'Manhood', p. 37.
52   Ibid., p. 37. And, to some extent, of adulthood or 'manhood', notably in
      the detailed accounts of dreams, which Leiris presents without any
      attempt at interpretation.
53   'Manhood', p. 37.
54   Ibid., p. 27.
55   Ibid., pp. 31, 27; Leiris's own italics.
56   Ibid., p. 31.
57   Jean Genet, 'The Thief's Journal', trans. Bernard Frechtman, Penguin,
      Harmondsworth, 1966, p. 98.
58   'Manhood', p. 28. Other 'jeux de mots' in 'Manhood' include courtesan/
      courtier (p. 51), La Guerre de Troie/détroit (p. 55), maîtres-chanteurs
      (p. 40).
59   'Manhood', pp. 130, 59, 42.
60   Ibid., pp. 100 (cf. 102), 120, 109, 121. Cf. Leiris's meditation on the fall
      of Icarus (p. 175).
61   Ibid., p. 69.
62   Ibid., p. 130.
63   Ibid., p. 144.
64   Ibid., p. 13.

65 Ibid., pp. 90-2.
66 Bréchon, p. 77.
67 Ibid., p. 41.
68 Projet de Préface dated 1932 of 'L'Afrique fantôme', Gallimard, Paris, 1934, p. 214.
69 Most accessible in Pierre Chappuis, 'Michel Leiris', Editions Seghers, Paris, 1973, p. 130.
70 Bataille is the dedicatee 'at the origins of 'L'Age d'homme' in a specific sense, as Leiris's interview with Madeleine Gobeil (Gobeil, p. 51) indicates. Leiris is the dedicatee of Bataille's 'L'Érotisme' (1957). Leiris's book of the same title is dated 1938.
71 'Manhood', pp. 161-2.
72 Ibid., p. 140. Cf. Michel Butor's 1955 Critique essay collected in 'Répertoire' (1960).
73 'Manhood', pp. 54, 186.
74 Ibid., p. 80.
75 Ibid., p. 194, cf. p. 89.
76 Ibid., p. 186.
77 Le Sacré dans la vie quotidienne, 'Nouvelle Revue Française', vol. 50, July 1938.
78 An irony that is doubtless not lost on Leiris is that the French word 'sacré' also designates the sacral region of the body, the seat of sexuality.
79 Boyer, p. 54.
80 'Manhood', p. 43.
81 Ibid., p. 43.
82 The eldest brother is also an important figure here, since he 'tells stories' about the more adult world he is on the point of entering.
83 'Manhood', p. 115. As a student of mythology (Leiris tells us in chapter two of how in the 1920s he drew up tables of concordance for the Greek, Latin and German pantheons) and indeed martyrology, Leiris would know the story of St Elmo (or Erasmus), whose 'fire' symbolizes protection.
84 'Manhood', p. 120.
85 Ibid., p. 48.
86 Ibid., p. 49. Leiris's 'taste for hermeticism' has been signalled earlier in the infinite regress of the image on the cocoa tin (in the prologue) and in his perplexity at the double plot of 'Pagliacci' (in the first chapter).
87 Ibid., p. 192. Leiris is particularly fascinated by nightgowns (see pp. 58, 104, 189) and tells in 'Biffures' (pp. 44-5) of how he first saw the female sex organ 'à travers un maillot mouillé devenu transparent'.
88 Ibid., p. 186.
89 Ibid., p. 181.
90 Ibid., p. 142.
91 Ibid.
92 Bréchon, p. 56. See Lejeune, p. 98, for a discussion of how the epigraph to chapter two relates to what follows it, and also pp. 100-3.
93 Boyer suggests that Leiris is not a memorialist but rather a genealogist in Nietzsche's sense of the word (p. 48).
94 'Manhood', p. 172.
95 Ibid., p. 170.
96 Ibid., p. 169.
97 Mehlman, p. 99.
98 'Manhood', p. 117.
99 Ibid.
100 The 'shouts exchanged' (p. 60) in the acoustical pipe of 'La Radieuse', for example.
101 'Manhood', p. 80.
102 'Cinq Etudes d'ethnologie', Gauthier, Paris, 1969, p. 26
103 'Brisées', Mercure de France, Paris, 1966, p. 173.

Chapter 6 Jean-Paul Sartre: 'Les Mots'
1 'Nausea', trans. Robert Baldick, Penguin, Harmondsworth, 1965, p. 248.

2 For a description of the composition of 'Les Mots', see the indispensable 'Les Écrits de Sartre', by Michel Contat and Michel Rybalka, Gallimard, Paris, 1970, pp. 385ff; hereafter Contat and Rybalka.
3 Dominick La Capra, 'A Preface to Sartre', Methuen, London, 1979, p. 25; hereafter La Capra.
4 Interview with Madeleine Gobeil partially translated in 'Sub-Stance', nos 11-12, 1975, p. 56. The sections of 'Being and Nothingness' that Leiris is referring to are part 1, chapter 2, ii and part 3, chapter 1, iv.
5 Interview with Olivier Todd, 'The Listener', 6 June 1957, p. 916; hereafter 1957 interview. Cf. Axel Madsen, 'Hearts and Minds; the Common Journey of Simone de Beauvoir and Jean-Paul Sartre', Morrow, New York, 1977 (hereafter Madsen), p. 13: 'Sartre had been writing since he was ten... and he never stopped telling girls he met that they should write. Only by creating works of the imagination could anyone escape from contingent life, he said'. Towards the end of his life blindness effectively stopped him writing: 'my occupation as a writer is completely destroyed' ('Life/Situations', Pantheon Books, New York, 1977, p. 1, hereafter 'L/S'); 'the only point to my life was writing' (L/S, p. 5).
6 'Nausea', pp. 9, 11.
7 La Capra, p. 128. La Capra's 'deconstruction' of the unfinished phrase seems to me highly questionable, however. Sartre was not much impressed by new formalist and/or structuralist approaches (see 'L/S', p. 126).
8 'Nausea', p. 61.
9 Ibid., p. 252.
10 'Existentialism and Humanism', trans. Philip Mairet, Methuen, London, 1968.
11 For a further instance of 'unfinishedness', cf. an interview of 1975: 'I will not finish my Flaubert. But I am not very unhappy because I think that I said essentially what I had to say in the first three volumes. Someone else could write the fourth on the basis of the three I wrote...the essential is done, even if the work remains in suspense' ('L/S', p. 56). The Tintoretto essay of 1957 was also left unfinished (see Contat and Rybalka, p. 314). An article of faith with the later Sartre is the notion that 'all works remain unfinished' ('L/S', p. 20).
12 Sartre and de Beauvoir have, however, attempted a kind of continuation (see Madsen, pp. 260ff. and 'L/S', p. 21: 'the book will not have as much style as "The Words" did, since I can no longer produce style').
13 Interview partially translated in the 'New York Review of Books', 26 March 1970, p. 30; hereafter 1970 interview.
14 Philippe Lejeune ('Le Pacte autobiographique', Seuil, Paris, 1975, p. 205; hereafter Lejeune) considers that 'the continuation is implied and already related.' But Sartre certainly intended at least two volumes at the outset, the first covering the period up to the age of twenty (see Contat and Rybalka, p. 313); 'Les Mots' actually covers the period up to the age of eleven-and-a-quarter.
15 See, e.g. B. Zimmerman ('Criticism', 6, Fall 1964, p. 320), J. Barish ('Wisconsin Studies in Contemporary Literature', 6, Autumn 1965, pp. 283, 284), J. P. Thody ('Southern Review', n.s.5, no. 4, Autumn 1969, p. 1032).
16 'L/S', p. 56.
17 Thody, p. 1030.
18 1957 interview, p. 915.
19 1970 interview, p. 30.
20 1957 interview, p. 915. Cf. an interview in 'Libération' (4 November 1953): 'Across my story I wish to transcribe that of my epoch' (quoted in Contat and Rybalka, p. 269); and a passage in the 'Critique de la raison dialectique', Gallimard, Paris, 1960, vol. 1, p. 67, quoted by Marc Bensimon ('Revue des sciences humaines', July-September, 1965, p. 430). Bensimon stresses Sartre's 'immolation de soi'. Cf. also 'L/S', p. 117 ('the self...is an object before us'), p. 16 ('a writer should talk about the whole world in talking about his whole self'), p. 44 ('(the) distinction between private and public life does not really exist') and also pp. 11, 12, 13. Cf. Madsen, p. 287 (' "We can only see the sombre recesses in ourselves if we try to

become transparent to others" '). We might say of Sartre, as he says of Merleau-Ponty, 'Unlike Stendhal, he was not trying to understand the individual he was, but rather in the manner of Montaigne [cf. 'Saint Genet', trans. Bernard Frechtman, Mentor, New York, n.d., p. 629n], to understand the person, that incomparable mixture of the particular and the universal' ('Situations', trans. Benita Eisler, Hamish Hamilton, London, 1965, p. 304).

21 Cf. La Capra, p. 36, where he proposes a three-fold structure to Sartre's life, a plausible and suggestive one but one that needs to be tested against Sartre's own explicit and implicit self-divisions.

22 In the 1957 interview, for example, entitled Jean-Paul Sartre on his Autobiography, Sartre spends more time talking about Flaubert.

23 1970 interview, p. 26. Cf. 'L/S', pp. 14 ('I wanted to write a fiction that was not a fiction'), 15 (' "Words" is not truer than "Nausea" or "Roads to Freedom"..."Words" is a kind of novel also - a novel that I believe in, but a novel nonetheless') and 17 ('By means of a true fiction...I would take up the actions and thoughts of my life again in order to make them into a whole'). Cf. 'L/S', p. 112.

24 'L'Idiot de la famille', Gallimard, Paris, 1971, vol. 1, p. 139.

25 E.g. by Lejeune, p. 234. Sartre himself suggested that his lack of personal experience also played a part, in an interview in 'Le Monde' for 17 September 1959; quoted by Contat and Rybalka, p. 329.

26 A less well-known example is Sartre's 1954 review of a book by Julius Fuc̆ík, which begins 'This book is not a novel' (most accessible in Contat and Rybalka, p. 709). But the purely documentary work that offers itself as literature (Oscar Lewis's 'The Children of Sanchez', for example) does not appeal to him (1970 interview, p. 28). Lejeune, p. 242, compares the essays on Nizan and Merleau-Ponty to 'Les Mots' because of their 'density, concreteness and incisiveness'.

27 'Literary Essays', trans. Annette Michelson, Philosophical Library, New York, 1957, p. 41.

28 Ibid., p. 23.

29 Ibid., p. 89.

30 Ibid., p. 73.

31 Ibid.

32 1964 interview.

33 Cf. 'Words', trans. Irene Clephane, Penguin, Harmondsworth, 1964, p. 201 (hereafter 'Words') and La Capra, p. 193.

34 Contat and Rybalka, p. 72. This invites comparison with the Mauriac essay, where Sartre defines the novel as 'the testimony of a participant which should reveal the man who testifies as well as the event to which he testifies' ('Literary Essays', p. 15); with Sartre's 'Baudelaire' (trans. Martin Turnell, New Directions, 1967, p. 51: 'Baudelaire wrote his poems in order to rediscover his own image in them'); with 'Saint Genet', pp. 583 ('his book is himself') and 584 ('to compose is to re-create *himself*'); and with Madsen, p. 78, Sartre saying to de Beauvoir 'Why don't you put yourself into your writing?'

35 'Literary Essays', p. 73.

36 'Situations', pp. 178–9.

37 Ibid., pp. 42, 43.

38 Ibid., pp. 48, 49. Sartre's dislike of Titian dates from at least 1938 (see Madsen, p. 53).

39 Cf. 'Baudelaire', p. 38: 'No one understood better than he that man is "a being of distances" ' (the quotation is from Heidegger), and 'Saint Genet', p. 17: 'that strange impression of being *kept at a distance*' (Sartre's own italics).

40 Contat and Rybalka, p. 388. La Capra, who does not cite this preface to the Russian translation of 'Les Mots', points out that 'the myth...of self-genesis' is not destroyed (p. 185). Lionel Abel ('Partisan Review', 32, Spring 1965, p. 267) sees the myth in 'Les Mots' as a secular version of the old Protestant myth of destiny and successful vocation.

41   Contat and Rybalka, p. 385. Lejeune, p. 206, calls it a 'conversion auto-
     biography'; Abel, p. 261, stresses that the author is 'a new Sartre risen
     from a long dying'. Cf. the 'funeral oration' 'Saint Genet' and Sartre's
     essay on Nizan, referring to Nizan's 'funeral oration' 'Antoine Bloyé'
     ('Situations', p. 173).
42   Cf. Madsen, pp. 70ff, for other 'madnesses'.
43   Contat and Rybalka, p. 387.
44   Cf. 'Critique de la raison dialectique', vol. 1, pp. 62-3, n.2: 'neither men
     nor their activities are *in time*, but rather time, in its concrete character
     as history, is *made* by men'; and 'Being and Nothingness', part 2, chap-
     ters 2 and 3, iv. De Man ('New York Review of Books', 5, November 1964,
     p. 10) calls 'Les Mots' 'a combination of two not altogether compatible texts,
     written several years apart' but stresses 'the extraordinary tightness and
     rigour of composition'.
45   1970 interview, p. 28.
46   1964 interview. Cf. 'Saint Genet', p. 330: 'One of Genet's most constant
     traits...is his contempt for anecdote.' Paul de Man points out that 'Les
     Mots' lacks the improvisatory air of Montaigne and Rousseau, and Jonas
     Barish (p. 283) adds that it 'lacks the gratuitous incident...that would
     guarantee the disinterestedness of it as memoir.'
47   1964 interview.
48   Cf. the 1957 interview. La Capra, p. 184, distinguishes it from them by
     stressing the role of parody and self-parody, but Abel (p. 260) and Bar-
     ish (p. 283) stress the connections. Bensimon (passim) compares it with
     the 'Critique of Dialectical Reason'.
49   Sartre's dislike of Freud began early (see Madsen, p. 40) but was moder-
     ated in the 1950s (see ibid., pp. 209ff.). As many critics have pointed out,
     Sartre's 'bad faith' is essentially a variant of Freud's unconscious; see,
     for example, La Capra, p. 131.
50   Cf. the 1957 interview. The fullest discussion of how important this is for
     'Les Mots' is that by J. Arnold and J.-P. Piriou, 'Génèse et critique d'une
     autobiographie: "Les Mots" de Jean-Paul Sartre', Minard, 1937, pp. 40ff.
     (hereafter Arnold and Piriou).
51   Cf. Lejeune, p. 234. Bensimon, p. 417, suggests that Sartre is anti-
     anthropology as the word is normally understood.
52   'Questions de méthode', Gallimard, Paris, 1967, p. 149.
53   'Words', p. 158.
54   Cf. 'Situations', p. 308.
55   Cf. 'Baudelaire', p. 25; 'Baudelaire's famous lucidity was nothing but an
     attempt at *recovery*. The problem was to recover *himself* and - as sight is
     a form of appropriation - to see himself. But he could only have seen
     himself if he had been two people.' But compare ibid., p. 84: 'a lucidity
     which is a method of punishment', and 'Saint Genet', pp. 264-5: 'It is a
     supreme lucidity which watches its own destruction.'
56   Barish, pp. 283-4.
57   O'Brien, 'New Statesman', LXVIII, 9 October 1964, p. 538.
58   Zimmerman, p. 320.
59   E.g. Maurice Cranston: 'one feels that a man for whom atheism is such a
     cruel and difficult achievement cannot be a very good atheist' ('The
     Listener', 14 May 1964, p. 795); A. Alvarez: 'My guess is that his Oedipus
     complex was complete' ('Spectator', CCXIII, 2 October 1964, p. 441); Abel:
     'What...he has done fundamentally in "The Words" has been to indulge,
     beneath a cruelty to others and to himself which I cannot help but think
     partly pretended, the evident talent he showed as a boy for believing in
     his myths' (p. 261).
60   Sartre himself has effectively countenanced this by admitting in a 1975
     interview: 'you approach your text somewhat as if it were a magical puzzle
     ...in "The Words" I attempted to give multiple and superimposed meanings
     to each sentence' ('L/S', pp. 6, 7). Cf. Bensimon, p. 415: 'the clarity of
     the work is deceiving'; and de Man, p. 12: 'every detail is significant'.
61   La Capra, p. 192.

62 Cf. 'Baudelaire', p. 17: 'His mother's second marriage was the one event
    in his life which he simply could not accept.' Cf. Madsen, p. 37: ' "My
    mother's remarriage made me break off my inner relations with her. I felt
    she had betrayed me although I never told her that." '
63 Lejeune, pp. 207ff. Cf. 'Saint Genet', p. 29: 'time is only a tedious illusion,
    everything is already, there, his future is only an eternal present....'
64 Madsen, p. 230, calls the book 'a dialogue between the mature Sartre and
    his childhood'.
65 Arnold and Piriou, p. 29. Sartre has said 'I don't think a person's life is
    written in the sands of his childhood' (Madsen, p. 261). Cf. 'L/S', p. 44;
    but cf. also ibid., p. 116.
66 De Man, p. 12.
67 Lejeune, pp. 209, 243. On totalization see 'Situations', pp. 217, 368 and
    'L/S', p. 122: 'it is impossible to totalize a living man.'
68 On Sartre's relationship with his maternal grandmother, see La Capra,
    p. 189 and Madsen, p. 38.
69 Cf. Bensimon, pp. 422, 424 for the book's humour.
70 'Words', p. 10.
71 Ibid., p. 11.
72 Ibid., p. 12.
73 On choice, see 'Baudelaire', pp. 95, 120, 192 and numerous other instances
    in Sartre's oeuvre.
74 'Words', p. 9. Cf. 'Baudelaire', p. 107: 'What he could not abide about
    paternity was the continuity of life...which meant that the first begetter.
    ..went on leading an obscure and humiliating life in [his descendants]';
    and 'Situations', p. 157: 'Aeneas had grown weary of carrying the sad
    Anchises for so long' (cf. 'Words', p. 15, for the same image).
75 'Words', p. 13.
76 Cf. 'Baudelaire', p. 19: 'Each of us was able to observe in childhood the
    fortuitous and shattering advent of self-consciousness.'
77 'Words', p. 14. On freedom, cf. 'Baudelaire', p. 40: 'Baudelaire always
    felt that he was free,' and numerous other instances.
78 'Words', p. 16. Cf. 'Baudelaire', p. 53: 'It is true that everything is novel
    for the child, but this novelty has already been seen, named and classi-
    fied by other people. Every object comes to him with a label attached to
    it.' Cf. 'Saint Genet', p. 51: 'Genet is on the side of the object named, not
    of those who name them.'
79 'Words', p. 23.
80 Bensimon, p. 429, stresses that 'Les Mots' is 'not a picaresque adventure
    but rather a drama'.
81 'Words', pp. 17–18.
82 Ibid., p. 22.
83 Ibid., p. 24 et seq. Later, in part two of 'Les Mots', Sartre demonstrates
    ironically how the declaration of war in 1914 enabled everyone to make the
    'sheep and goats' distinction.
84 Ibid., p. 25.
85 Ibid., p. 27.
86 Ibid., p. 29. Cf. the description of Flaubert in 'Baudelaire', p. 142: 'the
    writer's nature seemed to him to be the exercise of a priestly office,' and
    of Genet in 'Saint Genet', p. 329: 'his poetry is not a literary art, it is a
    means of salvation.'
87 'Words', p. 49.
88 Ibid., pp. 31–2.
89 Ibid., p. 32.
90 Ibid., p. 35.
91 Ibid., p. 33.
92 Ibid., p. 34. Cf. a later ironic reference to his 'epic idealism' (ibid., p.
    74; cf. 'Saint Genet', p. 68) and an earlier reference to a book in his
    father's library, Max Weber's 'Vers le Positivisme par l'idéalisme absolu',
    roundly condemned as 'rubbish' ('Words', p. 15); also 'Baudelaire', p. 123.
93 'Words', p. 40.

94   Ibid., p. 42.
95   Ibid., p. 45.
96   Ibid.
97   Ibid., pp. 46–7.
98   Cf. 'Baudelaire', p. 99 and 'Saint Genet', pp. 273, 599.
99   'Words', p. 40. 'Correcting' is of course ambiguous; it could mean 'proof-reading' but it could also possess connotations of 'rendering more orthodox'. The remark is especially interesting in the context of the question of 'un-finishedness' that was discussed earlier.
100   Cf. 'Saint Genet', part 1, section 2, and ibid., pp. 302, 338, 424–34.
101   Cf. ibid., p. 175.
102   'Words', p. 51.
103   Ibid., p. 53.
104   Ibid., pp. 53, 52. The admission in the previous section – 'sometimes I am a Cartesian diver' (ibid. p. 40) – would seem to justify an interpretation of this madman as a Sartrian variant of Descartes's deceiving demon, with the difference that it does not, in the long run, deceive.
105   Ibid., p. 53.
106   Sartre stresses that he 'was not' at the end of the penultimate paragraph of this section of 'Les Mots', ('Words', p. 56).
107   Cf. 'Being and Nothingness', part 1, chapter 2, i.
108   Cf. 'Baudelaire', p. 135; 'his aim was to exist for himself as an object.'
109   'Words', p. 57.
110   Cf. 'Baudelaire', p. 170: 'his dearest wish was to be like the stone and the statue enjoying the peaceful repose which belonged to the unchange-able.'
111   The story of Saint Maria Alacoque ('Words', p. 63) is also referred to in 'Saint Genet', p. 144.
112   'Words', p. 65.
113   Ibid., p. 69. Cf. 'Baudelaire', p. 156 and 'Saint Genet', pp. 86ff. for other mirror confrontations.
114   'Words', p. 71.
115   Ibid., p. 71.
116   Ibid., p. 73.
117   This passion continued into later life, see Madsen, pp. 48–9, 60, 209ff.
118   'Words', pp. 76–7. Cf. 'Baudelaire', p. 149: 'Baudelaire, the man of crowds, was also the man who had the greatest fear of them'; and Madsen, p. 125: 'He was moved by the crowds in New York.'
119   Cf. 'Saint Genet', pp. 77–8.
120   'Words', p. 79.
121   Ibid., p. 78; Sartre's own italics.
122   Ibid., p. 80.
123   Cf. 'Baudelaire', p. 55: 'people have taken every opportunity of attrib-uting an unresolved Oedipus complex to him, but it matters little whether or not he desired his mother'; and 'L/S', pp. 114ff., on Flaubert's mother. De Man, p. 12, says that the mother remains a scarcely real fig-ure throughout the book; Arnold and Piriou give the fullest Oedipal account. Sartre's mother has been recorded as saying: 'Poulou hasn't understood anything of his childhood' (Madsen, p. 231).
124   'Words', p. 81.
125   Cf. 'Baudelaire', pp. 192: 'the free choice which a man makes of himself is completely identified with what is called his destiny'; p. 161: 'He spared no pains to transform his life in his own eyes into a destiny'; and 'Situ-ations', p. 246: 'the gentle contingency of birth is changed, by its very irreversibility, into destiny.'
126   'Words', p. 82.
127   Ibid., p. 84.
128   Ibid., p. 90. Cf. 'Baudelaire', p. 82: 'man is never anything but an imposture.'
129   'Words', p. 93.
130   Ibid., pp. 93, 92.

131 Ibid., p. 94.
132 Ibid., p. 97.
133 Ibid., p. 107. Cf. 'Situations', p. 370: 'today, there are only two ways to speak of oneself, the third person singular of the first person plural.'
134 'Words', pp. 107ff. Cf. Lejeune, pp. 215ff., and 'Baudelaire', p. 43: 'He admitted that there were "three sorts of beings who are respectable: the priest, the warrior and the poet." ' 'Saint Genet' is also organized around a triad of sorts.
135 Cf. 'Baudelaire', p. 165: 'Baudelaire chose to live his life backwards.'
136 'Words', p. 125. Cf. 'Baudelaire', p. 162: 'the very fact that it was bound to end made his existence appear as though it had *already* ended.'
137 'Words', p. 128.
138 Ibid., pp. 70ff.
139 Ibid., p. 134.
140 Ibid., p. 136.
141 Ibid., p. 137.
142 Lejeune, p. 222.
143 'Words', p. 139.
144 Ibid., p. 142.
145 Ibid., p. 143. Cf. 'Being and Nothingness', part 3, chapter 1, iv; 'Baudelaire', p. 25: 'sight is a form of appropriating'; ibid., p. 89: 'the poet felt that he was *look* and freedom' (Sartre's own italics); 'Saint Genet', p. 139: 'Genet, who has withdrawn from the cycle of praxis...is here pure gaze'; ibid., pp. 296, 297.
146 'Words', p. 145.
147 La Capra, p. 192: 'Sartre at one point states that he believed in the myth of literature until the age of twenty....This would imply that he was already growing out of it by the time he wrote his well-known works...He also, however, discusses "Nausea" as if, while writing it, he was still prey to the myth in all its force.'
148 'Words', p. 156.
149 Ibid., p. 148.
150 Ibid., p. 157.
151 Ibid., p. 158.
152 La Capra, pp. 192, 193.

Chapter 7 Vladimir Nabokov: 'Speak, Memory'
1 'Speak, Memory', Gollancz, London, 1951, p. 7. Cf. 'I am an ardent memoirist with a rotten memory' ('Strong Opinions', Weidenfeld & Nicolson, London, 1974, p. 140). Jane Grayson's 'Nabokov Translated', Oxford University Press, 1977, pp. 141ff., deals fully with the way Nabokov has tried to remedy this defect in the 1967 'Speak, Memory'.
2 'Speak, Memory', Weidenfeld & Nicolson, London, 1967, p. 11 (hereafter 'Speak, Memory').
3 Cf. 'facts are never really quite bare' ('Nikolai Gogol', Weidenfeld & Nicolson, London, 1971, p. 119). See 'Strong Opinions', pp. 10ff. for what Nabokov understands by 'reality'.
4 This title would remind a Russian of Alexander Herzen's 'From the Other Shores', written in exile in England.
5 'Speak, Memory', p. 12.
6 Ibid., p. 12.
7 Ibid., p. 16.
8 Ibid., p. 290.
9 The last problem, appropriately enough, is Nabokov's index, by no means as 'useless' (Andrew Field, 'Nabokov: his Life in Art', Hodder & Stoughton, London, 1967, p. 371) as that at the end of 'Drugie Berega', but not quite as helpful as that which concludes 'Pale Fire'. But cf. Dabney Stuart's The Novelist's Composure: 'Speak, Memory' as Fiction, Modern Language Quarterly, vol. 36, June 1975, pp. 189-92.
10 'Speak, Memory', p. 9.
11 Ibid.

12 Ibid., p. 15.
13 Ibid., p. 10. Nabokov makes a similar claim, with more obvious justification, regarding 'Pnin' (serialized in 'The New Yorker') in 'Strong Opinions', p. 84. Cf. 'Strong Opinions', pp. 16, 31–2, 69, 99–100.
14 'Speak, Memory', pp. 13, 12.
15 Ibid., p. 13.
16 Ibid., p. 11.
17 Ibid., p. 12.
18 'Eugene Onegin', Routledge & Kegan Paul, London, 1964, p. 8. Nabokov habitually relates art and science (cf. e.g. 'Strong Opinions', pp. 16, 44, 79 and 'Speak, Memory', 1951 edn, p. 159) like the good monist he claims to be ('Strong Opinions', pp. 85, 124). As a teacher, he stressed details and encouraged students to draw maps ('Strong Opinions', pp. 22, 55 (cf. p. 90 where he brings the two together in relation to 'Speak, Memory'), 168, 186 – the latter in the context of being a memoirist). 'Speak, Memory' suggests that Dobuzhinski was influential in this regard ('Speak, Memory', pp. 92–3).
19 'Speak, Memory', p. 139.
20 Ibid., p. 21.
21 Cf. 'Strong Opinions', p. 197 ('My sense of places is Nabokovian rather than Proustian.')
22 Nabokov hints that he has inevitably failed by adding to the 1951 version an account of how he tried 'in vain to reach the sub-base of Pushkin's "Exegi monumentum"' (Cf. 'Strong Opinions', p. 76) which also provides him with a link to the 'Eheu, fugaces' paraphrase which opens the final chapter.
23 'Speak, Memory', p. 20.
24 In the 1951 edn (p. 9), Nabokov is much vaguer: 'a sensitive youth'. For the changes in Nabokov's perspective on time between edns of 'Speak, Memory', see Grayson, pp. 150–1.
25 'Speak, Memory', p. 20.
26 Ibid., pp. 22, 21. Cf. Stuart, p. 192 and Elizabeth Bruss, 'Autobiographical Acts', Johns Hopkins, Baltimore, 1976, pp. 130 (on the general problem of time for any biographer), and 147 (on 'Speak, Memory' specifically).
27 'Speak, Memory', p. 13.
28 Ibid., p. 73.
29 Ibid., p. 10.
30 Cf. Grayson, p. 139, for what Nabokov does not mention in his foreword.
31 'Speak, Memory', p. 12.
32 Ibid., p. 11. Concentric rings or nimbuses seen (chiefly in alpine or polar regions) surrounding the shadows of an observer's head projected on a cloud or fog bank opposite to the sun.
33 Ibid., p. 27.
34 Ibid., p. 233. Cf. 'Strong Opinions', p. 14 ('I don't think in any language. I think in images'). In the foreword to 'The Gift' and elsewhere, Nabokov bemoans his loss of Russian as a creative medium. The photographs in the 1966 'Speak, Memory' are presumably designed to recall things more vividly than mere words can. But the young Nabokov also had a fondness for illustrated books ('Speak, Memory', pp. 195, 244).
35 'Speak, Memory', p. 27. Stuart, p. 179, sees this as 'one of the basic perspectives from which the autobiography is constructed.'
36 Ibid., p. 309.
37 Nabokov seems, however, to have been fascinated by the imperative mood; see Andrew Field, 'Nabokov: his Life in Part', (Viking Press, New York, 1977, p. 293) on the possible title of a second volume of memoirs: 'Laugh, Memory', 'Smile, Memory', 'Speak, America'; cf. 'Strong Opinions', p. 294.
38 Bruss, p. 152, stresses that 'the final words of the autobiography catch consciousness in the act.'
39 'Speak, Memory', pp. 309–10.
40 Ibid., facing page 129.
41 Bruss, pp. 150ff., interprets the fifteen chapters of 'Speak, Memory' as a triad of five chapters each.

42 W. W. Rowe, 'Nabokov's Deceptive World', New York University Press, 1971, p. 153, says of these pages that they 'contain a sustained potential sexual analogy'; Bruss, p. 136, explores this further. Nabokov vigorously pooh-poohed this ('Strong Opinions', p. 304–7). On combinations and deceptions see 'Strong Opinions', p. 12; on 'Lolita' as at once composition and solution see 'Strong Opinions', p. 20.
43 'Speak, Memory', p. 293.
44 Ibid., p. 291.
45 'The good writer is first of all an enchanter' (Nabokov, in a letter of 27 November 1946 to Edmund Wilson); A. Field, 'Life in Part', p. 268.
46 'Speak, Memory', p. 25.
47 Ibid., p. 11.
48 See 'Strong Opinions', p. 129, for Nabokov's dislike of mystery fiction.
49 'Speak, Memory', p. 86. See Stuart, p. 180, for a different interpretation of the last words of this quotation.
50 Ibid., pp. 24–5.
51 Ibid., p. 31.
52 Stuart, pp. 184ff., analyses chapter 6 of 'Speak, Memory' (originally entitled 'Butterflies') fully. Cf. Grayson, p. 146.
53 'Speak, Memory', p. 32.
54 Ibid., p. 31.
55 Ibid., p. 50.
56 'Speak, Memory', p. 77. Bruss, p. 149, relates the beginnings and ends of chapters (stressing the present-tense aspect) and, p. 150, suggests that the first five chapters all end 'on a note of childish defenselessness and trust'.
57 'Speak, Memory', p. 193. Cf. Stuart, pp. 183–4, for another important approach to Nabokov senior's death.
58 'Speak, Memory', p. 137.
59 Ibid., pp. 208ff.
60 Ibid., p. 236.
61 Ibid., pp. 229, 241.
62 Ibid., p. 238.
63 On the love and literature question see also Stuart, p. 189 and Grayson, pp. 157–8. One can be forgiven for being momentarily reminded, at the beginning of chapter 12, of Proust's 'jeunes filles' at Balbec as Tamara 'catches up with two other, less pretty girls who were calling to her' ('Speak, Memory', p. 230).
64 'Speak, Memory', p. 193.
65 For other patterns, see Stuart, pp. 178–9.
66 'Speak, Memory', p. 11.
67 Cf. Bruss, pp. 160–2. 'Strong Opinions', p. 40 shows that Nabokov thinks of writer and reader as co-operative. But in more arrogant moods he thinks otherwise ('Strong Opinions', pp. 114, 117).
68 'Speak, Memory', p. 227.
69 There are other deaths that Nabokov dwells on in 'Speak, Memory'. One curious network of relationships involves the Hanged One (pp. 63, 156, cf. 'Eugene Onegin', vol. 2, p. 434), and the headless horseman (195, 200; cf. Pushkin's 'Bronze Horseman', p. 166). Cf. also pp. 278, 303.
70 'Speak, Memory', p. 149.
71 Ibid., p. 216.
72 Nabokov himself is a great rereader, as his forewords indicate; see also 'Eugene Onegin', vol. 1, p. 17. He is also, as 'Speak, Memory' is not alone in proving, a great rewriter (cf. 'Strong Opinions', p. 4). Stuart's essay on 'Speak, Memory' ends by inviting the reader to reread it.
73 Cf., in this respect, the dead leaves of 'Speak, Memory', p. 152 (Nabokov and Colette) and also p. 162 (Lenski and his fiancée).
74 Ibid., p. 216. Cf. Bruss, pp. 153ff., and Stuart, pp. 189ff.
75 'Speak, Memory', p. 93.
76 Stuart, p. 182, also stresses how dramatic 'Speak, Memory' is.
77 'Speak, Memory', p. 227.
78 Cf. 'Imagination is a form of memory' ('Strong Opinions', p. 78).

79   'Speak, Memory', p. 40.
80   Cf. Grayson, p. 155 on Nabokov's 'increase in humour' between editions
     of 'Speak, Memory'. Nabokov himself stresses that it was 'a happy expat-
     riation' ('Strong Opinions', p. 218) and many times speaks of America as
     a second home.
81   'Speak, Memory', pp. 308-9.
82   Cf. Bruss, p. 152, for a different interpretation of the implications of this
     event.
83   'Speak, Memory', p. 298.
84   Ibid., p. 22.
85   Ibid., pp. 259, 273.
86   Cf. Grayson, pp. 147ff.
87   'Speak, Memory', p. 275.
88   Ibid., p. 40.
89   Ibid., p. 39. Cf. Stuart, p. 179, for a different approach to this pencil.
90   'Speak, Memory', p. 39.
91   Cf. Stuart, pp. 186-8, on the importance of high perspectives in 'Speak,
     Memory'. Analogous images may also be found on pp. 25, 146, 148, 240,
     244.
92   Ibid., p. 50.
93   E.g. 'Speak, Memory', pp. 73 ('the sense of receding endlessly, as if this
     was the stern of time itself'; cf. 'Strong Opinions', p. 72), 85.
94   Ibid., p. 90.
95   Ibid., p. 267.
96   Ibid., p. 251. Cf. Grayson, p. 161: 'Nabokov's treatment of the corres-
     pondence with Tamara can also be read as a retrospective commentary on
     "Mashenka".'
97   'Speak, Memory', p. 75.
98   Ibid., p. 77.
99   Ibid., p. 95. Cf. Bruss, p. 135.
100 Ibid., p. 92.
101 Ibid., pp. 99-100. Stuart, p. 183, relates this to the child's fairy-tale.
102 Ibid., p. 153.
103 The image recurs in the poem 'In this life, rich in patterns....'
104 'Speak, Memory', pp. 170-1.
105 Cf. ibid., p. 186 ('I viewed his activities through a prism of my own.')
     The camera-lucida (see p. 113) operates by means of a peculiarly shaped
     prism (cf. Sebastian Knight's 'book' 'The Prismatic Bezel').
106 See his 'Nabokov's Dark Cinema', Oxford University Press, New York,
     1974, passim.
107 'Speak, Memory', p. 213.
108 Ibid., p. 222.
109 Ibid., p. 232.
110 Cf. Stuart, p. 181; Grayson, pp. 156-9, 227-31, 165 (relating 'Ada' to
     chapter 12 of 'Speak, Memory'; cf. also 'Strong Opinions', pp. 120ff);
     Rowe, p. 139n., who adds other parallels with 'Mary'; Appel, preface to
     'The Annotated Lolita', (McGraw-Hill, New York, 1970) who sees 'Lolita'
     as in part a parody of the 1951 'Speak, Memory'; and Proffer, 'Keys to
     Lolita' (Indiana University Press, 1968), pp. 150-2, proposing parallels
     between 'Lolita' and Colette, vigorously denied by Nabokov ('Strong
     Opinions', pp. 24, 83).
111 'Speak, Memory', p. 256.
112 Ibid., p. 167.
113 'Eugene Onegin', vol. 2, p. 314.
114 Cf. V's discussion ('The Real Life of Sebastian Knight', Penguin, Harmonds-
     worth, 1964, p. 79) of Knight's 'methods of composition', often applied to
     Nabokov's works.
115 'Speak, Memory', p. 290.
116 Quite unlike Sebastian Knight's 'autobiography', 'Lost Property', in fact,
     which V. considers 'his easiest book' ('The Real Life of Sebastian Knight',
     p. 95).

117 'Speak, Memory', p. 288.
118 Luzhin, in Nabokov's 'The Defence', goes insane 'when chess combinations pervade the actual pattern of his existence' ('Speak, Memory', 1951 edn p. 216).
119 'Speak, Memory', p. 245.
120 Ibid., p. 275.
121 Cf. 'Strong Opinions', pp. 52, 127
122 'Speak, Memory', p. 240.
123 Ibid., p. 230.
124 Ibid., p. 145.
125 Ibid., p. 152.
126 Ibid., p. 308. Cf. Rowe, p. 63, for two other occasions where the reader is invited to collaborate.
127 'Speak, Memory', p. 278. Cf. Nabokov's own 'Invitation to a Beheading', described in the 1951 edn as 'the most haunting of Sirin's works' (p. 215) and the headless horseman of the 1967 'Speak, Memory', pp. 166, 195, 200, 278, 303.
128 In the first version of 'Speak, Memory', Nabokov again stresses the motifs of love and literature by suggesting that his writing was 'talentless and derivative' until 1925, 'the year I met my present wife' (p. 183). (Cf. Bruss, p. 160, on the role of Véra). Interestingly, Nabokov tells us in chapter 12 of the 1967 'Speak, Memory', that 'until the writing of a novel ['Mary'] relieved me of that fertile emotion, the loss of my country was equated for me with the loss of my love' (p. 245). 'Speak, Memory', by contrast, clearly does not relieve 'all the pangs of exile' (ibid., p. 244).
129 Not, of course, in the same sense as Nabokov's novel 'The Gift', which contains a brilliant 'biography' of Chernyshevsky to which Nabokov alludes obliquely in 'Speak, Memory'.
130 Cf. Bruss, p. 156, on the artistic effect of disguising oneself as Bloodmark; also Stuart, p. 182, on the artistic effect of 'disguising' oneself as 'Sirin'.
131 'Speak, Memory', 1951 edn, p. 189.
132 'Speak, Memory', p. 218.
133 Bruss, p. 157, would restrict the title 'memoirist' in a pejorative sense to Humbert Humbert in 'Lolita'.
134 'Speak, Memory', p. 269. Cf. 'Ada', part four and also 'Strong Opinions', p. 184.
135 'Speak, Memory', p. 269.

Conclusion
 1 Irving Horowitz, Autobiography as the Presentation of Self for Social Immortality, 'New Literary History', vol. 9, no. 1, Autumn 1977, p. 178.
 2 See Michel Foucault, 'L'Ordre du discours', Gallimard, Paris, 1971, pp. 30-1.
 3 See, for example, Roland Barthes, The Death of the Author in 'Image-Music Text', trans. Stephen Heath, Fontana, London, 1977, pp. 142-8.
 4 'Safe Conduct', p. 61.
 5 J. Sturrock, The New Model Autobiography, 'New Literary History', vol. 9, no. 1, pp. 55, 56.
 6 Jean Starobinski, The Style of Autobiography, 'Literary Style; a Symposium', ed. Seymour Chatman, Oxford University Press, London, 1971, pp. 286, 289.
 7 Stephen Shapiro, The Dark Continent of Literature; Autobiography, 'Comparative Literature Studies', vol. 5, 1968, p. 448.
 8 'Literary Style', p. 296.
 9 Ibid., p. 296.
10 See ibid., pp. 287ff. Philippe Lejeune ('New Literary History', vol. 9, no. 1, p. 27) has found an analogous idea in Paul Valéry's 'Cahiers', Gallimard, Paris, 1973, vol. 1, p. 488.
11 Louis Renza, The Veto of the Imagination; a Theory of Autobiography, 'New Literary History', vol. 9. no. 1, p. 22.
12 Michael Cooke, Modern Black Autobiography in the Tradition, in

'Romanticism; Vistas, Instances, Continuities', ed. D. Thorburn and Geoffrey Hartman, Cornell University Press, 1973, p. 259.
13 William L. Howarth, 'New Literary History', vol. 5, Winter 1974, p. 377.
14 Richard M. Dunn, 'Les Mémoires d'outre tombe': Chateaubriand's Alter Ego, 'Genre', vol. 6, no. 2, June 1973, p. 180.
15 Cf. Mutlu Konuk Blasing, 'The Art of Life', University of Texas Press, 1977, p. xxvi: '[the reader] must act and try to become the ideal audience that a particular work is addressing. In effect the reader attempts to become the author's first reader - the author.' This invites comparison, despite its differences of emphasis, with the Henry Adams letter cited on p. 16.
16 Dunn, p. 186.
17 Blasing, p. xxi.
18 Robert F. Sayre, 'The Examined Self: Benjamin Franklin, Henry Adams, Henry James', Princeton University Press, 1964, pp. 180-1, 182.
19 Shapiro, p. 449.
20 Blasing, p. xxvii.
21 Sturrock, p. 51.
22 A number of critics have suggested that Yeats's autobiography effectively ends after 'The Trembling of the Veil'.
23 See James Olney, 'Metaphors of Self' (Princeton University Press, 1972); and John Morris, 'Versions of the Self' (New York University Press, 1966).
24 The substantiality of Stendhal's self has often been called into question, see Robert Martin Adams, 'Stendhal: Notes on a Novelist', Merlin, London, 1950, pp. 223ff.
25 Christine Vance, Rousseau's Autobiographical Venture: a Process of Negation, 'Genre', vol. 6, no. 1, March 1973, p. 109.
26 Renza, p. 19.
27 'The Ambassadors', Macmillan, London, 1923, p. xxi.
28 Renza, p. 18.
29 Cf. David Gervais, Leonard Woolf's Autobiography, 'Cambridge Quarterly', vol. 7, no. 1, Spring/Summer 1970, p. 98: 'good autobiographical literature leads us back to life in an especially intimate way.'
30 'Letters of Henry James', ed. Percy Lubbock, Macmillan, London, 1920, vol. 2, p. 373.

Appendices
1 For a good study of English diaries, see Robert A. Fothergill, 'Private Chronicles', Oxford University Press, London, 1974.
2 See, for example, Edward Stokes, 'The Novels of Henry Green' (Hogarth Press, London, 1959); and John Russell, 'Nine Novels and an Unpacked Bag' (New Jersey, 1960); and Keith C. Odom, 'Henry Green' (Twayne, Boston, 1978).
3 'Pack my Bag', Hogarth Press, London, 1952, p. 5.
4 Ibid.
5 Green's real name was Henry Vincent Yorke.
6 'Pack my Bag', p. 7.
7 Ibid., p. 8.
8 Ibid., p. 93.
9 Ibid., p. 47.
10 Ibid., p. 32.
11 Ibid.
12 Ibid., p. 40.
13 Ibid., pp. 64-5.
14 Ibid., p. 188.
15 Ibid., p. 67.
16 Ibid., p. 88.
17 Ibid., p. 80.
18 Ibid., pp. 79-80.
19 Ibid., p. 80.
20 Ibid.

21 Ibid., p. 145.
22 Ibid., pp. 146-7.
23 Ibid., p. 148.
24 Ibid., p. 40.
25 Ibid., p. 166.
26 Ibid., p. 10.
27 Ibid., p. 37.
28 Ibid., p. 91.
29 Ibid., p. 120.
30 Ibid., pp. 119, 122.
31 Ibid., p. 123.
32 Ibid., p. 151.
33 Ibid., p. 211.
34 Ibid., p. 43.
35 Ibid., p. 175.
36 Ibid., p. 185.
37 Ibid., pp. 143-4.
38 Ibid., p. 152.
39 Ibid., pp. 152-3.
40 All the quotations in this paragraph are from 'Pack My Bag', p. 88: 'Prose is not to be read aloud, and it is not quick as poetry but rather a gathering web of insinuations which go further than names however shared can ever go. Prose should be a long intimacy with strangers with no direct appeal to what both may have known. It should slowly appeal to feelings unexpressed, it should in the end draw tears out of the stone....'
41 See, for example, the special Stokes supplement to 'Poetry Nation Review' (vol. 7, no. 11, 1980), and the widespread critical response to the three-volume 'Critical Writings of Adrian Stokes' (hereafter 'CW'), Thames & Hudson, London, 1978.
42 Richard Wollheim, Introduction to 'The Image in Form: Selected Writings of Adrian Stokes', ed. Richard Wollheim, Penguin, Harmondsworth, 1972, p. 10.
43 'CW', vol. 2, p. 141.
44 Ibid.
45 This and the other phrases of Stokes's quoted in this paragraph are taken from his Notes Towards a Book Beginning August 1943, 'Poetry Nation Review', no. 15, pp. 41-2.
46 Stokes began to be analysed by Melanie Klein in the mid-1930s ('CW', vol. 1, p. 10); Stokes says in 'Inside Out': 'I say this after a seven years' analysis' ('CW', vol. 2, p. 163; all subsequent quotations from 'Inside Out' are from this printing.) For a serviceable account of the ideas of Melanie Klein see Hanna Segal, 'Klein', Fontana, London, 1979 and Wollheim's Penguin introduction.
47 Stokes's antipathy to conventional rational thinking can be found as early as his first two books, 'The Thread of Ariadne' (1925) (especially pp. 59ff) and 'Sunrise in the West' (1926). In the preface to 'The Thread of Ariadne', Stokes has his character the Sceptic say 'Only the mad are sane', an idea echoed thirty years later in 'Michelangelo' ('CW', vol. 3, p. 32).
48 The young Stokes was particularly impressed by the ability of the modern novel to 'uncover the subtle interconnections of significance, madeira cake and guiltiness, green bottles and penguins' ('Sunrise in the West', p. 93). Cf. 'The Thread of Ariadne' (pp. 175-6) where Stokes has been reading Virginia Woolf's 'Jacob's Room'.
49 'CW', vol. 2, p. 142.
50 Cf. Stokes's 'Colour and Form', (1937) and the 1950 text published in 'CW' vol. 2.
51 For a similarly decisive thunderstorm, see 'Sunrise in the West', p. x: 'at the first clap of thunder, the tired countryside, overcome by a thousand repetitive memories...suddenly leaps from this nightmare'; and cf. 'CW', vol. 1, pp. 31-3, 72, 299.
52 Stokes's prose is so fluid that a musical metaphor seems appropriate. But

the young Stokes distinguished himself from Pater's Symbolist demand that all art should aspire to the condition of music, see 'CW', vol. 1, pp. 20, and cf. pp. 17, 55, 103, 139, 184, 266. Later Giorgione is praised for perceiving 'the interval of silence' ('CW', vol. 2, p. 208) and Stokes dwells on 'the huge silence of the lagoon' in Venice ('CW', vol. 2, p. 115). 'CW', vol. 1, p. 139 is Stokes's most sustained attack on Symbolism. Stephen Bann's comparison of 'Inside Out' to a Paterian 'imaginary portrait' ('Poetry Nation Review', no. 9, 1979, p. 8), seems to me misguided.

53 'CW', vol. 2, p. 143.
54 Cf. 'A Game That Must Be Lost', Carcanet, Manchester, 1973. The quotation is from Beaumont and Fletcher's play 'Philaster' and refers to life.
55 'CW', vol. 2, p. 144.
56 Ibid., p. 163.
57 Ibid., p. 144.
58 The early paragraphs of 'Inside Out' are too full of battle imagery to require illustration.
59 Cf. the 'water pellets' of 'CW', vol. 2, p. 144.
60 Ibid., p. 145.
61 Cf. the peacock cry that acts, like the barrel-organ, to synthesize effects into a unity ('CW', vol. 2, p. 245) and two references in 'Colour and Form' ('CW', vol. 2, pp. 40, 44) which see the peacock's tail as an image of art.
62 Cf. 'The Thread of Ariadne' (p. 89): 'I am a fanatic without a creed.'
63 'CW', vol. 2, p. 146. Cf. 'A Game That Must Be Lost' (p. 110): 'The face is...[an] indispensable metaphor for the work of art.'
64 Cf. 'Smooth and Rough': 'A house is a womb substitute in whose passages we move with freedom' ('CW', vol. 2, p. 241); also a later section of 'Inside Out' ('CW', vol. 2, pp. 160ff). The absence of any account of his actual home life in 'Inside Out' is not irrelevant here.
65 'CW', vol. 2, pp. 146-7.
66 Cf. 'The Quattro Cento': 'The aesthetic sense cries out for emblem, an aspect of art that is a proper substitute for literature' ('CW', vol. 1, p. 41; cf. pp. 53, 153).
67 Stokes's life is very much 'at sea', as the cliché has it, in his childhood. His fondness for clichés and nuggets of familiar wisdom is exemplified in the first essay in 'A Game That Must Be Lost', 'Listening to clichés and individual words', and earlier in 'The Thread of Ariadne', p. 199 and 'Sunrise in the West', p. 103. 'Smooth and Rough' contains many descriptions of Stokes's experiences beside the sea in Cornwall.
68 'CW', vol. 2, p. 147.
69 Ibid., p. 148.
70 Ibid., p. 149.
71 Stokes's second book, 'Sunrise in the West', is sub-titled 'A Modern Interpretation of Past and Present'. 'Smooth and Rough' is more emotional: 'An early passion for history was an antidote to imaginative despair' ('CW', vol. 2, p. 227). By the time of 'The Invitation in Art' Stokes had come to believe that 'there can be no history without a potential history of ourselves' ('CW', vol. 3, p. 298).
72 'CW', vol. 2, p. 149.
73 Ibid., p. 150.
74 Ibid., p. 151.
75 Ibid., p. 153.
76 Cf. Stokes's other references to Renoir: 'CW', vol. 1, p. 244 (where he is compared unfavourably with Piero della Francesca); vol. 2, p. 40 (where he is seen as comparable to Piero and Giorgione); and the many references in Stokes's writings on Monet and Cézanne. Stokes never lost his affection for the Quattro Cento, but obviously the Impressionists came to matter more and more to him as he grew older.
77 'CW', vol. 2, pp. 151-2.
78 Ibid., p. 153.
79 Ibid., p. 154. Cf. 'Sunrise in the West', p. x: 'should a barrel-organ start to grind an unrecognizable tune, should the air be pricked by barrel-

organ noises, then the neighbourhood is transformed, lives, has a present'; and also 'Tonight the Ballet', p. 13: 'Think how the streets spring to life when the bolder kind of barrel-organ grinds its tune. At once the streets become a *mise-en-scène*, the movement of passers-by and of traffic becomes a ballet of a sort. So many things that lay in pieces in the mind... are gathered together, organized.' Stokes never tired of attacking what he called in a late lecture 'the loss of textures in our streets' ('A Game That Must Be Lost', p. 155) and had a particular antipathy to Oxford Street (see 'Sunrise in the West', p. x and 'CW', vol. 2, p. 245).

80 See Wollheim's Penguin introduction, p. 21 and also 'The Thread of Ariadne', pp. 64ff., 'A Game That Must Be Lost', p. 122, and 'CW', vol. 2, pp. 31-4.

81 'CW', vol. 2, p. 156.

82 Ibid., pp. 156-7.

83 Ibid., p. 157.

84 Ibid., p. 158.

85 Cf. Geoffrey Hartman, 'Beyond Formalism', Yale University Press, 1970, pp. 311-36.

86 'CW', vol. 2, p. 159.

87 Previous to this, Stokes makes the network of railways equivalent to the network of correspondence in the Unconscious: 'We are always making up new trains within' (ibid., p. 167).

88 Ibid., p. 159.

89 I.e. after Stokes had divorced his first wife and married her sister. Richard Read tells me that the original drafts of 'Smooth and Rough' were titled 'Outside In', as if it were to be a more obvious sequel.

90 'CW', vol. 2, pp. 234ff.

91 'CW', vol. 1, p. 71. The context is interesting, for in talking about Verrochio Stokes makes a remark that we might well apply to the Hyde Park section of 'Inside Out': 'in the case of stresses and strains an ever increasing complication in correspondence is necessary to avoid their cancelling each other out, instead of enhancing one another.'

INDEX